The Impact of Technology on Library Instruction

Papers and Session Materials Presented at the Twenty-First
National LOEX Library Instruction Conference
held in Racine, Wisconsin
14 to 15 May 1993

edited by
Linda Shirato, Director
LOEX Clearinghouse
University Library
Eastern Michigan University

Published for Learning Resources and Technologies
Eastern Michigan University
by
Pierian Press
Ann Arbor, Michigan
1995

The Pierian Press
Box 1808
Ann Arbor, Michigan 48106

LIBRARY ORIENTATION SERIES
(Emphasizing Information Literacy and Bibliographic Instruction)

*   Pierian Press's ISBN identifier is 0-87650. This identifier should precede the number given for a book (e.g., 0-87650-327-X).

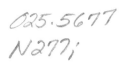

Table of Contents

Articles

Instructive Sessions

Poster Sessions

Bibliography

Roster of Participants

PREFACE

Is there any area of library work that has not been changed by technology? Technology is changing libraries, and with them library instruction. The term "bibliographic instruction" is being debated, and perhaps will be discarded, in part because so much of what we teach daily are no longer books. This year, for the first time ever and at the specific request of conference participants, e-mail addresses are included along with the mailing addresses of those who attended the conference. In short, the ways we work and communicate have been changed forever, and this change has had a major impact on library instruction.

Carol Tenopir, our keynote speaker, addressed the changes that electronic resources have made on the reference area and on instruction activities. Her research indicated that technology has resulted in a busier reference area with more ad hoc teaching, and consequently an increased work load as well as a strengthened instructional role for reference. While stress and burnout have become more likely, the increased teaching role also has made librarians' jobs "livelier" and "more fun"!

Diane Nahl discussed guidelines for doing this instruction in the new technological/electronic environment which were based on several research studies including her own. While much of her talk presented the theory on which these guidelines are based, she also gave a list of specific recommendations that can be put into immediate practical use.

Not all change in instruction is a result of technology, however. New ways of teaching and learning such as cooperative learning are being explored and used. We at the LOEX Conference had the opportunity to experience a morning-long workshop on this method of learning presented very successfully by four able practitioners, Lori Arp, Sharon Mader, Lizabeth Wilson, and Mary Jane Petrowski. We all wondered just how successful "active" learning would be in a large ballroom with 180 participants, but the results were overwhelmingly positive. We came away having experienced cooperative learning and with considerable knowledge for incorporating it into our teaching.

As always, our main speakers were supplemented and enhanced by an array of excellent short sessions. These sessions ranged from graphic design to the Internet, each demonstrating the wide spectrum of change propelled by technology from desktop publishing to World Wide Web. Six excellent poster sessions completed a full and lively conference, which was, for the first time in several years, away from Ypsilanti in Racine, Wisconsin. Thanks are due our Wisconsin hosts from the University of Wisconsin-Parkside and Carthage College for helping to make this an excellent conference.

Linda Shirato
Director

IMPACTS OF ELECTRONIC REFERENCE ON INSTRUCTION AND REFERENCE

Carol Tenopir

Two years ago a librarian colleague and I started surveying academic research libraries to find out how the growing use of electronic reference sources has affected the jobs of librarians.[1] Although we didn't focus on instruction librarians in particular, many of our responses came from instruction librarians or from reference librarians with instructional duties. We used a mailed questionnaire, followed up with several rounds of in-person or telephone interviews. Many people have continued to contact me with updated information or stories about their experiences.

Not surprisingly, in this survey and subsequent follow-ups we found many different types of impacts both in the day-to-day jobs and in the perceived roles of the librarians. We also found things that have not changed.

We found impacts or changes in budgeting and in collection development procedures, more emphasis on software evaluation and design, the addition of a new set of technician duties such as changing ink cartridges and fixing jammed printers, rearrangement of physical workspace, and so forth. We found no change in the concern for stretching budget dollars as far as possible, for choosing the best resources for the collection, and for providing the best possible service for the greatest number of people with limited staff and limited hours.

But, by far, the most profound (and I think the most interesting) impacts came in the instructional role and duties of the public services librarians.

Instructional librarians know that, but judging from the responses I got to our articles, many administrators, database producers, and librarians in other parts of the library do not realize it.

One university library director expressed surprise that electronic reference sources didn't solve the instructional "problem," as he called it; a head of public services, while recognizing the importance of instruction with electronic resources, thought perhaps the solution was to focus on just one or two options (such as CD-ROM, for example) and let someone else on campus or other libraries cope with other electronic options; more than one database producer or software vendor offered the solution of purchasing only their products or their search software.

Instructional and reference librarians realize that there is not one easy answer. You also realize, I think, that instruction with electronic resources is not so much a *problem*, but an opportunity. An opportunity to reach more students, faculty, and other users than ever before, an opportunity to try new methods, an opportunity to get out of any instructional ruts you may have found yourselves in.

Of course opportunity means change, or at least examining what you do and how you do it with the possibility of change. Any type of change means a certain amount of stress.

Tenopir was professor, School of Library and Information Studies, University of Hawaii at Manoa. She is now professor, School of Information Sciences, University of Tennessee.

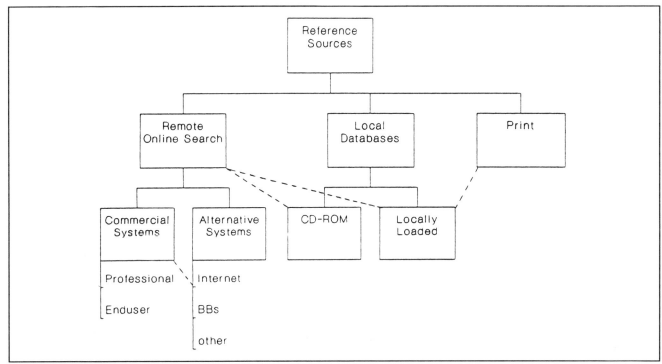

Figure 1: Reference Options

I would like to share with you some of the data, plus reactions, comments, and ideas that I have gathered from your colleagues around the country. What electronic options are being used? How is electronic reference changing instruction (and how is it not)? What does that mean in your daily jobs as well as in your future role? How are some of you adjusting?

Let me also say that you don't always offer the same options, have the same approach, or agree about what is the best approach. I can offer you no one *right* answer—because there isn't one. But by sharing what others are doing and feeling perhaps you can rethink what is right for you and your library.

I have separated my remarks into two parts: first factual information on electronic options, and second comments and reactions to the impact on library instruction and reference services. Factual information shows why instruction has gotten more complex (not necessarily more difficult) in the last few years.

In our survey and in other surveys of different types of libraries, the pace at which electronic reference is taking hold becomes evident in the many options now available that were added in the last decade or two.

Figure 1 shows the three main reference options—remote online, local databases, and print—in libraries today.[2] Remote online services, those services where the information itself is housed in another location that you get access to by dialing in, can be split into commercial systems and what I've called alternative systems.

Commercial systems can be those for the intermediary searcher or professional in the workplace (such as DIALOG, BRS, and EPIC) and those for end-users (such as BRS/After Dark, FirstSearch, CompuServe, Prodigy, and America Online). Some can fit in either box (such as Dow Jones News/Retrieval or Mead) depending on how they are being used.

Alternative online systems include the many information resources created by libraries and universities that are accessible over the Internet, bulletin boards, and other often free state or local options. In Hawaii, for example, we have a service called FYI that provides access to all the state legislative actions and many other state procedural documents.

On the other main branch are local databases—meaning the library or user purchases or leases the information in electronic form and brings it inhouse. You have the responsibility for providing adequate hardware for the data and you pay for it upfront for usually unlimited use. The two main local access options are, of course, CD-ROM and locally loaded tapes.

Actually, the boundaries between options are not as clear as implied in an organizational chart. Internet can be used as a method to access commercial services; CD-ROM databases are connected through networks so branch libraries or dial-in users can access them remotely; print gets scanned and made available online or CD; locally loaded tapes may be put up on an OPAC accessible over Internet so even separate library systems can access other libraries' local databases remotely.

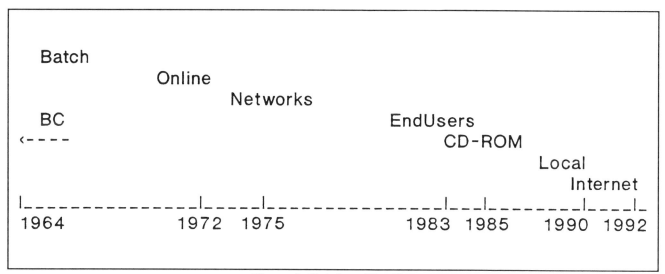

Figure 2: Database Timeline

What is remote for you is local for someone else. Look for more blurring of lines in the future as we all try to maximize access opportunities.

It is helpful to put all of this into historical context to see where we've come from and maybe where we are going. A database searching timeline, as seen in figure 2, can help with both.[3]

Everything before 1964 we can call BC (before computers) or "The Age of Print." Electronic reference began on a small scale almost thirty years ago with the National Library of Medicine's development of the Medlars system. Medlars was first available for batch searching in 1964: some of you may have a hard time imagining the process of submitting a search request in writing to NLM, then waiting a week or two to finally get a printout of citations on your topic.

This changed to interactive online like we know today in the early 1970s with NLM, DIALOG, and ORBIT, the first publicly available remote online systems. Online searching became much more common after the first packet-switching networks such as Tymnet became available in 1975. Online users no longer had to make a long distance call, so online began to get a bit more affordable.

For its first ten years of development, online was pretty much the domain of librarians and other professional searchers as intermediaries (with some exceptions in the workplace, such as lawyers). The first active marketing to widespread numbers of end-users came in the early 1980s (after IBM introduced the PC) with systems like CompuServe, BRS/AfterDark, and Knowledge Index.

CD-ROM came on the scene starting in 1985 and local loading of database tapes took off in a big way just a few years ago. Internet is the online phenomenon growing the most right now. Although Internet has been

around in one form or another almost as long as commercial online, it wasn't until just about a year ago, when Internet was opened up to a wide user community, that it began to have a profound impact.

What is interesting about this timeline is that, with the exception of batch searching, none of the options disappears when a new one comes on the scene. The new options just get piled up on top of the older ones and all become part of the information access scene.

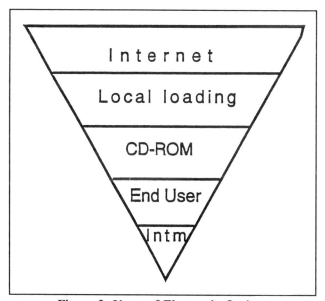

Figure 3: Users of Electronic Options

Actually it is more like an upside-down pyramid in terms of the number of users or number of people affected by each option (see figure 3). The newer electronic options affect many more people and are expanding electronic information access to tens of thousands and even millions (and perhaps should be

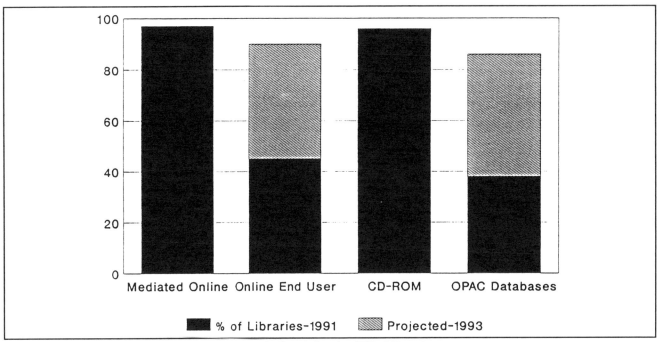

Figure 4: Searching in ARL Libraries

occupying a larger percentage of your instructional efforts, although they don't seem to yet).

Research libraries are often the leaders in implementing new things. Members of the Association of Research Libraries (ARL) are often early and enthusiastic adopters of new technologies. In research libraries, as you would expect, multiple electronic options are the rule. Figure 4 shows that in mid-1991 97 percent offered intermediary online, 96 percent offered CD-ROM, 45 percent offered end-user online, and 38 percent offered locally loaded databases. An additional 48 percent planned to have locally loaded databases up by mid-1993.[4] This survey was conducted before OCLC FirstSearch and before the heavy involvement in Internet that there is now, so I suspect the end-user online is now up with the others (or should be.)

Although the amount of emphasis on some of these options such as intermediary online may go down as new options are added, very few libraries have eliminated or are seriously thinking of eliminating options.

The American Library Association gathers statistics from all types of academic ibraries, as shown in figure 5.[5] Although fewer libraries support all of the electronic options found in academic research libraries, there is still an impressive variety of options in libraries from two-year colleges to Ph.D.-granting institutions. The Public Library Association gathers statistics for public library systems broken down by size of user population and overall.[6] Figure 6 summarizes the overall numbers for use of electronic reference options.

It is harder to get good numbers for special and for school libraries. Special libraries have long been the biggest users of commercial online systems, and many use the other electronic reference options as well, but in smaller numbers. School libraries are enthusiastic users of CD-ROM and are a fast growing segment of online use (but they account for very little in terms of online revenues).

As I said in the May 1992 *Online* magazine, "The bottom line is not surprising: *more* electronic reference options are being added in libraries and are being used by *many more* library patrons, to conduct a *greater* number of searches, resulting in retrieval of a *much greater* amount of information."[7]

How is the increasing diversity of options affecting instructional and reference librarians? Our follow-up interviews identified many impacts. All quotes given here are from the survey and follow-up interviews.[8]

The comments on impacts can be separated into two instructional areas:

1)   point-of-use instruction; and
2)   formal bibliographic instruction classes.

The first thing that almost everyone told us in our surveys is that the reference area where the workstations are has become busier. Most say that the reference desk is busier as well.

The increase in point-of-use instruction is almost all due to one technology: CD-ROM. The need for developing (and sometimes interpreting) customized printed instructions (that SOME people use), more time required to help each new user not only to get started but often throughout the search, and troubleshooting

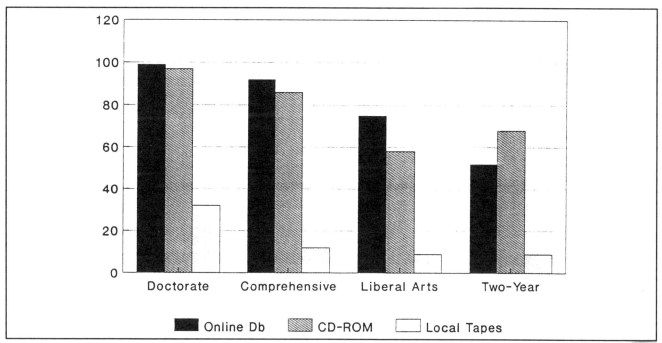

Figure 5: Academic Libraries

hardware and searching problems make the hours on the reference desk fly by!

Part of that has to do with the still relative newness of CD-ROM for many users. One librarian said, "I spend a lot more time answering CD-ROM questions as opposed to paper index questions, because I spend more time explaining things pertaining to CD-ROM such as Boolean, what is an index, etc. I assume people have used paper indexes, but perhaps not CD-ROM."

That is an impact that will certainly change over time as more public libraries and school libraries have more CD-ROMs. It is certainly in the best interests of academic and special libraries to encourage libraries and electronic resources in schools.

Already, after a few years with CD-ROM some librarians find that people are doing more independently. (A librarian from a private technical university told us, "Our users are quite sophisticated computer and database users...they don't need too much handholding...Most prefer searching on their own." In her case requests for help had decreased with increased CD-ROM use.)

But be careful. In the library mentioned above, the traffic in the reference area and the use of materials have gone up dramatically, even though the users aren't requesting much help. Another library admitted to us that CD-ROM hasn't had much of an impact on instruction *or* on the business of the library because "We haven't really pushed public access to many of the CD-ROMs. Nobody in the library seems to be able to figure them out." What people don't know about

they can't use and what the library staff can't figure out they may be reluctant to let others know about.

But back to the majority that are finding more time spent on point-of-use reference with CD-ROM. In some cases there may be more users and more questions, but in most it is that librarians are spending more time with each individual. One library that felt particularly busy found that the number of reference questions went up just 1.5/hour, but it seemed like much more to the staff because they spent more time with each questioner.

This taking of more time with each user of CD-ROM indexes was found to be true in many libraries. Instructional librarians often stay with a user until a search is complete or at least until the user has retrieved a manageably sized set. Although it takes more time for each question, from an instructional viewpoint some very positive things have been happening.

According to one librarian: "CD-ROM has increased my workload, because instead of paper I send them to CD-ROM. Now it is more important to find out what they need—I don't want to overwhelm students." "We are guiding/assisting the students more, because the technology has forced us to do that."

Another said, "I tend to spend more time helping people with the CD-ROMs, I think because it is technology-based, but actually people using paper sources need more help because they have less success. Now I see that I should have spent much more time with the students at the paper index, while now, I think most of us take the time at the CD-ROM to see what the results of the students' searches are."

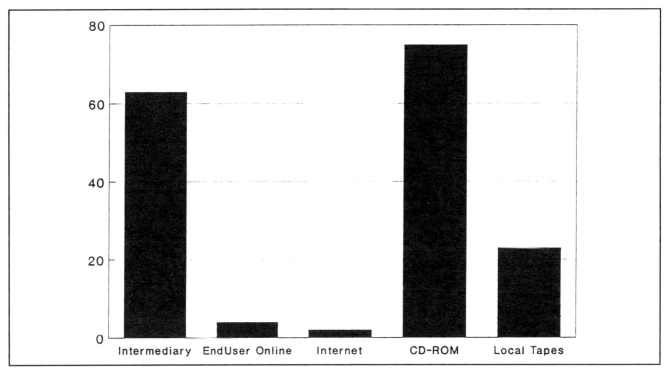

Figure 6: Public Libraries

The instructional role at reference has been strengthened. These librarians feel technology helped get them out of a bad habit of assuming everyone was getting satisfactory results once they had been directed to a resource or taught the rudiments of its use.

This leads to another fairly raging debate about point-of-use instruction. Besides having good printed materials or on-screen tutorials (that people may or may not use), what is the librarian's obligation to help or instruct those users who don't actually ask for help or instruction? Last year I wrote one of my most popular *Library Journal* columns, titled "Is It Any of Our Business?," after one respondent to our survey wrote some very thought-provoking comments questioning just this.[9]

You probably can all relate tales like that of the Sociofile searcher looking through over 11,000 hits for the search term "children" for those few on parental authority; or of the ERIC user searching for "schools and drug-truncated" and printing out all 800 citations on the library-supplied printer and paper.

If users are satisfied, the argument goes that it is not our business to interfere or to impose our notion of effective searching. Some librarians argue that since we have never worried about how good the strategies are when people are using printed resources, why should we start with electronic?

The fact is that with electronic resources it is much easier to do a really bad (and more time-consuming or more paper-consuming) search than it is with paper. Just because we have failed some users in the past with paper resources, it is no excuse to continue to fail users.

So it is our business, but up to a point. You all know better than I that you can't shove help down an unwilling throat. Some people will flee at the first approach of an authority figure. Peer tutors help in some cases, but not in all. Increasingly those reticent to ask for or take help if offered never even have to set foot in the library. There is a huge and growing group of users librarians never see.

Locally loaded databases and access to Internet are having much less impact on point-of-use instruction than CD-ROM. This is for two main reasons: 1) many users are accessing these systems from remote locations (almost all research libraries have dial-in access to OPAC and databases on it so users aren't the captives of the library building anymore), and 2) the interface to get to these resources is often consistent (even if the search system when you reach a remote site isn't) and users find it easier to get started. With Internet, another reason is that in many cases the users just don't think it has anything to do with librarians or libraries.

The lack of impact is most certainly *not* because of what several respondents to our follow-up surveys told us when they said "not that many people are using these dial-up databases" because "most people are not willing to explore." Usage figures show quite the opposite. These resources are indeed being used and they are being used thousands or tens of thousands of times per week.

Not many libraries offer the opportunity to ask questions while remotely connected. Very few users will hang up, dial a reference department, and ask a question (especially in the middle of the night). More libraries need to rethink this role of point-of-use reference for remote systems. I'm glad to see that a few libraries are adding SOS services modeled after the EasyNet gateway's service where a librarian will immediately respond to an SOS command typed in by a user.[10] More libraries need to do this.

Better modeling of reference interactions into software design will help as well. With CD-ROM the librarian who saw the user reading through thousands of citations could offer to help; for locally loaded databases the software should offer to help. Design of better software that incorporates more of the librarian is becoming an important part of the instruction librarian's role.

Formal instruction is less reactive and more proactive than individualized point-of-use and more under the librarian's control in terms of content. All of the librarians we talked to have changed their formal instruction; in most cases they now spend the bulk of class time on CD-ROM, locally loaded databases, end-user online, and/or Internet instruction. All of these options may be incorporated into one comprehensive class or special short courses may cover only one or two options at a time.

Some libraries have taken another tact and have eliminated formal instruction. Let me elaborate on both of these approaches to change. There are three main ways formal instruction has changed. These are: 1) content of instruction; 2) facilities for instruction; and 3) effectiveness of instruction.

Almost all of you have rethought what content should be in instruction. The big debate here seems to fall between teaching procedural things (how does this software work, what keys do I press to do a search on this system) vs. searching conceptual things (effective search strategy, Boolean logic, how to choose an appropriate database).

As with most things in life a balance of both seems to be best. One librarian told us, "I first teach the basic features of the software and the use of the equipment; then I teach them concepts, Boolean, and thinking creatively about terms." Not every software package or even every option can be taught at once; people simply cannot remember that much detail.

Also, teaching every feature of every software package is counterproductive at best. Students need enough practical information to get them started and then follow-up classes, reference assistance. Good written instructions take over from there as the need arises.

Most respondents agree that effectiveness of content absolutely relies on hands-on practice. Enough to get them started includes supervised hands-on practice of basics. This requires adequate facilities.

The best facilities include a lab where student pairs can do the hands-on as part of the instruction. More than one librarian commented, "We are beginning to set up a classroom-kind of arrangement for the CD-ROM and OPAC terminals. We will be able to do more and more hands-on instruction, where you can immediately find out what the problems are."

Lots of hands-on exercises, a mix of concepts and practical aspects, and direct student involvement are improving bibliographic instruction for these students and for the librarians. Words I hear are "livelier," "more interactive," "easier," "better," "more effective," and, last but not least, "more fun."

There are a few librarians who say electronic resources make instruction obsolete. One who feels this way is in a library with no special facilities for instruction and no access to a lab with workstations for instruction. Rather than trying to do instructional classes with no hands-on, she decided to stop formal classes altogether.

Another feels students do better if they ask questions when they really need the information. This goes for printed instructional materials as well. One says, "We offer a minimum of printed and verbal instructions. With things changing so fast, what's the point of wasting time teaching people how to do this and that?" These seem to be minority opinions.

Even without a big laboratory, though, instructional librarians are making classes livelier. With just one workstation, some are doing interactive demonstrations where the students pose questions and the librarian searches. Others have students work in pairs with paper and pencil and print thesauruses to develop a search strategy. Then, in turn, each pair searches their topic for the class. Instructional materials include many practice exercises as well as short cheat sheets for various software.

I've talked a lot about what has changed, but what hasn't changed? The fundamental nature of the role and responsibility of the reference and instructional librarian has not changed, as many librarians told us. "The basic concepts of reference service have not changed; the *format* of the sources has" and "How we interact with the patrons hasn't really changed. We try to help the individual at the desk and the group in classes, where we emphasize that they should come back to the desk for more help."

The methods may be different, but the responsibilities are the same—it is just a whole lot more fun for everyone concerned!

Notes

1. Carol Tenopir and Ralf Neufang, "Electronic Reference Options: How They Stack Up in Research Libraries," *Online* 16:2 (1992): 22-28 and Carol Tenopir and Ralf Neufang, "The Impact of Electronic Reference on Reference Librarians," *Online* 16:3 (1992): 54-60.

2. Carol Tenopir, "Choices for Electronic Reference," *Library Journal* 118:12 (July 1993): 52,54.

3. Tenopir, "Choices for Electronic Reference." For another timeline, see Charles T. Meadow, "Online Database Industry Timeline," *Database* 11:5 (1988): 23-31.

4. Tenopir and Neufang, "Electronic Reference Options."

5. Mary Jo Lynch, project director, *Alternative Sources of Revenue in Academic Libraries* (Chicago: ALA, 1991) 10-11.

6. Public Library Association, *Public Library Data Service Statistical Report '92* (Chicago: ALA, 1992), 133-163.

7. Tenopir and Neufang, "Impact of Electronic Reference" 54.

8. Tenopir and Neufang, "Impact of Electronic Reference."

9. Carol Tenopir, "Is It Any of Our Business?" *Library Journal* 117:6 (1 April 1992): 96,98.

10. Cynthia Schoenbrun, "EasyNet: What Has Become of the Small Giant?" *Online* 17:1 (1993): 52-56.

GUIDELINES FOR CREATING USER-CENTERED INSTRUCTIONS FOR NOVICE END-USERS

Diane Nahl

Today it is common to find complex information retrieval systems in academic libraries, and we are faced with the prospect of increased numbers of novice end-users who need instruction. The new challenge for BI librarians, brought on by the technological environment, is how to deal with an entirely new species of search behavior. When you wander around the terminals you can hear people talking to the computer, saying things like:

- Why can't I print?
- Do I have my own printer?
- Why am I getting a disc error message?
- Why is this taking so long?
- Oh, NO, zero again!
- Oh, NO, 640, I don't want that many!
- How does this thing work?
- Can't I search just one newspaper?

In this technological, and even technophobic, environment, each system has different interfaces for conducting searches, with different types of search capabilities, commands, and screen layouts, among other things. Librarians in academic libraries everywhere are being deluged with requests from people using the system for on-the-spot instruction. Individualized instruction at the terminal can take on the average 20 minutes per searcher.[1] Despite well-designed course-

Nahl is assistant professor, School of Library and Information Studies, University of Hawaii.

integrated instruction, live interactive demos, hands-on practice exercises, and workshops, novice end-users still need help during their own searches.

THE SEARCHER'S MICRO-INFORMATION NEEDS

The help users need while searching involves micro-information needs about how to search and how to interpret search results. If one studies the search process, the magnitude of these micro-information needs becomes apparent. In one study,[2] we asked 10 novice searchers to think aloud while they searched a full-text magazine database, so that we could study their decision-making strategies and relevance judgments. We tape recorded them as they searched and spoke their thoughts out loud. These searchers were faculty, graduate students in other fields, and undergraduates. Over a period of three weeks, they each spent a total of about five hours searching in the full-text magazine database. To prepare them for this experience, we designed a 2.5-hour hands-on training session and trained five to six searchers at a time in the sessions. Then they scheduled themselves and were allowed to search for anything they wanted. We had graduate student monitors on hand to help them out of difficulties, to answer questions, to tape record the searchers' comments throughout their searches, and to print out a transaction log, which served as a permanent record of the searchers' actions that went along with their tape-recorded verbalizations.

We discovered, among other things, that despite the 2.5-hour hands-on training session, these searchers addressed the monitor with an average of 53 questions per hour, mostly about how to use the system for a given purpose. They actually asked around 90 questions the first hour, and around 20 questions in their final hour of searching. Still, for the five sessions combined, they asked on the average a question almost every minute, despite the 2.5 hours of training. As Dervin[3] points out, questions that derive from situations that people find themselves in represent information needs, and that gives us an additional direction for BI: the questions searchers have about how to search represent *micro-information needs* that instruction could respond to.

Using an online search tool generates a large quantity of new micro-information needs related to

- advice on how to use the system;

- help in translating a query into a search statement;

- explanations on finding information both in records and on screens;

- developing a conceptual model of what the system is designed to do;

- understanding Boolean search logic;

- information on what topics the database contains; and

- reassurances that the searchers are "doing it right."

There is thus a magnitude of difference in the options for searching electronically versus searching in print. To me this means that, in the technological search environment, we need to discover exactly what type of online instruction is needed, at what level, and how frequently.

In an interesting study with similar findings, Stewart[4] tape recorded 19 novice searchers interacting with "library staff coaches" while they searched BRS Menus. She discovered that these novices asked an average of 31 questions in one 30-minute coaching session, and that the coaches averaged 250 comments each 30-minute session. The novices asked questions about

- search strategy;
- which database to search for a given topic;
- which vocabulary to use;
- which commands to use;

- advice about printing; and
- advice about reviewing results for relevance and access points.

Stewart[5] also found that feelings of self-confidence as a searcher are important to success in searching because anxiety interferes with the learning process, so that anxious novices have less success than the self-confident novices. Only half of her subjects described themselves as "confident." In a study I did, which is described below,[6] I also found that self-confidence as a searcher is a significant factor in success and in search style.

These findings reveal the complexity of online searching. Sitting down at a search workstation in a library is a fateful act for the searcher who now becomes embroiled in a world of dilemmas, worries, elation, and other intense feelings. The students in Stewart's study were positive about the personalized assistance, but some wanted more control in the interaction so that they could reject some suggestions of the coaches and speed or slow the pace of the search at will. Obviously, independent operation of the system, following one's own voluntary decisions, is the state that searchers find most congenial and rewarding. However, interactive systems seem to encourage impulsivity. Since it is hardly feasible to provide a librarian at the elbow of every novice searcher, BI efforts have gone into the mass development of written point-of-use instructions to give people the information they need at the time they need it, to help guide them in the use of a retrieval system.

HELP IN USING POINT-OF-USE INSTRUCTIONS

When observing end-users searching, I have been struck by their avoidance of available point-of-use instructions and online help. Written instructions are important in the technological information environment, and they will become more important as the information retrieval environment becomes increasingly complex. The growing numbers of remote users of electronic sources must rely on written instructions since there are few online reference librarians to help searchers out of deadends.[7] Why do novice searchers avoid the very source where their questions can be answered? To solve this puzzle, I decided to get some data on this phenomenon.

Library and Information Studies (LIS) students in the library instruction course I teach did an informal field study working with end-users at the University of Hawaii in Hamilton Library's CD-ROM reference area. There are eight workstations on a LAN with 11 databases on the menu from Wilson, SilverPlatter, and

UMI, and other databases on two stand-alone workstations. The LIS students spent over 200 hours as volunteer CD-ROM assistants by stationing themselves near the computers and announcing to the searchers that they were available for help and questions. Part of their class assignment was to keep notes on the questions the searchers asked and the spontaneous evaluative comments users made. Searchers asked questions like:

- Which database do I use?

- I've never used CD-ROM before; can you just do it for me?

- What if I don't know the author's full name?

- Why is there so little on my topic in this database?

- Just what is this thing good for?

- But how can I print just this one record?

- How can I find articles about patent rights in Japan?

- How do you mark records in ERIC?

- How do you return to the main menu?

- Does the database tell you if Hamilton Library has the journal?

- How do you get to a specific record in sociofile?

One interesting finding is that end-users needed instruction in how to incorporate Help screens and written point-of-use instructions into their search repertoire. In other words, we can't just assume that people will know how to make use of Help screens or point-of-use instructions. In fact, they need help in using Help. My students found that Help screens and instructional materials are often quick and useful, but that users have an aversion to accessing them. Perhaps this is due to bad past experiences with such facilities or simply an impulsivity promoted by online interactive systems. In any case, this is an affective information problem that may be related to an emotional symptom of information overload, or the law of least effort in operation.

Part of writing instructions in a technophobic environment should perhaps include statements of encouragement to motivate users to read and consult instructions. Students may be more likely to use these materials if we legitimize Help screens and written

point-of-use instructions by including them in BI sessions and personal instruction at the workstation. The LIS students discovered that it was not enough to make the point-of-use instructions available by pointing them out or mentioning them; they must be integrated into the search process. We also discovered that, despite the fact that the end-users were making errors, having difficulty using the various search systems, and despite their openly expressed frustration, they did not ask for help. Even those who needed it but said they didn't want help did not look at the written instructions or the online Help instructions. They were making major errors, such as trying to combine two set numbers in SilverPlatter without using the #, so they were caught in very long searches that retrieved a jumble of topics.

It is apparent that in a technophobic environment, searchers need instruction in how to use Help facilities and point-of-use instructions. Although point-of-use instructions are available in most academic libraries, a search of the literature revealed few studies on the efficacy of written point-of-use instructions or of the online Help facilities that are available on many CD-ROM and online retrieval systems.

EFFICACY OF POINT-OF-USE INSTRUCTIONS

Bostian and Robbins[8] did a study of the effectiveness of different forms and quantities of CD-ROM instruction with 93 students who all searched the same question. One group only received access to the written documentation published by the database producer. Another group was given, in addition to that, printed point-of-use instructions. A third group had, in addition to written plus point-of-use, a lecture on search strategy; and a fourth group had all of that, plus a live demo of the database, so that the last group had the most instruction. This last group was the only one that differed significantly in satisfaction, search strategy, and use of written instructions. Bostian and Robbins[9] tallied the number of printed search aids used by all of the groups. On the average, they used fewer than one aid per person. In other words, the typical student did not use any of the available instructions. The groups that received the most instruction were the least likely to use the printed instructions. The groups with the most instruction may have had a false sense of security about their knowledge of searching, or may have learned enough to become independent searchers. In either case, we are reminded once again that searchers who need instructions fail to use them if left on their own.

Bucknall and Mangrum[10] surveyed 1,135 library users on their CD-ROM use, including their use of written point-of-use instructions. About 21 percent (225) of users reported that they had used printed instructions, and only 8 percent (88) had used Help to assist them with their searches, so that 313 in all used written instructions. About 25 percent used experimentation and only 5 percent said they had no problems. The point-of-use instructions answered the commonly asked questions about the CD-ROM databases, and the authors were expecting the written instructions to reduce the traffic at the reference desk, but 40 percent of users (410) routinely asked the librarians for help. In other words, roughly one out of three users look at instructions if available, one out of four experiment on their own, and most of the rest consult a librarian. Thus, written instructions do help a significant proportion of the user population, about 1 in 3, but they are undervalued by the majority of end-users and need to be changed and be incorporated into BI sessions in order to reach more searchers.

Markey[11] did a study of online and offline user assistance for online catalog searchers. She found that all of the 33 libraries in the survey provided printed instructions or brochures for the catalog, along with personal assistance from librarians. When she asked end-users in six libraries how they learned to use the catalog, 37 percent said they had used printed instructions, and 14 percent used the instructions on the screen. So, in this case 51 percent of searchers were able to learn by using the written instructions. Markey[12] makes suggestions on how to prepare useful printed materials, which have since been incorporated by many BI librarians. Appendix A summarizes her suggestions.

Naismith and Stein[13] did a test of the popular handouts in their library. They studied how well students could comprehend the library terms used in printed instructions and guides and in reference interviews. Their study included terms such as: "citation," "microform," "search term," "catalog screen," "online database searches," "search statement," "command search," "online catalog," and others. They constructed a multiple choice quiz of the words and definitions. Out of 20 terms, the students answered half (10) correctly. Think about this: half of the terms we normally use in instructions are without meaning to the users!

Naismith and Stein subsequently tested another group of students by asking them to think aloud as they tried to answer the questions. They discovered that people used a number of strategies to figure out definitions for unfamiliar terms. Most students relied on existing mental schemas, and in many cases these were unsuccessful. For instance,

• A citation is like a traffic ticket that involves a fine; or

• Interlibrary loan means you can go there and borrow books.

Naismith and Stein make recommendations for improving instructional materials and the language of interviewing. These recommendations are designed to help close the 50 percent communication gap that they have identified. They present these options in a list from least to most accommodating to library users. Examples include

• use terms without defining them (that's the least accommodating);

• use terms without defining them, but be alert to verbal and non-verbal cues indicating confusion (that is a little more accommodating to the user);

• define terms the first time they are used (still more accommodating); and

• avoid jargon altogether (that's supposed to be the most accommodating to users).

They present other intervening steps not listed here. They acknowledge that neither end of the continuum is ideal, and that the intermediate options may be useful in different situations with different types of searchers. However, their study reveals that it is important to test instructional materials to discover whether they are suitable and comprehensible to users, and why they are effective or ineffective in helping end-users become independent searchers.

AFFECTIVE AND COGNITIVE BEHAVIORS OF NOVICE SEARCHERS

Ensor[14] studied how much library users at all levels understood about how to do keyword searching in an online catalog. Her survey listed 10 statements that were *true* about keyword searching, and her 400 subjects either agreed or disagreed with each statement. On the average, these subjects answered about 43 percent of the statements correctly. Only 2 of the 10 statements received 50 percent agreement.[15] She cites other studies that found similar low levels of online search knowledge. Those who knew the most had used online help or had library instruction sessions. Incidentally, the faculty received the lowest knowledge scores. The data in my study with novice CD-ROM users show that after reading the point-of-use instructions, students were able to answer 55 percent of the 30 questions they needed to know to use the Wilson search software.[16]

Currently, written instructions contribute moderately to search knowledge and to success. We need to discover exactly what information users have trouble assimilating and applying to the search task. Ensor[17] found that the more satisfied end-users were with keyword search results, the more likely they were to answer correctly on the true/false knowledge quiz. In Markey's interview data,[18] end-users discussed what they would have liked the system to do; for example:

- When I have retrieved a lot of items, the computer would say, "Do you really want to know all about the United States or are you just looking for a state or a region?"

- After you've done a step, it could print out what you should do next.

In BI, we try to teach people search strategy so that they can ask themselves these questions as they proceed in their searches, but these comments reflect the need for specific answers at particular stages in the search process. The novice end-user needs personal assistance to solve very specific search problems.

The LIS students mentioned earlier, who volunteered to assist novice CD-ROM users, summarized their observations within the three behavioral domains identified in educational psychology: affective, cognitive, and sensorimotor behaviors.[19] Affective behaviors involve the searcher's emotional and motivational reactions to the informational demands of the technological environment. For example, getting through the steps of a search requires persistence to continue to exert the effort to stick with the task. Persisting at the search task, wanting to print something, and being careful to avoid typos are examples of affective behaviors.

One LIS student observed that a user was having trouble in a Wilson database but was unwilling to budge from Browse mode. The LIS student tried to show the person how to use Wilsearch to combine terms, but the person refused saying "No, no, this is fine, thanks." Being unwilling to change from what you are used to when it does not work is an affective error. Cultivating a willingness to learn new ways of searching is an affective skill. Another affective error that is commonly observed is users who feel that they are not competent enough and want to turn the keyboard over to the librarian to type in the appropriate commands for them. Acquiring the desire for mastery and the confidence to want to do it independently is an affective skill.

Cognitive behaviors involve the searcher's knowledge and decision making throughout the search activity. For example, in order to limit a set that is too large, a decision must be made on several available alternatives such as using more specific search terms, limiting by date, or limiting by language. Acting on a wrong assumption is a cognitive error. In one situation, a user hit every key trying to find the one to tell her if the library subscribed to the journal for the citation she found. Although this function is now being added to information retrieval systems, knowing that libraries have listings of the journals subscribed to is a cognitive skill. Another very common cognitive error is known as the conjunction fallacy. This occurs when a user ANDs too many words in a long string yielding an empty set, and then adds another term in order to retrieve more articles. The cognitive skill here involves thinking in Boolean. This is further discussed below.

Sensorimotor behaviors involve the searcher's sensory awareness and motor coordination. Examples of sensorimotor behaviors include perceiving where the cursor is currently located on the screen, finding information on screens, finding a needed explanation in the instructions, or operating the keyboard. When users hit the return key repeatedly because the screen seems stuck, they then have to sit through the display of the screen being refreshed over and over again. This is a sensorimotor error that could be remedied by inhibiting all finger movements during waiting time. Another common sensorimotor error is not looking at the screen when hitting the return key, so that the searcher is unaware of what action has taken place.

CONTENT ANALYSIS OF POINT-OF-USE INSTRUCTIONS

I analyzed a sample of CD-ROM instructions used in academic libraries that I requested from LOEX. I used the three behavioral domains to guide my analysis to see how instruction is provided for each domain. The purpose was to come up with an inventory (though not a complete one) of instructional speech acts commonly used in CD-ROM library instructions. "Speech acts" is a concept I am borrowing from philosophy of language and the field communications.[20] The idea is that an instructional sentence is an exchange between writer and reader and functions as a social act. I categorized the sentences in some of the LOEX sample. My purpose was not to develop a complete catalog of CD-ROM instructional speech acts but to inspect a range of them for the purpose of constructing a continuum without specifying all of the steps on it. Some examples include:

- Cognitive speech acts

define terminology and

explain the meaning of Boolean.

- Affective speech acts

alert users to check command statements for typos and

warn that library does not subscribe to every journal retrieved in a search.

I was interested in investigating the efficacy of two types of written point-of-use instructions for Wilson's Readers' Guide Abstract database. What emerged from my study is a more detailed view of what novices must face when sitting down at a search workstation. Becoming a searcher for a few minutes is to enter a dynamic world of interrelated concerns that must be solved. These concerns stem from the interactive technology itself. It's as if you came to a forest where someone has hidden a small object, which you must find by following some rules and tips. These rules are fairly complex, and some of them are hard to figure out. You are therefore searching with a handicap, without knowing how to follow all of the rules.

THE NOVICE SEARCHER'S DYNAMIC WORLD

The findings of the study reveal some of the factors in this dynamic world of searchers. They include success, satisfaction, frustration or stress, self-confidence as a searcher, helpfulness and clarity of point-of-use instructions, use of available search modes, number of strategies attempted per query, and total number of search moves. Note that in figure 1 there are seven layers of micro-information structure in the searcher's environment. This is as detailed as I can picture it now, and I have at least some findings in each layer. Beginning with the outer layer, SEARCH QUERY (layer 1), shows that the structure of the query derives from the searcher's INFORMATION NEED, which itself is grounded in CULTURAL TOPICS. The entry point to this connection is PRESEARCH REFOR-MULATION of the query, either with or without help from librarians or instructional interfaces. Query reformulation takes place through the language of SUBJECT HEADINGS and INDEXES as they are organized by disciplines into a THESAURUS or other structured list containing CROSS-REFERENCES, or through key natural language terms (layer 2).

The third layer (3) is made up of the SEARCH SOFTWARE, which is designed to aid recovery of a record through INFORMATION RETRIEVAL TECH-NIQUES, which require interactive decision making regarding selection of SEARCH MODE or other OPTIONS, such as SEARCHABLE FIELDS and various available SHORTCUTS. This also requires the use of LOGICAL and PROXIMITY OPERATORS and special features like TRUNCATION. Layer 4, as we proceed inward toward the searcher, concerns TEACH-ING METHODS used in the POINT-OF-USE IN-STRUCTIONS FOR SEARCH SOFTWARE, or other ONLINE HELP facilities, including bottom-of-the-screen option lines. What these teaching methods should be and how to write more effective user-centered instructions are two issues that my research has addressed.

Note that as we come to layer 5 we are reaching the limits of the searcher's boundary as an individual. My findings led me to the principle that point-of-use and other instructions on search software need to address directly and explicitly the layers of concerns that searchers have. Using the taxonomic approach within a behavioral perspective, three layers of the individual searcher are addressed in instruction: the SENSORIMOTOR environment (layer 5), the COGNI-TIVE environment (layer 6), and the AFFECTIVE environment (layer 7). Point-of-use and other instruc-tions (layer 4) address the AFFECTIVE ENVIRON-MENT of the searcher by giving ORIENTING INFOR-MATION, ADVICE, and REASSURANCES that legitimize common errors and bolster self-confidence.

The COGNITIVE ENVIRONMENT of the searcher is addressed in the instructions by providing definitions and explanations. The SENSORIMOTOR environment also needs to be addressed by the instruc-tions as novice users need practice in keyboarding skills and in becoming familiar with screen structures like menu commands, highlighted texts, and other aspects of screen reading ability.

Research shows that search style or INTER-ACTIVITY (the number and type of moves during a search) varies with individuals, even though the same search task or problem is involved. Excessive inter-activity is inefficient and less effective, so it may be that instructions should also address this feature of searchers. The seven layers of the searcher's world constantly interact. In my study of novice searchers of a CD-ROM database, SEARCH MODE (in layer 3) influenced success, but the more SELF-CONFI-DENCE searchers had (layer 7), the more they were successful and satisfied, and the less frustration they experienced.

Table 1 shows that novices who said they thought they could do three search tasks successfully had significantly higher scores in success and satisfaction with the retrievals when they actually did the searches,

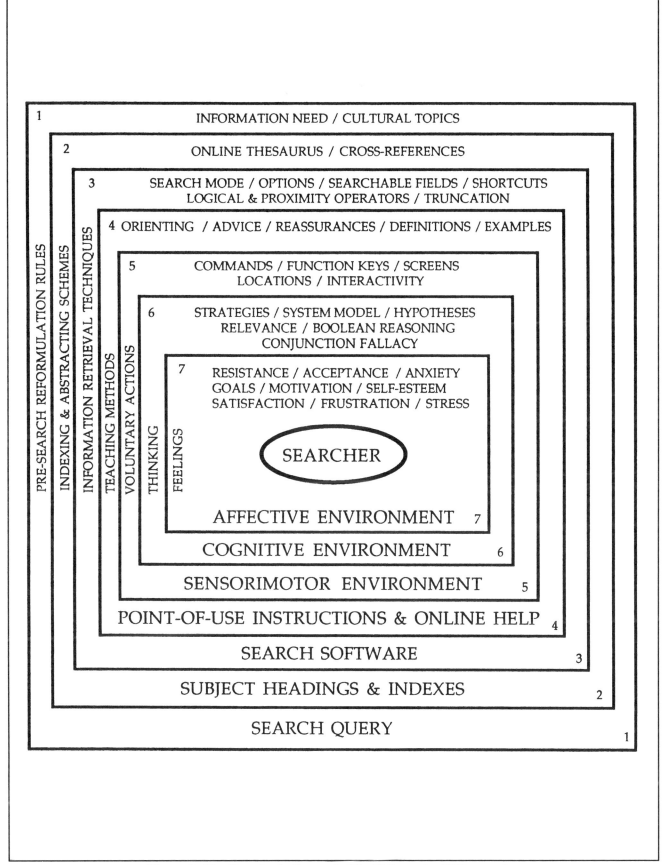

Figure 1: The Searcher's Dynamic World from the BI Perspective

Table 1: Perceived Self-Efficacy and Interactivity[1]

"I Think I Can Do 3 Tasks Successfully"	Mean for those saying Yes	Mean for those saying No	Significance F** p < .05
Overall success (all tasks and conditions) (max. =2)	1.3	0.8	19.9**
Satisfaction (all tasks) (max. =28)	17.6	11.9	23.9**
Frustration (all tasks) (max. =7)	3.3	4.0	3.1, p=.08
Number of conceptual moves (all 4 tasks)	24.6	32.6	5.2**
Number of strategies (all 4 tasks)	13.7	16.9	4.3**
Elapsed Time (all 4 tasks)	5.4	7.6	21.3**
Helpfulness ratings of instructions (max. =28)	19.5	16.2	8.4**

NOTE

1. Diane Nahl-Jakobovits, *CD-ROM Point-of-Use Instructions for Novice Searchers: A Comparison of User-Centered Affectively Elaborated and Unelaborated Text*. Ph.D. diss., 212. University of Hawaii, 1993.

and they had lower frustration scores during searching. At the same time, they were less interactive, used fewer conceptual moves and fewer strategies, and spent less time searching. They were thus *more efficient*, even though they were not more experienced.

Self-confident novices found the point-of-use instructions significantly more helpful than those who doubted their ability to do three searches successfully. This implies that if we intend to improve the search style of novices, we should turn our attention to the problem of building self-confidence in online search instruction sessions, and in written point-of-use instructions and Help facilities.

There are certain problems novices have that need particular attention. For instance, a pernicious problem for novice searchers is the CONJUNCTION FALLACY (layer 6). Many failures are due to ANDing too many search terms in one search statement. End-users frequently enter a specific phrase of several words, sometimes in sentence form.[21] For example, in my

study, one searcher trying to find "a review of the movie 'Ferngully' about the rainforest," entered

FERNGULLY MOVIES REVIEWS
RAINFOREST ANIMATED

which results in a disappointing announcement on the screen ("zero hits"). The novices are apparently unaware that their strategy of including all of the relevant words they can think of in one statement will have the consequence of reducing to zero the probability of finding a record that contains all of them. This is the conjunction fallacy in operation. The conjunction fallacy has been thoroughly researched in cognitive science and the conclusion is that the Boolean AND requires a reasoning process that must be taught explicitly.[22]

A related problem is the common strategy of entering a single term and retrieving hundreds or thousands of records and proceeding to look through them. Another problem is when novices turn simple search tasks into complex ones leading to less success and satisfaction, more frustration, and longer search times. An active searcher is not necessarily a successful searcher because making more moves than is necessary becomes a handicap.

All of these problems reveal that novices over-extend most of their strategies by using overly general terms, adding too many terms, using too many operators, and trying too many strategies. Explaining Boolean logic is therefore not enough; novices probably need to be taught to think in terms of logical operations before constructing search statements on their own. What might work is explaining it in terms of some metaphor they are already familiar with. For example, ask them to decide which is more likely, finding someone to go on a date with who is *tall*, *dark*, and *handsome* or finding someone who is *tall* and *dark* but not handsome. I am planning to investigate this part of the reasoning process that is so key to successful information retrieval by designing an exercise to teach the Boolean reasoning process, without regard to searching per se, then observing how search strategy is influenced. I think searchers need a workable SYSTEM MODEL (layer 6) or search metaphor which gives them the ability to "think in Boolean."

Saracevic, Mokros, and Su[23] studied 40 online searches with intermediaries and users by recording transaction logs and videotaping the interaction. Their most striking finding is that both the users and the intermediaries paid far greater attention to trying to reduce the size of the sets retrieved than to relevance. They refer to this search strategy as "reductionism" and "magnitude feedback." "Search tactics were reductionist first and precision-oriented second".[24] As they put it, the dread of information overload that searchers feel "makes for a confrontation...to defeat the size at any cost."[25] We need to acknowledge this dynamic in searchers and address it explicitly in BI. Why are many searchers so averse to looking at some retrieved records in a large set? Do they assume they must look through all of them?

Dalrymple[26] compared searchers of a card catalog to those who searched an online catalog and discovered that the reformulation process of translating the user's query into the terms of the system represented an important bottleneck. She recommends that "user supports" deal explicitly with this translation process to help searchers think in system terms. MARCIVE provides such a facility; after typing in a search term, it automatically displays a set of related terms.

WRITING USER-CENTERED DOCUMENTATION

A paradigm shift is taking place in the area of technical writing and user documentation for computer software. The shift is from a system-centered to a user-centered focus. Bradford[27] relates the recent emphasis in documentation on user-processes to the diversification of audiences for microcomputer documentation. As a result, he says,

> writers have begun to abandon the traditional posture and to establish themselves as teachers....We are often expected to encourage and entertain our audience. We are no longer playing technician; we are being forced to play the more appropriate role of educator.[28]

According to Bradford, the elements of the "user-friendly persona" include humor, irony, cartoon graphics, reinforcement, personification, pronoun voice (first vs. second person), and eloquence (analogy and metaphor).

Chavarria[29] warns writers that they need to be friendly without being "patronizing or cute." She refers to the "ease-of-use movement" that stresses

> simplifying messages and error recovery, adding procedures, and using headings and other information locators....This movement has been good for technical publications, because it has reminded us writers to think of the needs of the readers.[30]

She advises writers to consider the characteristics that make dialog friendly, and to apply these to instructional manuals:

- genuineness (the writer's involvement);
- self-revelation (or the writer's "presence");
- supportive psychological climate (tone);
- empathy (addressing readers' perspective);
- nonjudgmental (users are never blamed); and
- equality (vs. the attempt to manipulate).

The key, according to Chavarria, is to communicate a positive attitude in writing, using the following approach (see also appendix 1):

- Do not include information just to impress readers.

- Don't be "impersonal and machine-like in an attempt to sound objective."[31]

- Address users directly ("you").

- Ask them questions within the text.

- Be supportive by making information easy to understand (e.g., by the use of graphics and white space).

- Get to know the audience (their demographics, knowledge, needs, interests).

- Express liking for users: "We must affirm the worth of readers in our tone."[32]

- Avoid making novice users feel left out.

Bradford[33] asserts that "an important function of user-friendly documentation is to relieve anxiety that accompanies the novice's learning the computer or acquiring the synergisms required by a new system." He cautions against the inappropriate use of humor and does not recommend personifying the computer (as when the computer dialog display addresses itself as "I"), since a machine with an electronic brain or personality (complete with ego and motivation) could be seen by novice users as an adversary, rather than a friend. He recommends giving the machine a servant role instead of the role of an expert advisor (which is inauthentic). Neither should writers rely on the traditional conventions in technical writing—the passive voice, denotative diction, the absence of humor or of analogy. According to Bradford, "the alien task and complex hardware should not be described by the disinterested persona if we are to effectively engage the naive audience."[34] Once writers abandon the traditional objective persona, "they become a noticeable presence" and "the appropriateness of that revised persona to their audiences is as crucial to their success as is the accuracy of the information."[35]

In response to the wordiness of technical manuals, Carroll proposed some "General minimalist design tips":[36]

- Cut secondary features (overviews, introductions, summaries).

- Focus on what users need to know in order to immediately apply it to productive work.

- Test repeatedly during design.

- Use pictures of what the screen is supposed to look like so users may easily coordinate the documentation with the screen information.

- Link new information continuously to what users already know.

These suggestions and others from the BI literature are summarized in appendix A. They may prove useful to BI librarians who produce written documentation, Help screens, and point-of-use handouts.

CONCLUSION

One can conclude that point-of-use instructions, online Help facilities, and orientation classes for novices should try to address more directly the searcher's needs occasioned by the technical interface which surrounds the searcher, as the diagram details. Searchers exhibit different patterns in reacting to search results. For instance, some searchers in my study were successful and satisfied, but reported high frustration or stress; on the other hand, some successful searchers reported low frustration; others who were not successful nevertheless reported low frustration or stress. As BI librarians, how do we respond to these findings? Are we to take responsibility for dealing with a searcher's frustration level or whether they find the point-of-use instructions helpful and motivating, instead of an inconvenient step that interferes with the search?

I agree with Carroll[37] and Markey[38] that we have to test our instructions. We don't really know how well novices understand our instructions until we study the search process from their perspective. In order to discover how instructions may be misconstrued, we need to test them on novice end-users and elicit their comments on how they reason while searching. Those who see the dynamic world of searchers as they are continuously influenced by the workstation environment can factor themselves into the equation by taking the user-centered perspective in point-of-use instructions to respond to searchers' ongoing concerns and micro-information needs.

NOTES

1. Linda Stewart, "Helping Students During Online Searches: An Evaluation," *Journal of Academic Librarianship* 18:6 (January 1993): 348.

2. Carol Tenopir, Diane Nahl-Jakobovits, and Dara Lee Howard, "Strategies and Assessments Online: Novices' Experience," *Library and Information Science Research* 13:3 (1991): 237-266.

3. Brenda Dervin, "Information as a User-Construct: The Relevance of Perceived Information Needs to Synthesis and Interpretation," in S. Ward and L.J. Reed, eds., *Knowledge Structure and Use: Implications for Synthesis and Interpretation* (Philadelphia: Temple University Press, 1983), 173.

4. Stewart, 347-351.

5. Stewart, 349.

6. Diane Nahl-Jakobovits, *CD-ROM Point-of-Use Instructions for Novice Searchers: A Comparison of User-Centered Affectively Elaborated and Unelaborated Text*. Ph.D. diss., University of Hawaii, 1993.

7. Stewart, 351.

8. Rebecca Bostian and Anne Robbins, "Effective Instruction for Searching CD-ROM Indexes," *Laserdisk Professional* 8 (January 1990): 14-17.

9. Bostian and Robbins, 17.

10. Tim Bucknall and Ricki Mangrum, "U-Search: A User Study of the CD-ROM Service at the University of North Carolina at Chapel Hill," *RQ* 31:4 (Summer 1992): 542-553.

11. Karen Markey, "Offline and Online User Assistance for Online Catalog Searchers," *Online* 8:3 (May 1984): 54-66.

12. Markey, 61.

13. Rachael Naismith and Joan Stein, "Library Jargon: Student Comprehension of Technical Language Used by Librarians," *College & Research Libraries* 50 (September 1989): 543-552.

14. Pat Ensor, "Knowledge Level of Users and Nonusers of Keyword/Boolean Searching in an Online Public Access Catalog," *RQ* 32:1 (Fall 1992): 60-74.

15. Ensor, 70.

16. Nahl-Jakobovits, 145.

17. Ensor, 70.

18. Markey, 65-66.

19. For a full explanation of the behavioral domains and their application to BI, see Leon A. Jakobovits and Diane Nahl-Jakobovits, "Learning the Library: Taxonomy of Skills and Errors," *College & Research Libraries* 48 (May 1987): 203-214.

20. Nahl-Jakobovits, 60, 193-194.

21. John Maxymuk, "Considerations for CD-ROM Instruction," *CD-ROM Professional* 4:3 (May 1991): 4,750.

22. Nahl-Jakobovits, 155.

23. Tefko Saracevic, Hartmut Mokros, and Louise Su, "Nature of Interaction between Intermediaries in Online Searching: A Qualitative Analysis," *Proceedings of the 53rd ASIS Annual Meeting 27 Held at Toronto, Ontario, November 4-8, 1990* (Medford, NJ: Learned Information, Inc., 1990), 47-54.

24. Saracevic, Mokros, Su, 53.

25. Saracevic, Mokros, Su, 54.

26. Prudence W. Dalrymple, "Retrieval by Reformulation in Two Library Catalogs: Toward a Cognitive Model of Searching Behavior," *Journal of the American Society for Information Science* 41:4 (June 1990): 272-281.

27. David Bradford, "Persona in Microcomputer Documentation," *IEEE Transactions on Professional Communication* 27:2 (1984): 65-68.

28. Bradford, 65.

29. Linda S. Chavarria, "Improving the Friendliness of Technical Manuals," *Proceedings of the 29th International Technical Communication Conference: Technical Communication, Charting the Course of Technology 5-8 May 1982* (Washington, DC: Society for Technical Communication, 1982), W26-W28.

30. Chavarria, W-26.

31. Chavarria, W-27.

32. Chavarria, W-28.

33. Bradford, 66.

34. Bradford, 68.

35. Bradford, 68.

36. John M. Carroll, *The Nurnberg Funnel: Designing Minimalist Instruction for Practical Computer Skill* (Cambridge, MA: MIT Press, 1990).

37. Carroll.

38. Markey.

Appendix 1: Recommendations for Creating User-Centered Documentation from the BI and Technical Writing Literature

1) Eliminate overviews, introductions, summaries. (Carroll)

2) Focus on what users need to know in order to immediately apply it to their searches. (Carroll)

3) Test instructions repeatedly on end-users throughout the design phase. (Carroll)

4) Use pictures of what the screen is supposed to look like to make it easy for users to coordinate the instructions with the screen information. (Carroll)

5) Link new information continuously to what users already know. (Carroll)

6) Don't be impersonal and machine-like in an attempt to be concise or sound objective. (Chavarria)

7) Address users directly ("you"). (Chavarria)

8) Ask users questions within the text. (Chavarria)

9 Be supportive by making information easy to understand (e.g., use graphics and white space). (Chavarria)

10) Get to know the audience (their demographics, knowledge, needs, interests). (Chavarria)

11) Express liking for searchers and affirm their worth in your tone. (Chavarria)

12) Avoid making novice users feel left out, be nonjudgmental, do not blame users. (Chavarria)

13) Address the readers' perspective, not the system or librarian's perspective. (Nahl)

14) Avoid small print, footnotes, and unexplained library jargon; give the meanings of common acronyms and abbreviations. (Naismith & Stein, Markey)

15) Don't assume that users know about particular processes and terminology; find out first by pretesting materials. (Markey)

16) Prepare materials of varying lengths, with greater or lesser detail for different knowledge levels of users. (Markey)

17) Show command statement examples for various types of searches. (Markey)

18) Identify field labels in record structure. (Markey)

19) Highlight search strategy, finding new search terms in records, and basic search options. (Markey)

20) Remind searchers of the coverage of each database and the need to use other related databases. (Markey)

21) Direct searchers to controlled vocabulary thesauri for databases. (Markey)

22) Show searchers how to translate their information need or query into system terms using controlled vocabulary or natural language. (Dalrymple)

23) Show searchers how AND will narrow the search by including search examples with set sizes with and without AND. (Nahl)

24) Give searchers a conceptual model of the system so they can picture its screenflow structure. (Nahl)

25) Reassure users that they can be successful and that they are capable. (Nahl)

26) Give advice, tips, feedback, and examples. (Nahl)

27) Advise users of the consequences of trying certain options or strategies. (Nahl)

28) Orient users by letting them know how long things will take, identifying common errors, telling which are non-reversible actions, telling how to interpret error messages, telling where something needed can be found, and telling what is excluded. (Nahl)

29) Acknowledge the technical difficulty and the need to control the time overload of information retrieved. (Nahl)

COOPERATIVE LEARNING:
A GUIDED DISCOVERY WORKSHOP

Lizabeth Wilson, Sharon Mader, Lori Arp, and Mary Jane Petrowski

COOPERATIVE LEARNING:
A GUIDED DISCOVERY WORKSHOP

Lizabeth Wilson

These proceedings can be read in two ways. As a transcript of the workshop, they may serve as a model for those interested in conducting a local workshop for faculty or staff. On another level, this "transcript" offers an overview of cooperative learning, its rationale and research base, as well as an introduction to various techniques and implementation issues. The structure of this workshop is based on staff-development literature and our collective experience providing similar workshops at colleges and conferences.

INTRODUCTION

Good morning and welcome to "Cooperative Learning: A Guided Discovery Workshop." We hope you will find the next few hours, engaging, invigorating, useful, and fun!

Wilson is associate director of libraries for public services, University of Washington, Seattle, Washington. *Mader* is associate director of information and research services, DePaul University Library, Chicago, Illinois. *Arp* is head, central reference, Norlin Library, University of Colorado at Boulder. *Petrowski* is head of library instruction, Colgate University, Hamilton, New York.

Why cooperative learning (CL)? To return to Carol Tenopir's question: Is it any of our business? The demands on individuals to cooperate, to work in groups, to resolve conflict, and to reach understanding, are everywhere—in the workplace, in the home. But traditional methods of teaching are competitive and individualistic. In fact, collaboration and cooperation have been penalized. Thus, much of higher education uses methods completely foreign to the real world. We graduate students not prepared or able to function once they leave the hallowed halls. We are beginning to experience changes—driven by the marketplace especially in the fields of engineering, business, and medicine, by desired outcomes and achievement, and by the need to address diverse learning styles in the classroom.

I'd like to take a couple of minutes to look at the packet. On the agenda for today, you will see that the workshop is divided into two parts with a 10-minute break halfway through. We'll be using a variety of cooperative learning techniques—modeling as we go. You will experience firsthand small group work, group processing, and mini-lectures. We will be borrowing some graphic support from Roger von Oechs' *Creative Whack Pack*[1] and *The Far Side* of Gary Larson.[2] The workshop presents cooperative learning, a teaching method that we have found to be particularly successful.

Cooperative learning is a pedagogical method that can readily be used in teaching the use of technology and electronic resources. I'd like to ask you all to think of ways you might apply these techniques to teaching technology as the morning progresses. The goals for the workshop are enumerated on the first handout in your packet: you will 1) experience a variety of cooperative learning techniques; 2) reflect on the nature and value of cooperative learning; 3) gain an overview of cooperative learning; 4) discover ways to use cooperative learning techniques in libraries; and 5) focus on practical implementation issues. To achieve these goals, we will be predicating the workshop on small groups. We hope to demonstrate how small groups can be used with a large number of people. We will be working in two basic formations: the whole and quadrants. We will come together as a whole for instructions and mini-lectures. We will work in our quadrants of seven or eight tables when we are doing small group work. Each workshop presenter will be a quadrant facilitator.

Today, assistance is being provided by Ann Scholz, Judith Pryor, Linda Piele, Pat Berge, and Abbie Loomis. Perhaps our most important assistant today is Keith Stanger—the keeper of time. We have a few rules and guidelines. You will have a set number of minutes for each segment. When time is up, Keith will raise his hand. As soon as you see him raise his hand, stop talking and raise yours. Are we all agreeable to this? Great! Let's get rolling!

FORMING COOPERATIVE GROUPS: FAMOUS PAIRS

Lizabeth Wilson

The first order of business is to form our groups. We're using a technique today called Famous Pairs. Take a card from the center of the table. Find your pair. For example, if your card says Adam, you would probably be looking for Eve. Once you have found your pair, go to the table that matches the number in the right-hand corner. You will be forming a group of six, made up of three pairs. One of you will have a star on the card. You will serve as the first recorder.

Early in CL workshops it is important to spend some time setting the climate for cooperative group interaction. Considerations in forming groups include size, composition, and duration. The smallest group is two; the largest recommended is six. Groups of six were necessary to accommodate the large workshop audience within a relatively small space. Larger groups generate more ideas, handle complex ideas more easily, and reduce the number of group reports made to the entire group.

In the classroom setting, groups may work together for five minutes or several times a week for an entire course. This workshop provided three hours of concen-trated group experience. Working together for a short period of time allows participants to get to know more colleagues and practice group formation skills.

Unless there is an overwhelming reason to use homogeneous groups, research favors making groups as heterogeneous as possible with regard to academic achievement, gender, ethnicity, task orientation, learning style, ability/disability, and learning style. Heterogeneous groups promote more elaborate thinking and explanations and provide opportunities for students to develop feelings of mutual concern. There are many ways to form heterogeneous teams. See appendix 11 for additional suggestions.

Cooperative Learning Strategy #1: Three-Step Interview

(See appendix 1 for directions.)

To further promote team building and trust and to establish cooperative norms, participants conducted "Three-Step Interviews." To break the ice, partners took turns interviewing each other regarding their experience with cooperative learning. Partners then introduced each other to the larger group, sharing new information and knowledge gleaned from the interview. Learners can use this technique to share hypotheses or reactions. Opinion or evaluation questions also work well. This exercise provides an excellent opportunity to practice active listening skills.

PETALS AROUND A ROSE: COOPERATIVE VERSUS COMPETITIVE LEARNING

Lizabeth Wilson

Now it's time for a party game. It is called "Petals around a Rose." As with all good party games, some of us are going to have to leave the room. I need one game leader from each group. If any of you have ever played this game before, I'd like you to volunteer to be your group's leader. The leaders and I will go out in the hall and we'll be back in a few minutes.

In order to experience the difference between cooperative and competitive learning environments, groups played different versions of "Petals around a Rose." Coordinators were selected from each group, taken out of the room, and given five dice and one of two sets of instructions. (See appendix 2 for directions.)

[Game is played.]

Now that everyone has had a chance to play the game, you'd probably like to know the solution. Dice with center dots are counted as roses. The number of dots outside of the center dot are counted as petals. So, ones have no petals, threes have two, and fives have four petals. The number of petals is the total number of petals per each roll.

You all had the same clue as to how the game is played. The name of the game, "Petals around a Rose," tells you more or less how the game is played. However, there were two sets of rules. Some groups had competitive rules—they played against each other, did not share information, did not talk. The winner of the game was the first person to solve the puzzle. Other groups had cooperative rules—they played together, shared information, and vocalized their strategies. The game was over for these groups when everyone understood the solution. In the group processing, you identified how the two different sets of rules affected outcomes, tolerance, self-confidence, and group interaction.

Reactions to the competitive game were largely negative. Recorders noted that players displayed tense body language; experienced frustration; became agitated, confused, introspective, or withdrawn. Many groups were unable to find the answer. One group reported that it was "frustrating not being able to share." Reactions to playing the cooperative game were mixed. Many group members shared information directly, which allowed the group to find and understand the solution quickly. Many experienced the cooperative game as a "safe environment" where "ideas were shared" and "knowledge was pooled." Other groups had difficulty playing cooperatively, despite explicit directions to do so. Some participants confessed that they didn't know how to share, preferred the competitive mode, or "mentally withdrew" in a cooperative environment because it was unfamiliar. Your students might react in similar fashion when you implement cooperative learning.

WHAT IS COOPERATIVE LEARNING?

Sharon Mader

If we asked everyone in this room to provide a definition of cooperative learning, the result would be similar to asking everyone for a definition of critical thinking: there would be almost as many variations as there are people present.

To what can cooperative learning be compared? There are two basic approaches to learning: learning alone or learning together. These are manifested in three common classroom structures: individualistic, competitive, and cooperative. The first approach, learning alone, is characteristically individualistic or competitive. Learning together is characterized by cooperation. In each of these, the measure of success is different, as is the nature of the interdependence among learners.

1. Individualistic or Individualized Learning—You are working by yourself and against yourself. You are not being measured against others. There is no interdependence.

2. Competitive—You are working against others. My success is your failure and vice versa. There is negative interdependence.

3. Cooperative—We are working together. We sink or swim together. There is positive interdependence.

You have just experienced the contrast between competitive and cooperative structures during the last exercise. Keep in mind, however, that competition can be used as a technique with both individualized and cooperative learning.

A succinct definition to start with is that "cooperative learning is a structured systematic instructional strategy in which small groups work together toward a common goal."[3] Though much of the research and practical applications to date have been done with levels K-12, cooperative learning has tremendous potential for higher education and for bibliographic instruction. In the past, education became increasingly competitive as one advanced to higher levels. Now, as teamwork is becoming the norm in the world of work, it is essential that colleagues and universities prepare students for this collaborative mode of interaction.

Let's look at an illustration of how collaboration might work in a traditional learning setting. Kenneth Bruffee, a leading figure in cooperative learning circles, credits a book that was influential in shaping his view of university instruction.[4] In *The Anatomy of Judgment*, M.L.J. Abercrombie describes her research in the late 1950s with medical education at the University of London.[5] A standard pedagogical approach in medical school is to have students gather around a bed in a hospital ward with a teaching physician and then to offer individual diagnoses of a patient. Abercrombie made a slight change in this process by having the whole group work together to discuss the case and arrive at a single diagnosis by consensus. What she found was that students who learned diagnosis collaboratively acquired medical judgment faster than students working alone. Bruffee credits her with being one of the first educators to realize that "learning...judgment is not an individual process, but a social one."[6] The learning process occurs not between people and things, but among people.

The significant finding for teaching librarians is that people learn judgment best in groups "because we tend to talk to each other out of our unshared biases and presuppositions."[7] As one of our goals as instruction librarians is to develop students' skills in exercising judgment about information resources and strategies, collaborative learning could help us to realize this aim.

Bruffee also singles out William Perry's work on stages of development in college students as a significant contribution to our understanding of the nature of knowledge. Not only the way we view knowledge but also the way we think about the acquisition of knowledge has changed. Bruffee cites Perry's conclusion that learning, as we view it today, does not involve people's assimilation of knowledge, but rather "involves students' assimilation into communities of knowledgeable peers."[8] These communities are not created spontaneously but as part of a structured university education. This is a liberating concept of education. Knowledge becomes something that is created by the community, not just something transmitted from teacher to learner. Thus, construction of knowledge is a social process.

Critical Attributes of Cooperative Learning

There are five attributes of cooperative learning that must be present for success. The instructor must incorporate all of these elements into the learning activity:

- Positive interdependence—Let's start with positive interdependence. Learners must feel that they need each other in order to complete the group's task, that they sink or swim together. Some ways to create this feeling are through establishing 1) mutual goals; 2) joint rewards (for example, if all group members achieve above a certain percentage on a test, each will receive bonus points); 3) shared materials and information (the instructor can provide one set of instructions per group, or each member receives only part of the information needed to do the assignment); 4) assigned roles (such as recorder, encourager, and elaborator).

- Face-to-face communication—The second attribute is face-to-face communication or promotive interaction. Positive interdependence alone is not enough. Beneficial educational outcomes also derive from interaction patterns and verbal sharing among students. Also as part of this process,

learners challenge each other's conclusions and reasoning. Oral summarizing, giving and receiving explanations, and elaborating (linking new knowledge to previous learning) are important types of verbal exchanges.

- Individual responsibility—A third attribute is responsibility. No one rides for free; group members must realize they cannot succeed unless other members of the group do, too. The group must promote individual accountability. It's also necessary to assess the performance of each individual student This can be done, for example, through individual exams or by randomly selecting one member to give an answer for the entire group.

- Social skills—The fourth attribute is social skills or interpersonal/small group skills. Learners do not come with the social skills they need to collaborate effectively with others. Teachers need to teach the appropriate communication, leadership, trust-building, decision-making, and conflict-management skills. Social skills are linked to group productivity.

- Time for reflection—The last attribute is time to think or group processing. This means giving learners the time and procedures to analyze how well group members are working together and how well they are using the necessary social skills. What actions by group members are helpful or unhelpful? What needs to be changed to improve the group's effectiveness?

There are a variety of ways to organize and motivate groups. In the literature of cooperative learning, you will encounter descriptions of the following CL structures, which have been used extensively at the K-12 level: Student Teams and Achievement Divisions (STAD); Teams-Games-Tournaments (TGT); Learning Together (LT); Jigsaw (JIG); Jigsaw II (JIG II); and Group Investigation (GI). The information packet included in the workshop folder (see appendix 11) describes various strategies that can be adapted for higher education.

Remember that cooperative learning requires training and practice, for both teachers and learners. Hands-on experience is essential. Be aware that putting students into groups to learn is not the same thing as structuring cooperation among students.[9] During this workshop you will have a chance to experience cooperative learning and work through some of these strategies so that you can develop a clearer sense of what cooperative learning is and how you can apply it to your own institution.

Cooperative Learning Strategy #2: Talking Chips

(See appendix 3 for instructions.)

The rationale behind incorporating small group experiences into the workshop design is that people do not learn how to implement cooperative learning just by listening to lectures about it. Participation in group experiences during the learning process models the philosophy of CL, gives participants an experiential, tactile-kinesthetic sense of the procedures, shows how the procedures actually work, and raises issues for discussion, questions, and reflection. It is very important to give participants time for reflection after each group activity.

Groups were given an opportunity to identify the benefits of cooperative learning using a brainstorming technique called "Talking Chips." This strategy insures that all members of a group are involved. The question or problem posed to the group is very important: it must have multiple answers and offer a high probability of success to all participants. Almost 70 benefits were identified in five minutes. The groups in all quadrants agreed that cooperative learning increases self-esteem and confidence, promotes retention, and is a less-pressured way for students to learn and teachers to teach. A complete list of responses appears in appendix 4. All participants were able to contribute and experience working productively as a group.

WHAT DOES RESEARCH SHOW ABOUT COOPERATIVE LEARNING?

Lizabeth Wilson

You've identified the possible benefits of cooperative learning. But what does the research tell us? In this mini-lecture, I will highlight the major findings. For specific studies, please consult the excellent bibliography compiled by Mary Jane Petrowski that is in your packet *(see appendix 12).*

There are three major areas of research with regard to cooperative learning: 1) cooperative learning and social development; 2) cooperative learning as compared to competitive and individualistic learning environments; and 3) cooperative learning and the instructor.

Cooperative Learning and Social Development

- Respect for others—Cooperative learning engenders greater tolerance for diversity in other's learning style, ethnic and racial background, gender, and mental and physical disabilities. Students in a cooperative learning environment engage more readily in helping and tutoring behaviors.

- Increased self-esteem—Learners in a cooperative environment gained an increased sense of self-confidence and decreased feelings of alienation.

- Improved attitudes—Cooperative learning results in improved attitudes toward the class, the subject matter, and learning in general. These improved attitudes result in improved attendance, motivation, and enthusiasm.

- Greater trust of other people—Students in cooperative learning environments learn to support one another and demonstrate increased concern for others and the learning community.

- More effective communication—Cooperative learning teaches students to disagree without being destructive, resolve conflict, find consensus, and move a group forward.

- Performance—Through cooperative learning, individuals learn how to tolerate situations that present more than one solution.

Cooperative Learning as Compared to Competitive and Individualistic Learning Environments

Studies show no significant difference in student achievement between competitive and individualistic learning environments but significant differences between competitive/individualist and cooperative learning.

- Increased cognitive skills—Cognitive skills improve to a greater degree in cooperative learning environments. We know how important these skills are to critical thinking.

- Peer acceptance and support—Supporting and accepting peers is much more evident in cooperative learning. Such behavior is critical to an individual's success.

- Group cohesiveness—Through reciprocal interaction, group members develop a greater liking for others than in either the competitive or the individualistic environment.

- Positive attitudes—Cooperative learning increases motivation and attitudes toward learning. Competitive/individualistic learning shows no significant impact on attitude.

- Communication skills—In cooperative learning, students with diverse learning styles learn from one another, something not possible in competitive/individualistic environments.

- Overall achievement—Student overall achievement is higher through cooperative learning. This result holds across age groups, ability levels, background, and subject disciplines.

Cooperative Learning and Instructors

- Antidote to burnout—Anecdotal evidence suggests that cooperative learning methods alleviate instructor burnout.

- Instructor's role—Instructors find the new role of "guide on the side" refreshing, invigorating, and satisfying.

- Enthusiasm for shared responsibility—Instructors demonstrate greater enthusiasm for sharing the responsibility for the student's success with the learner.

- Caveat—Instructors need to watch out for "half-knowledge." Knowing a few techniques does not mean you will be successful using cooperative learning in the classroom.

In summary, the research results concerning cooperative learning are positive:

1. Cooperative learning promotes active learning and achievement.

2. Cooperative learning creates a sense of community, critical to knowledge transfer.

3. Cooperative learning enhances student and instructor self-esteem and self-confidence.

4. Cooperative learning locates knowledge in the community (the learners) rather than in the individual (the instructor).

Student/Teacher Reactions to Cooperative Learning: The Video

Participants viewed a 10-minute segment from "Thinking Together: Cooperative Learning in Science," which demonstrated the implementation of cooperative learning in a large physics class.[10] It also featured testimonials from Harvard University students and professors regarding the effectiveness of cooperative learning.

WHY DOES COOPERATIVE LEARNING WORK?

Lori Arp

Why are cooperative learning techniques effective? To a large extent, they are based on and validated by current views of thinking and learning advocated by cognitive and social psychologists. Cooperative learning reflects a new tradition or paradigm in educational theory.

Older traditions of learning in vogue until the eighties had certain characteristics.[11] These included the following:

1. The student was seen as an empty vessel or blank slate.

2. Knowledge and learning were seen as "additive" processes.

3. Learning could be measured by behavior.

4. The teacher was viewed as the "absolute authority."

The student, then, came to the classroom with no preconceived view of a topic. Knowledge was dispensed incrementally by the teacher, or expert authority, and was assimilated. Pieces of knowledge were sequentially added until a whole view of a topic was reached. External observation of behavior was used as proof that learning had occurred. In the older traditions, the teacher was to dispense all knowledge; the student could only hope to emulate the expert.

By the late 1970s, however, learning theorists became disenchanted with the older traditions, and new and alternative learning traditions began to emerge.[12] Many principles in these traditions refuted earlier thought on learning. In the new traditions:

1. The student is not a blank slate, but comes to the learning environment with preconceived views based

on previous experience. These views are often called schemata or mental models.

2. The student actively participates in the learning process and transforms schemata. Learners can and do construct and transform knowledge. In fact, new knowledge may be created which goes beyond the material taught.

3. Learning is not an additive process, in which each piece of knowledge is incrementally added to create a whole. In the new view, learning is seen as holistic. Students go back and forth between parts and the whole to understand a topic.

4. There is no absolute authority. In this tradition, the teacher is viewed as a coach, moderator, or facilitator who encourages and guides the learning process.

The newer traditions reflect views that thinking and learning are intertwined and complex processes. Raymond Nickerson, in one of the most extensive review articles on this topic, states "research is revealing deep and unbreakable connections between thinking, knowing, and learning."[13] Nickerson's article provides an excellent overview to the research and theories presently advocated in learning.

An important goal of newer learning traditions is to educate students to be expert reasoners in a given domain (or discipline). What exactly constitutes expert reasoning was studied and commented on by Robert Gloser. In his studies, he found that expert reasoners

1. Have coherence of what is known (i.e., they understand the relations between topics and points);

2. Have knowledge of domain-specific patterns or principles;

3. Use these patterns and principles in problem solving;

4. Recognize situations and conditions for using knowledge;

5. Exhibit highly efficient performance;

6. Use self-regulating skills (such as metacognitive strategies).

Novice reasoners do not display these traits.[14]

Cooperative learning techniques, then, are based on cognitive learning traditions. They actively engage students in creating and transforming knowledge. They

are designed to develop expert reasoners. The teacher serves as coach, modeler, and facilitator rather than expert authority.

Cooperative learning also reflects theories developed by social psychologists, who view knowledge not as absolute but as constructed socially. Interaction is critical to learning in these views.[15]

Johnson, Johnson, and Smith, while examining the benefits of cooperative learning, outline many points which review the social psychology approach to learning.[16] They found that in cooperative learning

1. Individuals directly learn attitudes, values, and skills previously unobtainable through isolated learning situations;

2. Support, opportunities, and models for prosocial behavior are provided;

3. Students learn to view situations and problems from perspectives other than their own;

4. The techniques influenced the development of autonomy;

5. Peers became modelers of behavior;

6. Self-identity and awareness in the individual is raised;

7. Productivity and greater achievement occurs;

8. Educational and social aspirations become greatly influenced by pairs.

Cooperative learning techniques, then, are practical translations of the theoretical views being advocated by cognitive and social psychologists. In this case, practice has informed theory.

Cooperative Learning Strategy #3: Group Brainstorming with a Recorder

(See appendix 5 for group instructions.)
Research on faculty development for cooperative learning in higher education shows that time needs to be spent openly addressing the concerns of participants with respect to barriers and resistance. Participants used "Group Brainstorming with a Recorder" to identify the potential resistances they might encounter when implementing cooperative learning. Brainstorming is a highly effective method of generating ideas provided that participants defer judgment, strive for unique ideas, aim for quantity rather than quality, and seek to build on or "hitchhike" onto ideas of others. Thirty-

two problems were identified in five minutes. Participants in all quadrants were worried about loss of control, about improvising, and about managing group processing. Also mentioned frequently was the difficulty of re-educating faculty to appreciate the cooperative learning approach. Concerns centered around students, curriculum, and administrative issues. See appendix 6 for a complete list of responses.

Cooperative Learning Strategy #4: Pass a Problem

(See appendix 7 for group problem-solving instructions.)

To demonstrate the importance of support systems and follow-up, groups were given the opportunity to share problem areas and brainstorm possible solutions within their quadrants. Each group identified a particular problem using the list generated in the previous exercise. Problems chosen by the groups fall into six broad categories: concerns related to control issues, student resistance, time, content, teaching faculty, and group learning. Because time did not permit sharing solutions in the workshop, all problems and solutions appear in appendix 8.

COOPERATIVE LEARNING AND BI:
APPLICATION AND IMPLEMENTATION

Mary Jane Petrowski

In previous workshops on cooperative learning, we've left the twin issues of application and implementation to the imagination of our audience. We've since realized that librarians are very interested in knowing how one proceeds to fit cooperative learning into existing programs and teaching styles. I'd like to discuss some key implementation issues with respect to my own experience at the University of Illinois Undergraduate Library.

- Getting started—You will need a support system to implement cooperative learning successfully. Find an interested colleague or two to assist with the transition. Enlisting the help of colleagues is critical to one's ability to implement and sustain cooperative learning. Learning to use CL effectively requires a willingness to change, time (2 to 3 years), planning, effort, and moral support. A support group can share successes, exchange ideas, discuss problem areas, and brainstorm possible solutions.

- Content—In the summer of 1991, we began revamping our instruction program to include cooperative learning. Our goal was to include CL in every instruction session. We had to accept the fact that lecturing less can, in fact, enable students to learn more. Perhaps the most difficult challenge was deciding exactly what we wanted students to learn and designing CL tasks that required students to learn something, not simply do something. It was a question of balancing breadth and depth. After much discussion, we were able to identify several content areas where CL applications could help students learn. Some examples: in a transition class, students now use CL to explore the differences between journals and magazines; in classes on finding contemporary materials, students work in pairs to develop keyword Boolean subject searching skills; in online catalog workshops, students work in teams to complete a hands-on subject searching exercise. *(See appendix 13 for copies of scripts.)*

- Structure—It is important to realize that the amount and type of cooperative learning one can introduce will depend to a great extent on local circumstances. A semester-long course affords more opportunities than a single-shot session. Remember that cooperative learning is only one of several ways of learning. It can be mixed and matched as needs warrant. At Illinois, we developed an instructional template that includes the following elements: mini-lecture (no more than 10 minutes), demonstrations or modeling, and small group work. This template allows us to incorporate individualized learning (mini-lecture) as well as cooperative learning (small group work). Determining how much time to allocate for each teaching method is important. It is easy to miscalculate how much time an activity will take. Adjustments are inevitable and a natural part of the implementation process.

- Preliminary organization—Once you've identified your objectives with respect to content and teaching methods, the next step is to organize the setting. This involves determining the size of groups, arranging furniture, planning for interdependence, and developing staff training.[17]

- Decide on group size—In determining the size of a group, keep in mind that as the size of the group increases, the number of solutions/ideas will increase; however, it also becomes more difficult for all group members to participate equally and reach consensus. Time on task also decreases.

Practical experience shows that as the length of class time decreases, the size of the group should shrink. Most important: when students and teachers are inexperienced in cooperative group work, the group size should be kept to 2 or 3.[18]

- Arrange the room—Room arrangements send messages about the kind of interaction that is expected between students and teachers. Chairs in straight rows facing the front of the classroom signal one-way lines of communication between teacher and learner. In cooperative work groups, students sit at tables (preferably round). The closer students are to each other, the better they can communicate. Students are expected to work together, sharing ideas to create knowledge within the group. At Illinois, rectangular study tables replaced rows of chairs facing the "sage on the stage."

- Set the lesson—Plan for interdependence when designing group assignments. This insures that all students will participate and contribute. A popular technique is to give an assignment where each student is responsible for a part of a whole. Another approach involves assigning roles or indicating that each group member is responsible for helping other members to understand the material.

- Train the teachers—As cooperative learning becomes more widely used in higher education, there is an increasing need for teacher development with respect to this method. What constitutes effective staff development? At the University of Illinois, an abridged version of this workshop is presented each fall to the new teaching staff. Other options include the use of video workshops (available commercially) or presentations by staff from a local instructional resources office. Regardless of how the staff training is done, it is important to include a presenter with experience in applying CL methods who can explain in a clear and convincing way the rationale for the use of CL in higher education. It's also important to include an overview of CL theory and research along with demonstrations/modeling, group experiences, and time for reflection. Planning for team teaching, peer observations, or coaching are additional types of support.

- Practice new roles in the classroom—Your role as instructor will change from being the "sage on the stage" to the "guide on the side".[19] It will take some practice to become comfortable with this new role. Small groups don't function well automatically. You will have to spend time initiating activities, structuring the work, and specifying criteria. This means explaining the task clearly, emphasizing that everyone is responsible for the work, and making sure students understand how results will be measured. Once group work is underway, your role changes from presenter to facilitator as you walk around the room observing behavior and providing assistance if necessary.

- Evaluate the process—In CL, each group evaluates the quantity and quality of learning. Groups also evaluate how well members functioned socially as a group. In actual practice, we evaluate group learning through group processing wherein individual group members report on group findings. The instructor is able to provide clarification and amplification, and solicit additional commentary at this point.

- Take a whack at it—In summary, our experience at Illinois reinforces the wisdom of starting small. Introduce one activity per class until everyone is comfortable and feels successful facilitating group work. Invite feedback and retool if necessary. Resist the temptation to fall back into lecture mode, but give yourself permission to fail. Research shows that for innovative teaching strategies to become internalized it requires the professional to systematically apply the new strategy more than 15 times over a three-month period.[20] Draw support from the literature. Above all, share your success with colleagues! The literature in our field with respect to implementation is sparse. Your contributions are both welcome and needed.

Cooperative Learning Strategy #5: Roundtable

(See appendix 9 for group instructions.)
To provide a final opportunity to reflect on what was learned, participants were instructed to identify the most important things they learned during the workshop using a brainstorming technique known as "Roundtable." One hundred sixty-one responses were generated in five minutes. Participants felt the most important things they learned had to do with the benefits of cooperative learning, implementation issues, and application to BI. All responses appear in appendix 10 by category.

NOTES

1. Roger von Oech, *Creative Whack Pack* (Stamford, CT: U.S. Games Systems, 1992), cards 5, 32, 52, 57, 59, and 64.

2. Gary Larson, *The Far Side* (San Francisco: Chronicle Features, 1982), 58, 92.

3. Jim L. Cooper and Randall Mueck, "Student Involvement in Learning: Cooperative Learning and College Instruction," *Journal on Excellence in College Teaching* 1 (1990): 68.

4. Kenneth A. Bruffee, "Collaborative Learning and the 'Conversation of Mankind'," *College English* 46 (November 1984): 636-637.

5. Minnie Louie Johnson Abercrombie, *The Anatomy of Judgment: An Investigation into the Processes of Perception and Reasoning* (New York: Basic Books, 1960).

6. Kenneth A. Bruffee, "The Art of Collaborative Learning: Making the Most of Knowledgeable Peers," *Change* 19 (March/April 1987): 42-47.

7. Bruffee, "The Art," 45.

8. Bruffee, "The Art," 45.

9. David W. Johnson, Roger T. Johnson, and Karl A. Smith, *Cooperative Learning: Increasing College Faculty Instructional Productivity* (Washington, DC: The George Washington University, School of Education and Human Development, 1991), iv.

10. *Thinking Together: Collaborative Learning in Science*, videorecording, prod. The Derek Bok Center for Teaching and Learning, Harvard University, 1993 (18 min.).

11. Glenda B. Thurman, *The Evolution of Behavioral Objectives*, Ph.D. diss., University of Colorado at Boulder, 1982.

12. Rao Aluri and Mary Reichel, "Learning Theories and Bibliographic Instruction," in *Bibliographic Instruction and the Learning Process: Theory, Style and Motivation*, ed. by Carolyn Kirkendall (Ann Arbor: Pierian Press, 1984), 15-25.

13. Raymond S. Nickerson, "On Improving Thinking through Instruction," *Review of Research in Education* 15 (1988-89): 3-57.

14. Nancy S. Cole, "Conceptions of Educational Achievement," *Educational Researcher* 19 (April 1990): 2.

15. Bruffee, *College English*, 636.

16. David W. Johnson, Roger T. Johnson, and Carla A. Smith. *Active Learning, Cooperation, and the College Classroom* (Edina, MN: Interaction Book Co., 1991).

17. A good overview of implementation issues can be found in Richard M. Henak, "Cooperative Group Interaction Techniques," in *Instructional Strategies for Technology Education* (Mission Hills, CA: Glencoe Publishing, 1988), 143-165.

18. D.W. Johnson, R.T. Johnson, E. Johnson-Holubec, and P. Roy, *Circles of Learning: Cooperation in the Classroom* (Alexandria, VA: Association for Supervision and Curriculum Development, 1984), 26-27.

19. Barbara J. Millis, "Helping Faculty Build Learning Communities through Cooperative Groups," in *To Improve the Academy: Resources for Student, Faculty, & Institutional Development,* ed. by Linda Hilsen (Stillwater, OK: New Forums Press, 1990), 48.

20. Bruce Joyce and Beverly Showers, "Improving Inservice Training: The Messages of Research," *Educational Leadership* 37 (February 1980): 379.

3-Step Interview

▶ Form pairs

▶ A interviews B (2 minutes)

▶ B interviews A (2 minutes)

▶ Rehearse (1 minute)

▶ Pairs form groups of 6

▶ Share introductions (1 minute)

Petals Around a Rose

▶ Petals Around a Rose: Competitive Version
Instructions for Coordinators
Each Coordinator gives the group the following information: "Petals Around a Rose" is a dice game. There is one clue to the game: the name of the game tells you, more or less, how the game is played. There is one rule to the game: the game is played against other people. Whoever gets the solution first is the best and smartest. Therefore, you never reveal the solution to anyone else. Once you have solved the problem, you let the Coordinator know by simply giving the correct answer several times.

To Coordinator: Throw the dice and, depending on the roll, say out loud: "There are (blank) petals around the rose." Do this a couple of times giving the right answer. Then start going around the circle, throwing the dice and asking each player in turn, "How many petals are there around the rose?" Tell the player either, "No, there are no/(number) petals around the rose;" or "Yes, there are (number) petals around the rose." Continue until time is called. As Coordinator, do not tell the solution.

Petals are determined visually. If a die has a center dot and has dots around it, each surrounding dot is counted as a petal. Dice rolls are counted as such:

1 : no petals	4 : no petals
2 : no petals	5 : 4 petals
3 : 2 petals	6 : no petals

If six dice are thrown and the roll results in two 2's, one 6, two 5's, and one 3, there would be 10 petals around the rose.

To Recorder: Observe the action and make written notes of behaviors.

▶ Petals Around a Rose: Cooperative Version
Instructions for Coordinators
Each Coordinator gives the group the following information: "Petals Around a Rose" is a dice game. There is one clue to the game: the name of the game tells you, more or less, how the game is played. There is one rule to the game: the game is over when everyone understands how it is played. Group members are encouraged to verbalize their strategies to others in the group. Once the group has solved the problem, let the Coordinator know by simply giving the correct answer several times.

To Coordinator: Throw the dice and, depending on the roll, say out loud: "There are (blank) petals around the rose." Do this a couple of times giving the right answer. Then start going around the circle, throwing the dice and asking each player in turn, "How many petals are there around the rose?" Tell the player either, "No, there are no/(number) petals around the rose;" or "Yes, there are (number) petals around the rose." Continue until time is called. As Coordinator, do not tell the solution.

Petals are determined visually. If a die has a center dot and has dots around it, each surrounding dot is counted as a petal. Dice rolls are counted as such:

1 : no petals	4 : no petals
2 : no petals	5 : 4 petals
3 : 2 petals	6 : no petals

If six dice are thrown and the roll results in two 2's, one 6, two 5's, and one 3, there would be 10 petals around the rose.

To Recorder: Observe the action and make written notes of behaviors.

Talking Chips

Each group member volunteers one idea about the benefits of cooperative learning after placing a talking chip (pen/pencil) in the center of the group.

Retrieve chips to begin a new round after everyone has contributed.

Continue until time is called.

Benefits of Cooperative Learning

The recorded responses below were generated by all quadrants during a five-minute brainstorming session.

▶ More Effective Communication
- Face-to-face communication enables individuals to share and understand unique perspectives
- Chance for communication
- Increases communication and interaction between diverse populations (mentioned by 2 quadrants)
- Feedback: can discuss what students don't know (mentioned by 2 quadrants)
- Everyone contributes
- No sleeping
- Peer communication using familiar terms
- Students responsible for articulating issues
- Modeling of behavior
- Clarifies ideas

▶ Performance Improvement
- Development of problem-solving skills
- Good practice for real world
- Positive reinforcement for sharing
- Knowledge is personalized
- Deep learning
- Makes it easier to ask questions at Reference Desk
- Easier to learn concepts
- Students apply learning to other environments
- Transference of skills
- Fosters social skills
- Better retention (mentioned by 3 quadrants)
- Conclusions tested by group
- Higher level of success
- Brings creativity into group
- Sharing responsibility

▶ Improved Attitudes
- Eases reluctance
- Promotes connection
- Reduces discipline problems
- Generates enthusiasm
- For instructor, it's invigorating
- Increases self-esteem and confidence (mentioned by 4 quadrants)
- Comfort with peers
- Show interest
- Peer pressure keeps group on track
- Students pay more attention
- Tolerance for diversity of ideas

▶ Better Learning Environment
- Energizing situation
- More fun (mentioned by 2 quadrants)
- Students deal with frustration in less threatening environment
- Develops ownership of their own learning
- Creates ownership of ideas
- Collective IQ bigger than that of single individual
- Less need for lecturing
- Smaller more effective
- Humanization of technology through groups
- Synergy
- Counteracts teacher "entertainment" or passive learning
- Saves time
- More interesting for instructor because each class varies
- Cooperative experience can use aggression (or lack of it) for positive gain
- Equalizes status
- Teaches the teacher
- Balances differences
- Creates safe environment
- Builds on fullness (what students bring to class)
- Positive interaction; enjoyable
- Active learning (mentioned by 2 quadrants)
- Teacher not "source of knowledge"
- Conducive to different learning styles
- Adds variety
- Gains support of administration
- Peers work as peers in natural environment
- More like "real life"
- Focuses instructor
- Less risk of failure for group members
- Less pressure/stress for students & instructor (mentioned by 3 quadrants)
- Meeting other students

Group Brainstorming with Recorder

▶ Select a Recorder

▶ Generate many wild and crazy ideas about why there might be resistance to cooperative learning

▶ Recorder captures responses

▶ Criticism not allowed

Resistance to Cooperative Learning

The recorded responses below were generated by all quadrants during a five-minute brainstorming session.

▶ Students
- Students have traditional attitudes and expectations
- Students perceive this is not the teacher's role
- Students like more structure
- Personality differences in groups
- Different learning styles
- Students get off track
- Students see activities as contrived
- Students see this as loss of individuality
- Introverts don't like groups
- Students don't want to admit ignorance
- Individuals not responsible
- Students don't see value in process

▶ Curriculum
- Overuse of cooperative learning techniques
- How to cover all instructional goals
- Belief that some concepts can't be taught by this method
- Less content is taught (mentioned by 2 quadrants)
- How to integrate cooperative learning into one-shot class
- Correct information may not be transmitted by peers
- Difficult to assess or measure learning (mentioned by 2 quadrants)

▶ Administrative Issues
- Costs more money (e.g., for things like staff development)
- The amount of time it takes (mentioned by 3 quadrants)
- Time factor: students can't get together after class
- Re-educating faculty to appreciate cooperative learning approach (mentioned by every quadrant)
- Facilities may be inadequate
- Pre-existing conditions (it's someone else's class)

▶ Instructor Inadequacies
- Inadequate understanding of cooperative learning techniques on part of instructor
- Old habits are hard to break on part of students and teachers; reluctant to change what's been done in the past (mentioned by 2 quadrants)
- Fear it won't work
- Teacher feels loss of control and fear of improvising/managing group process (mentioned by every quadrant)
- Teachers fear loss of authority
- Teachers not comfortable without scripts

▶ Philosophical
- American ethos values rugged individualism and competition more highly than cooperation

Pass a Problem

▶ Write group choice on envelope.

▶ Brainstorm and find consensus solution.

▶ Put idea in envelope.

▶ Repeat process 2 times. Return envelopes to home group.

▶ Read and prioritize solutions.

Responses to Pass a Problem

Below is a list of the problems chosen by each group along with solutions generated by the home group and other groups within the quadrant. Problems are grouped by broad areas of concern.

Problems Related to Control Issues
▶ Problem 1: Fear of losing control and/or authority.

Solutions
1. Get out there and **try** it and you'll not be so fearful. If you **know** what you're doing, you're still in a position to exercise control.
2. Team teach.
3. Structure class and roles so that there is assigned responsibility in tested tasks. Test your lesson plan in advance.
4. Plan your work and work your plan.

▶ Problem 2: The instructor fears a loss of control using the cooperative process, especially in the area of improvisation or thinking on one's feet.

Solutions
1. Training in role-playing practice for the instructors; confidence-building workshops.
2. Atmosphere set by supervisor that risk-taking and possible failure are acceptable.
3. Freedom to experiment on small-scale pilot projects.
4. Help teacher/facilitator learn alternative approaches to thinking on his/her feet; not to worry about being "wrong". Teacher-training workshops. Be willing to learn by doing.
5. Encourage instructor to relax and inform them it's OK to give up a certain amount of control. Do this through training sessions.

▶ Problem 3: Instructor's fear of losing control of the class, especially during student brainstorming periods.

Solutions
1. Well-conceived lesson plan with outcomes, objectives, and goals, all communicated to the group and then use periodic breaks to restate goals and objectives, summarize results.
2. Improve teachers' communication skills.
3. Observe colleague using similar method to reduce anxiety or change perspective.
4. Set time limit (so still have "control" through structure).

▶ Problem 4: Teacher's fear/insecurity in managing

Solutions
1. Team teach until all become comfortable with new methodologies.
2. Pair librarians with diverse backgrounds, diverse teaching styles, etc.
3. Encourage faculty to work together.
4. Evolution—gradually putting group activities into lectures.
5. Recognition—reward system.
6. Training workshops or in-house workshop that incorporates observing someone using cooperative learning.

▶ Problem 5: Teachers fear the loss of perceived authority.

Solutions
1. Have librarians work in pairs: the resistant one is coached by the secure one.
2. Build rapport and team approach with academic instructor.
3. Use combined approaches—lecture and cooperative learning.
4. Get student evaluation of the cooperative learning process success.
5. No sympathy! You lost it long ago. Don't sweat it; you never had it. Authority is an illusion. Authoritative model is not a requirement for learning.
6. Send them to a cooperative learning workshop.
7. Retrain through conferences and workshops—can draw on local expertise.

Problems Related to Student Resistance
▶ Problem 6: How can we overcome students' resistance to admitting possible ignorance or giving up prestige of possessing knowledge?

Solutions
1. Instructor must set positive, social attitude and over time (with practice) students will overcome resistance.

2. Emphasize that the goal is not (getting) the right answer, but rather the process of learning. Do this in a nurturing environment.
3. Create non-threatening atmosphere.
4. Use cooperative learning techniques only for non-graded activities.
5. Encourage anonymous contributions.

► Problem 7: Students' perception of what the instructor is "supposed" to do.

Solutions
1. Don't make entire session a cooperative learning experience. Combine with teacher as expert (mini-lecture).
2. Ease into this: start with *small, short, simple* cooperative learning activities then move to more complex, longer activities.
3. Instructor needs to articulate, explain the process and benefits at the beginning of the session.

► Problem 8: Students view the activities as too contrived

Solutions
1. Make the activity relevant to a practical application and subject specific (e.g., a marketing class would market sources to the class). Have them do the work.
2. Alert participants that it is a contrived situation.
3. Place ownership on group participants rather than on instructor ("How would you solve this?").
4. Explain why it is contrived, after all, lectures are contrived.
5. Choosing or selecting an appropriate class to ensure success.
6. Give students some choices and responsibility for the activity.

► Problem 9: Students don't see value of process, only results.

Solutions
1. Give students an incentive to participate in the process.
2. Discuss the value of the ability to work cooperatively in career.
3. Students still might enjoy innovation in spite of themselves and the resistance, try not to worry about this. Give students objectives at beginning and summarize at end and just proceed.

► **Problems Related to Time**
► Problem 10: Time factor: Not enough class time for teaching and not enough time for students to get together for group project.

Solutions
1. Precise planning by instructor.
2. Librarian's insistence to administration for additional class time.
3. Faculty cooperation and development, e.g., bringing in extra speakers.
4. Librarian seminars—learning more about cooperative learning.
5. Hard for freshmen; try with upper division (students) who have basic library understanding.
6. Identify most essential learning objectives and focus on those.
7. CD-ROM: use it to develop group search strategy.
8. Try the one-minute approach like the advantages of OPAC over card catalog with freshmen orientation.
9. Focus on a few key concepts and simplify to permit mastery.

► Problem 11: Time required for planning and implementation.

Solutions
1. Limit goals and structure planning.
2. Plan ahead
3. Teacher as coach must develop leadership skills.
4. Cooperative learning by instructors to share ideas, work, and materials.
5. Efficacy increases with practice.
6. Work together as a team to plan classes.
7. Ask for more time from faculty.
8. Plan and structure ahead.
9. Pre-assignments.
10. Write to LOEX for examples.
11. More than one person teaching.
12. Collaborative planning.
13. Get help from faculty development sources.
14. Role play among staff
15. Limit goals and objectives.
16. Replicate with other faculty.

▶ Problem 12: How can you make sure you cover all your goals for a class when using cooperative learning?

Solutions
1. Frequent checkpoints to be sure you are on target.
2. Build in progress checks in the form of questions and control the timing of the class carefully.
3. Alternate group work and mini-lectures.
4. One librarian can model the process for another one in a team-teaching approach.
5. Rehearse with colleagues, student assistants, and time it.
6. Re-examine objectives; stick to major goals.
7. Make a time diagram (clock face?) and stick to it.
8. Stress results at end of each class.

▶ Problem 13: Can't cover as much subject content.

Solutions
1. Turn it into an opportunity for a follow-up (second meeting).
2. Don't worry about it! Remember: students don't retain most of what we impart through traditional methods, so focus on most essential messages realizing that cooperative learning should lead to greater retention of these essential points.
3. Select the one, two, or three most important concepts you want them to go away with and reinforce them. You can expand upon these with handouts and by incorporating short lectures into the experience.

▶ Problem 14: Cooperative learning takes more time and effort to prepare on the instructor's part.

Solutions
1. Work as a team or as a team with classroom instructor. It **does** take time but it's worth it because students will learn more and that's your ultimate goal. (Preparing the old way took time, too, but is no longer effective.)
2. Share successes and failures with colleagues on regular basis (1/2-hour weekly meeting).
3. Dovetail with faculty member already using group learning methods.
4. Network ideas and share preparation with other librarians—either team teach, use suggested core strategies, check with LOEX.
5. Share resources, (e.g., LOEX) and work with a partner (e.g., the faculty member). Prepare them by discussing value of cooperative learning

▶ Problem 15: It's impossible or difficult to integrate into a one-shot time slot.

Solutions
1. Try to select 2 or 3 things (tasks) most important; work on those and groups and have additional task or exploration or assignment. Expand 50 minutes by collaborating on follow-up with professor.
2. Try one activity. Start small and don't try to do it **all** as cooperative learning.
3. Time it!
4. Wait for the right class to try it with as a group for whom the needs match the process.
5. It works best with one small specific assignment.
6. Gradually incorporate small changes.

Problems Related to Content
▶ Problem 16: Belief that there may be concepts that cannot be taught by cooperative learning.

Solutions
1. Analyze concept: break into parts and attempt this method on some of the *parts!*
2. Go ahead and give it a try. Take a risk. Don't be defeatist. It's OK to experiment and fail.
3. Admit that some concepts cannot be taught this way. Identify methods that can be taught and combine with other methodologies.

▶ Problem 17: Less content taught.

Solutions
1. Revise your expectations of what needs to be taught *in the classroom.*
2. Problem-solving processes are lifelong skills. Content evolves (becomes outdated), but process endures and is useful with difficult content.
3. Establish goals, evaluation, and assessments.

Problems Related to Teaching Faculty
▶ Problem 18: Instructor may not support librarian's cooperative learning approach.

Solutions
1.Target cooperative teachers and hope in time the word will get around and teachers resistant will cooperate (with) this teaching method.

2. Introduce the instructor to techniques, concepts, advantages of cooperative learning.
3. Show videotape of a cooperative learning session.
4. Discuss the issue with the instructor *before* the BI session and try to convince that the special nature of new technology in libraries lends itself to group work and hands-on.

▶ Problem 19: Re-educating faculty

Solutions
1. Sponsor a workshop on cooperative learning.
2. Get a copy of the assignment and tell them how your proposed technique will benefit the students in completing the assignment successfully.
3. Let faculty know that collaborative learning techniques can be matched with their objectives for the class and invite them in as peer collaborators.

▶ Problem 20: Resistance on part of teaching faculty.

Solutions
1. Start with a more willing faculty member and develop a base of *success*.
2. Meet with faculty member and cite research, outline goals and process. Suggest an experiment trying it with 1 or 2 sections.

Problems Related to Group Learning
▶ Problem 21: Penalizes individuals who are gifted, talented, shy, lazy, etc. (heterogeneous group)

Solutions
1. Form pairs.
2. Responsibility falls to the teacher/instructor to recognize individual differences and make sure each individual is encouraged to contribute.
3. Cooperative learning can have a balancing effect for those who are lazy, uncooperative, etc.
4. Acknowledge that there are differences in the group.

▶ Problem 22: Personality types don't work well in groups.

Solutions
1. Give an uncooperative learner more responsibility or a special assignment.
2. Give specific guidelines, group rules, feedback in a constructive manner.
3. Have students give feedback to each other after class toward improving future cooperative learning.
4. Possible monitoring.
5. Provide written rules for group behavior, have someone moderate or monitor group activity.

▶ Problem 23: Correct information may not be transmitted by peers.

Solutions
1. Frequent check-up by teacher. Teacher as ex-officio member of group. (This takes more time on behalf of teacher— (who) may not want or be able to do this much.)
2. If instructor hears an incorrect answer from the group recorder, then other groups can advise the group of the correct one.
3. Receive training on techniques to use to deal with incorrect answers such as asking students, "Under what conditions would this solution not work;" "Why wouldn't it work?".
4. Ask leading questions.
5. (Have) larger group evaluate the answers.

▶ Problem 24: Loss of student individuality

Solutions
1. Ground rules for opportunity to participate.
2. Incorporate individual problem solving, creativity; individual completes assignment, then come together as group.
3. Give each person in the group a responsibility.
4. Show that we value every one's ideas.
5. Eye contact.
6. Devise a way to encourage each individual to participate (e.g., "Talking Chips").

▶ Problem 25: Individuals are not responsible/accountable for their contributions (good, bad or none) to the group effort.

Solutions.
1. Assign responsibility for tasks to individual group members.

2. Method for assessing individual and group efforts.
3. Inform students beforehand that any student in each group may be called on to report.

▶ Problem 26: Difficult to evaluate learning.

Solutions
1. Evaluate student performance on post presentation quiz.
2. Ask student to write down the main point for the day and hand it in as they leave.
3. Oral feedback
4. Evaluation can be individual although learning is cooperative.

▶ Problem 27: Recreating the cooperative learning experience for a student who misses class legitimately.

Solutions
1. Provide session outline/objectives to the student and request peer assistance to help student complete worksheets.
2. Assign missing person to a group—make it the group's responsibility to bring student up to speed.
3. Have one member brief the student.
4. Try to better integrate the student into the group.
5. Stress how important it is that they attend.
6. Consider changing group meeting time given other conditions
7. Try to accommodate students' needs.

Miscellaneous Problems
▶ Problem 28: Inadequate understanding of cooperative learning techniques by instructor.

Solutions
1. In library BI, team-teaching.
2. For other teaching faculty, workshops and reporting back from meetings.
3. Attend workshops on cooperative learning techniques.
4. Mentoring—find someone successful.
5. Keep up-to-date on literature.
6. Rehearsal—could use videos.
7. Library puts together collection of materials on cooperative learning. Also, the library will create a bibliography on the topic.

▶ Problem 29: American society has an attitude that independence and rugged individualism are to be highly regarded. This is counter to cooperative learning concepts, thus there is "built-in" resistance.

Solutions
1. Acknowledge that this is a belief of American society, but stress advantages of cooperative learning approach. Tell students that their independent contributions are recognized and that the small group moves ahead just as the nation moves ahead.
2. Game or technique that promotes cooperation.
3. Start young.
4. Instructor needs to be sensitive to the students' personalities.
5. World is becoming smaller and smaller. People need to have this technique brought to their attention.

▶ Problem 30: Old habits are hard to break for students and instructors.

Solutions
1. Tell them: "Well. . . life's a bitch and then you die!"
2. Using cooperative learning techniques with each other and the staff. Consider team teaching and focus on one course.
3. Show results/success by example of how cooperative learning works.
4. A well-designed and enthusiastic presentation will likely be easily accepted.

Roundtable

▶ Purpose: To identify the most valuable thing you learned.

▶ One person writes task at top of pad.

▶ Next person writes 1 idea, reads aloud, passes pad to left.

▶ Brainstorm until time is called.

Roundtable Reflection

At the end of the workshop, all participants had an opportunity to reflect on what they had learned. Group members also shared their written responses with each other. The list below is a compilation of all the written responses we received arranged by broad category.

Most Important Things We Learned

▶ What Cooperative Learning Is
  • What cooperative learning really is.
  • Shared responsibility.
  • Have been doing several things cooperatively that I didn't think of at the beginning.

▶ Petals Around a Rose
  • Competitive behavior is difficult to suppress.
  • The obvious success of the cooperative learning groups in Petals Around a Rose vs. the failure of the competitive groups.
  • The Petals Around a Rose game proved the greater success of cooperative learning and made it clear also that learning by **doing** is most effective.
  • That groups working cooperatively solved problem better than those workingcompetitively.
  • Modeling of game approaches in a time frame (1-2 minutes)

▶ Theory of Cooperative Learning
  • The ed psych basis for successful cooperative learning.
  • Social construction of shared knowledge through cooperative learning.
  • The objective of the instructional sessions is to cause the students to learn, not for us to teach.
  • Need to expand by turning more learning over to students—user centered focus.

▶ Benefits of Cooperative Learning
  • I learned that research has shown that students learn more and more effectively through cooperative learning which is a strong argument for implementing it.
  • People learn better with cooperative learning; therefore, it's worth the effort!
  • The social research behind cooperative learning was especially interesting to me.
  • Working in small groups is possible, constructive, and fun.
  • That cooperative learning can be used to facilitate the teaching of many different concepts.
  • Group members have lots of good ideas and I can learn from them.
  • One is forced to look at concepts and/or knowledge from many different perspectives—not just one's own perspective.
  • Students will retain knowledge longer when they've participated in process.
  • Students learn and retain more when cooperative learning methods are used.
  • Active learners remember more.
  • This technique increases retention.
  • Learning sticks.
  • Cooperative learning can produce long lasting transfer of knowledge.
  • We also can teach social development.
  • Through our own experience at the table I learned that cooperative learning activities really engage the learners (us) and make lectures more effective.
  • Opportunity to use each person's contribution.
  • Everybody can express ideas.
  • Allows even shy members to express their ideas.
  • Students have more accomplishments.
  • Collective input provides a variety of ideas.
  • The group can often generate better and more creative ideas.
  • More work done when fun.
  • Creativity encouraged.
  • People will pay attention because they are involved.
  • Cooperative learning hopefully will eliminate the glazed look of students.
  • Increases attention.
  • More personal investment.
  • Sharing.
  • Solutions are reinforced when shared.
  • Face-to-face connections.
  • Interdependence
  • Breaks down resistance to stay within cultural group.
  • Reduces stress and competitiveness.
  • Easier for teachers.
  • Supportive
  • Don't have to carry the whole load.

- Enables librarians to see things from students' perspectives.
- Cooperative learning is fun for both teacher and student.
- Cooperative learning can/should be **fun.**
- Learning more fun.
- Cooperative learning is engaging and fun as well as instructive.
- Less for students/teachers to worry about.
- Stimulation
- Can be exciting for students and teachers.
- Cooperative learning techniques can increase effectiveness.
- Different ways of teaching that can be more interesting and productive.
- More spontaneity.
- Preparation more invigorating
- More honest process.
- Recognizing that sometimes "messy" process of cooperative learning can still convey important concepts.
- I learned that the technique of cooperative learning—if well done—will deepen the understanding of basic concepts on part of all students.
- Research validates the advantages of cooperative learning.
- That these techniques work—create enthusiasm and participation and engagement.

▶ Enthusiasm/Desire to Apply
- Discussion has given me the confidence to try this method of teaching.
- That cooperative learning has lots of positive points and is worth trying.
- That I am complacent about my success and must move on into cooperative learning.
- The most valuable thing I learned is the depth of ideas shared strengthens my outlook regarding a **new** teaching technique.
- Cooperative learning is a viable option to teaching students.
- Cooperative learning is a viable teaching tool.
- People **do** care to work cooperatively—give them a chance.
- My insecurities have been addressed and I learned that I can do it.
- Take ideas back to colleagues ("new concept"!)

▶ Implementation
- Cooperative learning is valuable, but time-consuming.
- Cooperative learning can be implemented—it can be done.
- Cooperative learning is doable.
- Cooperative learning is **doable.**
- The idea can work and you should try it.
- I learned that this kind of teaching takes time, planning, and lots of help in implementation and can be rewarding.
- How necessary pre-planning is to successful implementation of this method.
- Rules provide a good working framework.
- We can acknowledge the difficulties of cooperative learning strategies and reach cooperative solutions.
- Start small—one thing at a time.
- To implement, start simple and evaluate as you go to determine how it's working.
- Start out small incorporating cooperative learning ideas until comfortable with situation.
- Pick a "partner" at library to help in planning and implementing cooperative learning.
- Overcoming fear—can take small steps like finding colleagues.
- When implementing a cooperative learning workshop/program, don't go alone; good to have colleague to help.
- Cooperative learning requires a structure but that structures can be flexible.
- I learned that change need not be painful if approached with a cooperative spirit.
- The amount of planning and self-education needed to begin thinking about implementing cooperative learning.
- I will need to find out more about cooperative learning techniques before I utilize them.
- The importance of using checkpoints to gauge progress toward goals in cooperative learning.
- Reinforces choosing your key concepts in order to make cooperative learning possible.
- Group projects must have clear objectives and clear directions.
- Make sure every person in group contributes.
- To not forget basics in addition to doing cooperative learning, e.g., cooperative learning + effective handouts.
- Individuality can be suppressed—must keep this in mind when planning exercise.

▶ Specific Techniques
- I learned helpful specific techniques.
- I also learned more innovative techniques that I can try at home.
- Talking Chips technique for sharing ideas.
- The actual modeling of the technique
- Different ideas of group activities
- Learned particular methods of cooperative learning by having them modeled in this workshop and from the video.
- Am using some of the techniques already and have learned some interesting points on how to expand cooperative learning in my sessions.
- Some techniques for students sharing and teaching each other, not just me interacting with different groups.

▶ Group Formation
  • Group size and what works.
  • Form groups and structure them so that each member of the group is responsible for a task and can contribute to the group.
  • Size of group determined (in part) by instructor's newness to the techniques.
  • **Structuring** the group experience.
  • Size and mix of members in group must be considered; i.e., individuals within group cannot be glossed over.

▶ Application
  • Faculty can be targeted in workshops to show how cooperative learning produces skills useful in the classroom.
  • Cooperative learning is a technique which may or may not work, but can be applied in all classes.
  • Cooperative learning is a viable option for core courses as well as freshman English.
  • Cooperatively learning can work successfully in a variety of settings.
  • Cooperative learning can be accomplished in many settings and in many ways.

▶ Application to BI
  • I can see a variety of ways in which I can use cooperative learning in both my formal credit course **and** in one-shot BI sessions.
  • The practical examples of successful implementation of cooperative learning in **library** settings.
  • To see how others have used cooperative learning techniques in libraries and how comfortable and fun it is for the facilitators and participants.
  • Learning that cooperative learning is being successfully introduced in 50-minute one-shot sessions.
  • Cooperative learning can increase effectiveness of BI sessions.
  • I found the suggestions to use cooperative learning techniques in small doses (focused on a search strategy, for example) will make it possible to use the techniques in the 50-minute "one-shot" sessions I do, not just in the more extended sessions.
  • Hearing how other libraries are applying cooperative learning.
  • The most valuable thing was seeing the actual examples of use (University of Illinois scripts, video).
  • The fact that I might be able to do something in 50 minutes.
  • Suggestions for 50-minute presentation.
  • How to transfer cooperative learning to brief B.I. sessions. I've used it in a formal class.
  • Practical examples in the University of Illinois handouts.
  • Variety of cooperative teaching methods allows for a lot of flexibility in application to BI.
  • Good, effective BI takes time, thought, and effort.
  • During the actual BI session, to avoid group confusion leading to a less-than-meaningful experience, the instructor must clearly present instructions.
  • BI can be fun!
  • Cooperative learning **can** be done in BI.
  • A new way of doing the BI and test the impact on a particular class.

▶ Application to Large Groups (Harvard video)
  • The feasibility of cooperative learning for large classes.
  • Grads modeling of behaviors not seen in professors.
  • Simple small group tasks can be done in a few minutes.
  • Students prefer cooperative learning to lecture—(the Harvard video exemplified this).
  • Learning about applicability of cooperative and collaborative learning in large group situation.
  • Try the one-minute technique from the video.
  • Cooperative learning can be implemented in large groups.
  • Cooperative learning does work with large groups.
  • Specific cooperative learning techniques, e.g., the one demonstrated in video.
  • From the video, that students really **do** learn better and enjoy cooperative learning.

▶ General
  • Characteristics of cooperative learning and basic ways cooperative learning could be implemented.
  • I feel that my creativity in teaching has been stimulated.
  • I learned how **effective** cooperative learning was/is by seeing it work.
  • I learned how cooperative learning works by observing it in action.
  • LOEX Conference is a good example of cooperative learning.
  • Global implications.
  • Importance of **experiencing** cooperative learning rather than hearing about it, plus pros and cons of cooperative learning which will (potentially) help to think about prior to implementation.
  • I was convinced that cooperative learning can work because of the group I was with.
  • I got a feeling from experiencing cooperative learning for how successful it can be in learning.
  • Others believe in cooperative learning, too.
  • Many people are doing cooperative learning.
  • I learned what cooperative learning is and obtained some idea of how to do it and what its benefits are.
  • Cooperative learning is a whole new way of "teaching" as opposed to lecture. It's not easy but rewarding.
  • Cooperative learning needs to be done in conjunction with other methods—too much is too much. (This workshop was a little overwhelming—perhaps a bit shorter.)
  • I've learned what cooperative learning is and how to implement it.

COOPERATIVE LEARNING

INFORMATION PACKET

- **Forming Groups**

- **Techniques**

- **Suggestions**

WORKSHOP LEADERS

LORI ARP
SHARON MADER
MARY JANE PETROWSKI
BETSY WILSON

CONSIDERATIONS IN FORMING GROUPS

■ SIZE . . .

The smallest group is two. The largest recommended is six. The following are some generalizations which may or may not be true for your specific situation.

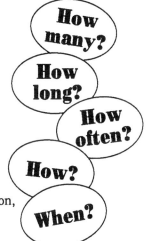

Advantages of smaller groups

- Each member participates more
- Fewer social skills required
- Require less time to form and reform (movement of people and chairs; selecting groups)
- Best for dealing with simple tasks and reaching consensus
- Can work quickly

Advantages of larger groups

- More ideas generated
- Can deal better with complex ideas
- Fewer group reports for large group to hear
- Work well with complex strategies such as Jigsaw, Group Investigation, and Co-op Co-op

Advantages of specific numbers in groups:

- **Two** – It's hard to get left out of a pair!
  – Pairs are easiest to form: "Turn to a neighbor" may do it.

- **Three** – Pairs can only interact one way. Triads can interact three ways.
  – Triads tend to surface issues. Two will reach consensus, then the third will say, "Yes, but . . ."
  – Triads are good for process observing: one observes two others.

- **Four** – Groups can easily form two pairs for Think-Pair-Share, interviewing, or tutoring.
  – Foursomes can interact six ways.

- **Six** – Six-somes can form two triads or three pairs for intra-group work.
  – There are fewer group reports to the class.

■ HOW TO FORM TEAMS . . .

Heterogeneous or Homogeneous

Unless there is an overwhelming reason to use homogeneous groups, research favors making groups as heterogeneous as possible with regard to academic achievement, gender, ethnicity, task orientation, learning style, ability/disability, and learning style. Heterogeneous groups promote more elaborate thinking and explanations, and provide opportunities for students to develop feelings of mutual concern.

Random, self-selected, or assigned

Student self-selection of groups is generally not successful, although there are ways for students to provide some input for teachers to consider in assigning groups.

Random selection or assigned groups are more likely to be heterogeneous. Whether to use random groups or assigned groups depends to a great extent on the duration of the task and the frequency with which groups are used.

If groups are used frequently or if the task is of short duration, then any difficulties arising from "unbalanced" teams will not be important over the long run . . . they will balance out.

If, on the other hand, groups are used frequently or the task is of some duration, it will become more important that the makeup of groups is seen as "fair," so the groups themselves should be carefully selected.

■ DURATION OF GROUPS . . .

Groups may work for as short a period of time as five minutes, or they may work together several times a week for an entire semester.

Short duration advantages

- Students have opportunities to get to know more classmates
- Group formation skills are practiced

Long duration advantages

- Students have practice with more complex collaborative skills
- Stronger bonds can form between students
- More complex tasks can be tackled

Note: Groups of long duration should work together at least once a week.

A rule of thumb is to allow groups to remain together long enough to feel successful, but not so long that bonds become counter-productive in the class. It is usually a mistake to break groups up because they are having trouble functioning, because members will then feel unsuccessful as group members and take that feeling with them to the next group situation. Try to find some measure of success!

■ FORMING TEAMS RANDOMLY . . .

Line up by some criterion and count off
  Students can line up by first name, last name, middle name, height, birthday, age, length of hair, color of eyes, or how much they like math.
Colored shapes method (e.g., use five kinds of shapes each in five different colors: group by color or shape)
Deuces Wild (uses a deck of cards)
Hum into groups (prepare index cards with the names of different songs)
Famous pairs (prepare index cards each with one name of a famous pair)
Puzzle pieces (students whose puzzle pieces go together form a pair or larger group)
Use your imagination!

■ FORMING HETEROGENEOUS TEAMS . . .

Especially for STAD, TGT, and Jigsaw

1. Rank students by academic achievement in the subject

2. Determine the number of teams. Divide the number of students by four to get the number of teams. The remainder, if any, tells you the number of 5-member teams.

3. If there was a remainder, reserve that many students from the middle of your list to be assigned to teams as 5th members.

4. Assign the highest student, lowest student, and two students closest to the middle of your list to the first team. Cross them off the list.

5. Assign from the remaining students the (now) highest, lowest, and two students closest to the middle to the next team. Cross them off.

6. Continue assigning teams until all students have been assigned except for those remaining from Step 3.

7. Check your teams for heterogeneity by gender, ethnicity, or other criterion. Balance them to the extent possible by adding 5th members or by swapping students who are of about the same ability academically.

8. Assign any remaining students that were not assigned in Step 7. Consider adding a 5th member to a team in which one member is frequently absent.

Example:

If you have 30 students, you will have 7 teams. Two teams will have 5 members. On your ranked list of students, make a note to reserve the 15th and 16th students until last.

Team #1 (tentatively) .... 1st, 30th, 14th, and 17th students
Team #2 (tentatively) .... 2nd, 29th, 13th, and 18th students, etc.

Compiled by Ellen Stine Miller • Howard County Staff Development Center • August 1988

SOME COOPERATIVE LEARNING STRATEGIES
THAT WORK WELL ON THE UNIVERSITY LEVEL

1. **THINK-PAIR-SHARE:** The instructor poses a question, preferably one demanding analysis, evaluation, or synthesis, and gives students about a minute to think through an appropriate response. This "think time" can be spent writing, also. Students then turn to a partner and share their repsonses. During the third step, student responses can be shared within a four-person learning team, within a larger group, or with an entire class during a follow-up discussion. the caliber of discussion is enhanced by this technique, and all students have an opportunity to learn by reflection and by verbalization.

2. **CORNERS:** Students divide into four large groups, based on a teacher-determined criteria, where they can discuss specific issues or join a partner and then form a new learning team.

3. **THREE-STEP INTERVIEW:** Common as an ice-breaker or a team-building exercise, this structure can be used also to share information such as hypotheses or reactions to a film or article. Students interview one another in pairs, alternating roles. They then share in a four-member learning team the information or insights gleaned from the paired interview.

4. **NUMBERED HEADS TOGETHER:** Member of learning teams, usually composed of four individuals, count off: 1, 2, 3, or 4. The instructor poses a question, usually factual in nature, but requiring some higher order thinking skills. Students discuss the question, making certain that every group member knows the answer. The instructor calls a specific number and the designated team members respond as group spokespersons. Again, students benefit from the verbalization, and the peer coaching helps both the high and the low achievers. Class time is usually better spent because less time is wasted on inappropriate responses and because all students become actively involved with the material. Because no one knows which number the teacher will call, all team members have a vested interest in understanding the appropriate response.

5. **ROUNDTABLE:** A brainstorming technique, students write in turn on a a single pad of paper, starting their ideas aloud as they write. As the tablet circulates, more and more information is added until various aspects of a topic are explored.

6. **TALKING CHIPS:** To structure discussion and encourage full participation, each team member shares information/contributes to the discussion after placing a talking chip (a pen, checker, index card, etc.) in the center of the group. After all students have contributed in random order, they retrieve their chips to begin another round.

7. **CO-OP CARDS:** Useful for memorization and review, students coach each other using using flashcards.

8. **SIMPLE JIGSAW:** The faculty member divides an assignment or topic into four parts with all students from each learning team volunteering to become "experts" on one of the parts. Expert teams then work together to master their fourth of the material and also to discover the best way to help others learn it. All experts then reassemble in their home learning teams where they teach the other group members.

9. **STRUCTURED CONTROVERSY:** Team members assume different positions on controversial issues, discussing, researching, and sharing with the group their findings. This technique allows students to explore topics in depth and promotes higher order thinking skills.

10. **GROUP INVESTIGATION:** Based on six successive stages, cooperative groups investigate topics of mutual interest, planning what they will study, how they will divide the research responsibilities, and how they will synthesize and summarize their findings for the class.

THINK-PAIR-SHARE
A COOPERATIVE LEARNING STRATEGY

■ WHY THINK-PAIR-SHARE?

Many teachers run their classrooms in the "share" mode. Basically this recitation model means that one student talks at a time. Though not fatal for the teacher who is proficient at this "uni-mode" strategy, it is not conducive to a high degree of pupil response, and for beginning teachers especially it can be a major source of control problems.

Think-Pair-Share is a "multi-mode" strategy developed to encourage student participation in the classroom. Students are taught to use a new response cycle in answering questions. The technique is simple to learn and is applicable across all grade levels, disciplines and group sizes. In some cases (K-12) students can facilitate the process themselves.

■ WHAT ARE THE COMPONENTS OF THINK-PAIR-SHARE?

- Students listen while the teacher poses a question.
- Students are given time in which to think of a response.
- Students are then sometimes cued to pair with a neighbor and discuss their responses.
- Finally, students are invited to share their responses with the whole group.

A time limit is set for each step in the process. Many teachers use cueing devices such as bells, pointers, hand signals, or cubes to move students through a cycle. Students may be asked to write or web (diagram) their responses while in the think and/or pair mode(s).

■ WHAT ARE THE BENEFITS TO STUDENTS?

Students have time to at least think through their own answers to questions before the questions are answered and the discussion moves on. They rehearse responses mentally, and sometimes verbally with another student, before being asked to share publicly. All students have an opportunity to share their thinking with at least one other student, thereby increasing their sense of involvement.

Think-Pair-Share is a Cooperative Learning strategy, and as such has advantages for students in the areas of acceptance, peer support, achievement, self-esteem, liking of other students, and liking of school. Cooperative Learning also has positive effects on mainstreaming and relationships between handicapped and nonhandicapped students.

■ WHAT ARE THE BENEFITS TO TEACHERS?

Students have been found to spend more time on task and to listen to each other more when engaged in Think-Pair-Share activities. Many more students raise their hands to respond after rehearsing in pairs. Students may have better recall due to increased "wait time," and the quality of responses may be better.

Like students, teachers also have more time to think when using Think-Pair-Share. They can concentrate on asking higher-order questions, observing student reactions, and listening to student responses. Class discussion can be a much more relaxing experience for teachers and students. Finally, Think-Pair-Share is easy to learn and easy to use!

Developed by Dr. Frank Lyman, Howard County Public Schools
and the Southern Teacher Education Center, University of Maryland

THINK-PAIR-SHARE STRUCTURES

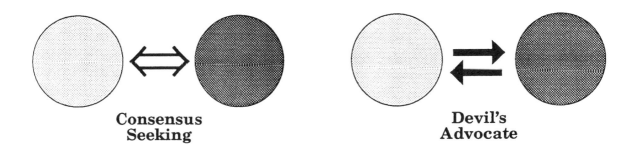

Consensus Seeking

Devil's Advocate

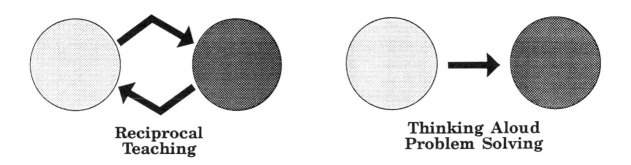

Reciprocal Teaching

Thinking Aloud Problem Solving

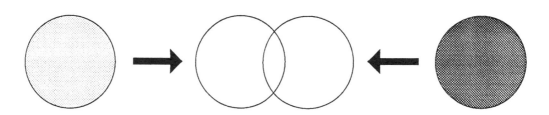

Pair Problem Solving

— LIZABETH WILSON AND OTHERS —

CORNERS

CORNERS can be used to gather data in a quick and visual way and to involve participants. It can be used as the basis for forming either homogeneous or heterogeneous groups around some theme. It provides for movement, and can be used for metaphorical problem solving.

Corners is designed to allow participants to more easily know and accept themselves and others. Any individual difference dimension can be the focus, such as favorite teaching strategies, favorite leisure activities, or favorite type of praise. Participants can also be grouped by favorite metaphors; for example, when you think of yourself as a teacher, are you most like an owl, a tiger, a dolphin, or a kangaroo?

TYPICAL SEQUENCE

1. Announce the corners; post a visual in each corner (or area in the room)
2. Provide think time for participants to choose a corner; ask them not to be swayed by other's choices
3. Participants go to corners
4. Brainstorm as a group:

   - Reasons for selecting that corner, or
   - Why that corner is best, or
   - Answers for some other question you put to them

5. Reach consensus on the best ideas
6. Select a spokesperson to share with the rest of the group

The leader or other members of the group can process the results.

For more information about Corners, see:
Spencer Kagan's *Cooperative Learning: Resources for Teachers*,
published by Resources for Teachers, San Juan Capistrano, CA (714) 248-7757.

Cooperative Structures for Administrators and Supervisors • Ellen Stine Miller & Karen Spencer • 6/90

THREE-STEP INTERVIEW

■ FORM PAIRS . . .

Use existing pair partners, or use cards or matched shapes to form participants into pairs, or tell participants to find someone they do not know.

■ A INTERVIEWS B . . .

In each pair, one participant interviews the other on a topic previously announced. Participant A should be reminded to use active listening skills. Give a time limit.

■ B INTERVIEWS A . . .

After the announced time has elapsed, participants reverse roles and participant B interviews participant A. Again, remind participant B to use active listening skills.

■ PAIRS PAIR TO FORM GROUPS OF FOUR . . .

You may continue your theme from forming pairs in the first step. For instance, if you used UNO cards to form your pairs, now the two pairs holding 3's would get together. If you asked participants to find someone they did not know to pair with, pairs should now find other pairs they do not know.

■ SHARE-AROUND . . .

Now participants take turns introducing their pair partners and sharing what they learned. They might use a formula sentence such as, "I'd like you to meet Saul. Something unusual about him is that . . ."

SOME HINTS

THE TOPIC: It is important to select a topic in such a way that each participant has a unique contribution (that is, so that the first participant does not give "the answer"). Opinion/evaluation questions work well.

> *Examples:* • Something about yourself others may not know (and you'd be willing to share)
> • A favorite book, and why
> • A current event
> • One thing I liked best about . . .

Another possibility is to have participants interview each other in roles, that is, assign each participant in established groups of four a different identity to research, and then do the interviews in those roles.

Time limits and clear transitions from one step to the next help the process run more smoothly.

INTERVIEW SKILLS: This is an excellent opportunity to practice listening skills. Participants can brainstorm skills, or you can introduce them a few at a time.

> *Examples:* • Take notes on what your partner is saying
> • If you are the interviewer, resist the temptation to talk. Use non-verbal encouragers (eye contact, nods, smiles, "um hm", etc.)

REHEARSAL: After the second interview and before participants move into groups of four, it sometimes helps to give participants a few seconds to mentally rehearse what they will say about their partner, and to check their recollections for accuracy with their partner.

From: Spencer Kagan, *Cooperative Learning: Resources for Teachers,*
published by Resources for Teachers, 27134 Paseo Espada #202, San Juan Capistrana, CA 92675

Cooperative Structures for Administrators and Supervisors • Ellen Stine Miller & Karen Spencer • 6/90

ROUNDTABLE

■ PURPOSE . . .

Roundtable is a technique that can be used for brainstorming, reviewing, or practicing a skill. Used in a contest fashion, it can also be an excellent teambuilding technique. Roundtable ensures that all members of a group are involved.

■ PREPARATION . . .

Roundtable requires groups of three or more seated around a common writing surface. Participants need a pencil or pen, and one piece of paper to be shared by the group. The leader should announce the question or problem. Groups should be told that their job is to brainstorm as many answers as they can to the question or problem. They must follow certain rules in answering:

- Group members must take turns writing answers on the piece of paper, passing the paper around the circle clockwise.
- Members must not skip a turn. (You may decide if helping allowed. If participants become stuck too often or too quickly, the problem was too hard.)
- Groups must stop when time is called (about one minute, depending on the task).

The key to Roundtable is the question or problem. It must be one with multiple answers and one which offers a high probability of success to all participants. You should relate the question to the purpose of the meeting or workshop, but keep it very simple so that all participants can contribute and experience working productively as a group.

When time is called, results will be handled according to your objective. If the objective was *teambuilding,* each team should score its own answer sheet and count the number of correct answers. The leader should reward the groups with the most answers and ask them to describe their methods. (Alternatively you can reward the most unusual or creative answers.)

If your objective was simple to *brainstorm* a variety of answers, a simultaneous sharing technique such as "Stand and Share" would be appropriate.

All groups should have an opportunity to reflect on what made them successful as a group, and how they might do better the next time.

SIMULTANEOUS ROUNDTABLE

When the answers are long, groups are larger, or production of ideas is more important, send more pieces of paper around at the same time.

Example 1: Have each participant begin to brainstorm answers to a question. Then have each pass his/her sheet to the left. Participants read and respond to the sheets they receive, then pass them on. Work continues until the papers have been passed completely around the table.

Example 2: Give each participant in a group a different category for a response. For instance, if working on a school climate plan, categories might be speakers, topics, sources of funds, and incentives for participating. Participants write one idea on their sheets, and then pass them to the left. They will have a new category to respond to as they receive each new sheet. Work continues until the papers have been passed around the group several times.

ROUND ROBIN

Have participants answer orally rather than in writing. You may use a recorder.

Cooperative Structures for Administrators and Supervisors • Ellen Stine Miller & Karen Spencer • 6/90

Send-A-Problem

1. PARTICIPANTS CREATE REVIEW QUESTIONS. Each participant in a group makes up a review problem and writes it down on a flash card. Encourage high-consensus problems which might have a right or wrong answer, verifiable by the text.

   The author of each question asks it of those in his or her group. If there is total consensus, the author writes the answer on the back of the card. If not, the question is revised so that it produces consensus. The side of the card with the question is marked Q and the side with the answer is marked A.

2. GROUPS SEND-A-PROBLEM. Each group passes its stack of review questions to another group.

3. GROUPS RESPOND. Each participant takes one question from the stack it receives. Participant 1 reads the first question. The group attempts to answer it. If they have consensus they turn the card over, to see if they agreed with the sending group. If not, they write their answer as an alternative. Participant 2 reads the next one, and the procedure is repeated. The stacks of cards can be sent to a third and fourth group, etc.

4. SENDERS CLARIFY. Stacks of cards are returned to the senders. Senders have an opportunity to discuss and clarify any questions indicated on the back of the cards.

From: Spencer Kagan, *Cooperative Learning: Resources for Teachers,*
published by Resources for Teachers, 27134 Paseo Espada #202, San Juan Capistrano, CA 92675

Variation: Send-A-Problem Problem-Solving

Each group reaches consensus on a real problem the group would like to have solved (e.g., what to do about people who arrive late for meetings or leave early.) The problem is written on a piece of paper and attached to the outside of a folder or envelope. Problems are then sent clockwise to the next group. Each group brainstorms for three minutes on solutions to the problem they receive, and then spends two minutes reaching consensus on their best 2-3 ideas. All work is put into the folder or envelope. Problems are then rotated to the next group, which also brainstorms and identifies best ideas without reading the previous group's work. This process may continue to one or more additional groups. The last group has seven minutes to read all of the previous group's ideas and develop a prioritized list of possible solutions, which is written on chart paper and presented publicly.

ALTERNATIVE: The leader can present a list of typical or previously generated problems and groups each select a different problem to begin work on. The number of problems should exceed the number of groups to permit choice. The class can also brainstorm a number of problems from which to select. Work proceeds as above.

Idea generated by the Howard County Staff Development Center. 1989

Cooperative Structures for Administrators and Supervisors • Ellen Stine Miller & Karen Spencer • 6/90

BRAINSTORMING

Brainstorming is a highly effective method of generating ideas. It is especially powerful when utilized by groups, although the process may be used by individuals as well. Unfortunately, the term, brainstorming, is often misused by many people who think of it as any open-ended discussion. Brainstorming is, in fact, a structured process with specific guidelines. Its effectiveness as an idea generating method is related to the degree to which groups understand and apply these guidelines.

THE D.O.V.E. RULE

The guidelines for brainstorming can be summarized by the acronym, D.O.V.E., as follows:

D EFER JUDGMENT
The judging or evaluation of ideas inhibits the flow of brainstorming and should be avoided. Ideas can be evaluated later. Participants in a brainstorming group should make a conscious effort to avoid judging their own ideas as well as those of others.

O RIGINALITY
Brainstorming is designed to stimulate original ideas. Brainstormers should strive for the unique. Even "wild and crazy" ideas are encouraged since these often lead to new insights.

V ASTNESS
Brainstorming groups should try to come up with as many ideas as possible. The more ideas available, the greater the probability of really good ideas emerging. Quantity breeds quality.

E LABORATE
In brainstorming session, one idea will frequently spark another. Participants should seek to build, or "hitchhike," on the ideas of others.

TEACHING BRAINSTORMING

Since brainstorming is a structured process involving specific rules, it is necessary to provide explicit instruction for its use. Many teachers have found it beneficial to introduce the brainstorming process to students by using "problems" of the type listed below:

What would be all the possible consequences if...

... people needed only two hours sleep each night?

... all home telephones had video screens?

... newspapers smelled like hamburgers?

... all the world's oil would be used up in one year at present consumption rate?

... the average daily temperature was 80 degrees?

... everyone in the world suddenly became six inches tall?

... all television stations stopped broadcasting for a year?

... students were only required to attend school until age 12?

... the average life expectancy increased to 120 years?

How many new ways can you think of to ...

... improve a bathtub?

... use a wire coat hanger?

... prevent a dog and cat from fighting?

... modify a popular game?

... use discarded automobile tires?

... improve a calendar?

... advertise a new breakfast cereal?

... improve a local recreation area?

Once students demonstrate an understanding of the D.O.V.E. rule and appear comfortable working in groups, the Brainstorming Process may be applied to a variety of subject-related and "real life" problems.

SUGGESTIONS FOR MANAGING
TEAM BUZZ SESSIONS & WHOLE GROUP DISCUSSIONS

1. After you ask a question allow wait-time.

   "Hold your responses/Don't begin your discussion until everyone has had 15 seconds to think."

2. When possible allow learners to respond first in pairs or small groups.

   "Tell your neighbor." "Buzz in small groups and then we'll discuss it as a large group."

3. Build in alternate response modes.

   "Thumbs up, thumbs down."

4. Use deadlines.

   "You have 30 seconds."

5. Use transition cues.

   "When you hear the bell, you have 10 seconds to finish talking to your partner/in your group."

6. Reduce sharing time.

   Instead of allowing eight participants to answer in the large group, allow three. Never have more than 6 groups report—find another way to share.

7. Provide alternative structures for sharing.

   "This time share your partner's/group's response." "This time try to reach consensus with your partner/group."

8. Use alternative pairs/groups.

   "This time share with the person across the table from you rather than the one next to you." "Sit with others with whom you don't normally work today."

9. Give auditory as well as visual directions.

   Written cues to the question provide focus for the discussion.

10. Be clear on your expectations.

    "Name three ways . . ." "Brainstorm as many ideas as you can."

11. Make it clear when or if you are looking for one answer.

    "There are many possible answers to this question." "We discussed this yesterday . . . you may want to review your notes."

12. Record answers on charts or overheads when appropriate.

    Charting helps visual learners, provides focus, lessens the likelihood that duplicate answers will be given, allows participants to build on others' ideas, and provides a reference for later discussion.

13. Encourage response from one participant or group to another.

    "Do you agree? Tell him/her/them why or why not."

Adapted from work by Frank Lyman
Howard County Public Schools/University of Maryland (1986)
by Ellen Miller, Howard County Public Schools (1990)

Cooperative Structures for Administrators and Supervisors • Ellen Stine Miller & Karen Spencer • 6/90

SUGGESTIONS FOR GROUP DISCUSSION

1. **After you ask a question allow wait-time:** *"No one may raise a hand until I give a signal."* *(Under no conditions let hands be raised until after all have thought and you have given a cue.)*

2. **When possible allow learners to respond first in pairs:** *"Tell your partner."*

3. **Build in alternate response modes:** *"Raise your yes or no cards." "Pick a shape and Think-Link your answer." "Thumbs up, thumbs down."*

4. **Use deadlines:** *"You have 20 seconds."*

5. **Use transition cues:** *"When you hear the bell, you have 10 seconds to finish talking to your partner."*

6. **Reduce sharing time:** *Instead of allowing eight children to answer in the large group, allow three.*

7. **Provide alternative structures for pairing:** *"This time you will tell the group what your partner said." "This time try to come to agreement with your partner."*

8. **Use prearranged pairings:** *"Today sit with your 'blue' partner."* *(Cue on the wall.)*

9. **Use wall-cues to provide common frames of reference:** *"Choose a story from the wall list and compare its setting to that of our book." "Pick an idea and give examples from some stories." "Choose a Think-Link shape and diagram your answer."*

10. **Make it clear when or if you are looking for one answer:** *"I have no idea what the best answers to this question are." "There are many possible answers to this question."*

11. **Encourage response from one learner to another:** *"Do you agree? Why?"*

12. **Use cues appropriate to the learner:** *Cubes, wheels, charts, hand signals for K-8; verbal or hand signals for high school.*

13. **Be clear on your objective:** *"That wasp flying around has nothing to do with gravity."*

14. **Flow from one thinking type to another:** *"What does that remind you of? Why do you think the did it? Should they have done it? Why?"*

15. **Allow students to make up their own questions:** *"Use the thinking type cues and make up a question for the class."*

By Frank Lyman • Published by the Howard County Public Schools Staff Development Center • 1986

COOPERATIVE LEARNING:
A SELECTIVE ANNOTATED BIBLIOGRAPHY

■ BIBLIOGRAPHIES

• Graves, L.N., & Graves, T. (Eds.). (1993). 1993 Resource Guide [Special Issue]. *Cooperative Learning*
12(4).

> An annotated bibliography of over 200 currently available books and videos on cooperative learning. Updated
> annually.

• Totten, S., Sills, T., Digby, A., & Russ, P. (Eds.). (1991). *Cooperative Learning: A Guide to Research.*
New York: Garland

> This evaluative annotated bibliography of 818 entries brings together relevant citations from the most commonly
> consulted educational bibliographic indexes. Cited items include research studies, dissertations, conference papers,
> reports, and numerous monographs. A handy and easy-to-use review of the literature on cooperative learning. The
> introduction provides a concise overview of the subject through 1990.

■ PERIODICALS DEVOTED TO COOPERATIVE LEARNING

• *Cooperation Unlimited Newsletter.* (Available from Educational Excellence, P.O. Box 68, Portage, MI
49081).

> Issued six times a year, it includes information by experts, practical tips by classroom teachers, lists of resources, and
> sample lesson plans.

• *Cooperative Learning Magazine.* (Available from the International Association for the Study of
Cooperation in Education (IASCE), Box 1582, Santa Cruz, CA 95061-1582).

> A quarterly magazine featuring resources for practitioners and research information on cooperative learning.

• *Our Link: Cooperative Learning Newsletter.* (Available from the Cooperative Learning Center,
University of Minnesota, 202 Pattee Hall, 150 Pillsbury Drive, Minneapolis, MN 55455).

> Addresses all aspects of cooperative learning and often includes short lesson plans, tips, and resource listings.

■ ORGANIZATIONS

• American Association for Higher Education (AAHE), 1 DuPont Circle, Suite 600, Washington, D.C.
20036.

> Founded in 1870, the AAHE seeks to "help resolve critical issues in postsecondary education through conferences,
> publications, and special projects." Within AAHE, the Collaborative Learning Action Community meets informally at
> the annual conference and provides a network for individuals interested in cooperative learning.

• Center for Social Organization of Schools, The Johns Hopkins University, Department L88, 3005 N.
Charles Street, Baltimore, MD 21218.

> Key research center headed by Robert Slavin. Publishes research findings, teachers' guides, and classroom materials
> on cooperative learning.

• Cooperation Unlimited, P.O. Box 68, Portage, MI 49081.

> Provides workshops on cooperative learning, including a half-day awareness session on cooperative learning
> strategies and a four-day in-depth training workshop.

• Cooperative Learning Center, 202 Pattee Hall, University of Minnesota, Minneapolis, MN 55455.

> Directed by David and Roger Johnson, the Center conducts research on cooperative learning, provides in-service
> programs, and publishes research findings, texts, and classroom materials.

• International Association for the Study of Cooperation in Education (IASCE), Box 1582, Santa Cruz,
CA 95061-1582.

> Founded in 1979, the Association investigates "the phenomenon of cooperation in educational settings," including the
> classroom, community school, professional training and cross-cultural settings. Sponsors biennial international
> conference on cooperative learning and numerous publications. Maintains a database.

■ INFORMAL SPECIAL INTEREST GROUPS

• Cooperative Learning: Theory, Research and Practice (AERA)

> Contact: Roger Johnson, Chair
> Cooperative Learning Center
> University of Minnesota, 202 Pattee Hall
> 150 Pillsbury Drive, S.E., Minneapolis, MN 55455
> Phone: (612) 624-7031

• Computers and Cooperative Learning

> Contact: Howard Budin
> Teachers College, Box 8
> 525 West 120th Street, New York, NY 10027
> Phone: (212) 678-3773

• Cooperative Learning in Higher Education

> Contact: Jim Cooper
> California State University Dominguez Hills
> 1000 East Victoria Street, Carson, CA 90747
> Phone: (310) 516-3810

■ GENERAL

• Adams, D.M. (1990). *Cooperative Learning: Critical Thinking and Collaboration Across the Curriculum.* Springfield, IL: C.C. Thomas.

> A fine introduction to cooperative learning and its relevance to teaching. Discussion of how to implement cooperative learning in major curriculum areas. Many useful ideas provided.

• Davidson, N., & Worsham, T. (Eds.). (1992). *Enhancing Thinking Through Cooperative Learning.* New York: Teachers College Press.

> A collection of essays by leaders in critical thinking and cooperative learning, including both theoretical and practical ideas.

• Graves, T. (1990). Cooperative Learning and Academic Achievement: A Tribute to David and Roger Johnson, Robert Slavin, and Shlomo Sharan. *Cooperative Learning,* 10(4), 13-16.

> An overview of the work and theories of three teams of researchers who have focused on cooperative learning. Cooperative learning has become the outstanding example of an educational innovation in which practice is informed by research and the collective leadership of these teams has advanced it use.

• Hertz-Lazarowitz, R., & Miller, N. (Eds.). (1992). *Interaction in Cooperative Groups: The Theoretical Anatomy of Group Learning.* New York: Cambridge University Press.

> This excellent collection edited by two pioneer researchers in cooperative learning brings together related research from developmental, educational, and social psychology for understanding group interaction and outcomes. The concluding chapter on implications for classroom application is particularly valuable.

• Johnson, D.W. (1991). *Learning Together and Alone: Cooperative, Competitive, and Individualistic Learning* (3rd ed.). Englewood Cliffs, NJ: Prentice Hall.

> A very practical text for teachers looking for guidance on selecting, implementing, and evaluating cooperative learning approaches. Discusses theories of social psychology with respect to classroom practice.

• Kagan, S. (1992). *Cooperative Learning* (8th ed.). San Juan Capistrano, CA: Resources for Teachers.

> Now in its eighth edition, this is the most comprehensive and eclectic manual currently available. Kagan is best known for his "structural approach" to CL, but this book also covers all the major CL approaches as well as several innovative adaptations, classroom climate and team building, coaching, and cooperative skills training.

• Manning, M.L., & Lucking, R. (1991). The What, Why, and How of Cooperative Learning. *Social Studies,* 82, 120-124.

> Article provides a clear definition of cooperative learning, examines reasons for and benefits to students working in cooperative teams, and provides an overview of eight selected CL methods that hold potential for middle and secondary schools.

• Sharan, S. (Ed.). (1990). *Cooperative Learning: Theory and Research.* New York: Praeger.

Sharan's book reflects the diverse research about many aspects of cooperative learning methods and instructional techniques. Cooperative learning is presented as a set of teaching models that can produce positive learning within the confines of a traditional classroom. Since presentation techniques for cooperative learning are different from traditional ones, design and procedures for implementation are discussed. The major key for cooperative learning success lies with the careful training of the teacher to understand the methodology necessary for successful implementation.

• Slavin, R.E. (1991). Synthesis of Research of Cooperative Learning. *Educational Leadership,* 48(5), 71-82.

For enhancing student achievement, the most successful cooperative learning approaches have incorporated two key elements: group goals and individual accountability. Positive effects have been consistently found on outcomes such as self-esteem, intergroup relations, acceptance of academically handicapped students, attitudes toward school, and ability to work cooperatively.

■ RESEARCH AND PRACTICE AT THE COLLEGE LEVEL

• Billson, J.M. (1986). The College Classroom as a Small Group: Some Implications for Teaching and Learning. *Teaching Sociology,* 14, 143-151.

A discussion of 15 principles concerning effective implementation of collaborative learning in the college classroom. Literature on group processes and development brought to bear on the subject in a very practical way.

• Bruffee, K.A. (1987, March/April). The Art of Collaborative Learning: Making the Most of Knowledgeable Peers. *Change,* pp. 42-47.

The latest of many articles by Kenneth Bruffee on cooperative learning.

• Cook, L. (1991). Cooperative Learning: A Successful College Teaching Strategy. *Innovative Higher Education,* 16, 27-38.

Based on a review of the literature, cooperative learning strategies seem to be effective in raising the level of university student achievement and attitude. Successful CL methodology characterized by positive interdependence, individual accountability, structured student interaction, instructor facilitation, and attention to social skills.

• Durrington, C. (1991). Cooperative Learning: What is It? Does It Work? *The Delta Kappa Gamma Bulletin,* 58, 43-6.

Article discusses two major approaches to cooperative learning and gives examples of author's use in the college classroom. Reviews research concerning effectiveness of cooperative learning.

• Gallien, L.B., Jr. (1988). *Cooperative Learning: Observations and Reflections in Context with Minority Achievement and Educational Reform.* Baltimore, MD: Johns Hopkins University, Center for Social Organization of Schools. (ERIC Document Reproduction Service No. 302 512)

This paper presents some observations on cooperative learning gathered from research in social and educational literature. Cooperative modes of learning seem to be more powerful in producing academic achievement in students.

• Lyons, P.R. (1989). *Implementing Cooperative Learning Methods.* Baltimore, MD: Johns Hopkins University, Center for Social Organization of Schools. (ERIC Document Reproduction Service No. ED 334 922)

This paper identifies the bases and rationale for the concept of cooperative learning, describes the dynamics of cooperative learning approach, and proposes methods that college faculty can use to enhance student motivation and learning.

• Sherman, L.W. (1991). *Cooperative Learning in Post Secondary Education: Implications from Social Psychology for Active Learning Experiences.* Baltimore, MD: Johns Hopkins University, Center for Social Organization of Schools. (ERIC Document Reproduction Service No. ED 330 262)

This paper briefly discusses pedagogical theory underlying the application of cooperative learning strategies in post secondary environments and describes nine specific cooperative pedagogical strategies at length. Appendix includes an annotated bibliography of 58 items.

■ COOPERATIVE LEARNING AND BIBLIOGRAPHIC INSTRUCTION

• Dickerson, M.J. (1989). *The Implications of Collaborative Writing: A Dialogue.* Baltimore, MD: Johns Hopkins University, Center for Social Organization of Schools. (ERIC Document Reproduction Service No. ED 305 644)

Dickerson's report is especially relevant to librarians because she describes how she uses learning groups to have students write collaborative papers on different aspects of library use. Student comments are included, most of which demonstrate outstanding understanding of the library as a result of this method of instruction.

• Fister, B. (1990). Teaching Research as a Social Act: Collaborative Learning and the Library. *RQ,* 29(4), 505-509.

Discusses the advantages of cooperative learning and includes specific examples from Fisher's BI classes.

• Osborne, N.S. and Wyman, A. (1991). The Forest and the Trees: A Modest Proposal on Bibliographic Burnout. *Research Strategies, 9*(2), 101-103.

Reports success using cooperative learning techniques, especially with regard to staff motivation.

• Ridgeway, T. (1989). Active Learning Methods in the One-Hour Bibliographic Instruction Lecture. In *Defining and Applying Effective Teaching Strategies for Library Instruction* (pp. 61-63). Ann Arbor, MI: Pierian Press.

Provides examples in an outline format that is easy to read and understand.

• Sheridan, J. (1988). The What, Why and How of Collaborative Learning and Its Importance for the Off-Campus Student. In *The Off-Campus Library Services Conference Proceeding* (pp. 365-373). Central Michigan University Press.

Provides an introduction to collaborative learning and gives suggestions for applying to bibliographic instruction.

• Sheridan, J. (1990). The Reflective Librarian: Some Observations on Bibliographic Instruction in the Academic Library. *The Journal of Academic Librarianship, 16*(1), 22-26.

Advocates the use of cooperative learning.

• Simmons-O'Neill, E. (1990). *Evaluating Sources: Strategies for Faculty-Librarian-Student Collaboration.* Baltimore, MD: Johns Hopkins University, Center for Social Organization of Schools. (ERIC Document Reproduction Service No. ED 309 405)

An interesting account of a successful collaborative learning assignment. Includes comments from students on collaborative learning.

• Warmkessel, M.M., & Carothers, F.M. (1993). Collaborative Learning and Bibliographic Instruction. *Journal of Academic Librarianship, 19* (1), 4-7.

After reviewing the history and philosophy of collaborative learning, the authors describe a project using a CL strategy known as "pairing" to introduce undergraduates to electronic database searching.

Compiled by Mary Jane Petrowski
April 1993

Appendix 13

First Session

▶ Mini-Lecture with Overheads (5 minutes)

OVERHEAD 1: "See the Big Picture" (have up as students enter)

I.   3-Step Research Strategy

OVERHEAD 2: 3-Step Research Strategy

A. Briefly introduce strategy and show how contemporary materials fit into overall strategy; define term.
B. Focus of both sessions will be on finding contemporary materials using a variety of access tools (print indexes, CD-ROM, IO+)

▶ Small Group Work (14 Minutes)

II. Identifying Characteristics of Periodical Publications

OVERHEAD 3: "Find a Pattern" (leave up while students work)

LOGISTICS: Distribute worksheets and explain purpose of exercise. Students will have 5 minutes to divide up responsibility for answering the 8 questions, pick a recorder, and record answers to designated questions.

When time is called, each student has 1 minute to report findings to the recorder who takes notes. Librarian and TA circulate, listening in on each group and coaching as appropriate. After 6 minutes, librarian calls time and summarizes findings by calling on different recorders for reports (4 minutes).

OPTIONAL HANDOUT: "What are the Differences Among Contemporary Materials?"

OVERHEAD 4: "Some Differences Between Journals and Magazines"

▶ Mini-Lecture (5 Minutes)

III. Access Tools: Print Indexes, Abstracts, Databases

A. The problem of information scatter: since access is scattered, it's necessary to use several different indexes or one index in more than one format.

OVERHEAD 4: "Look Somewhere Else"

Question: Ask students to reflect on all the sources they consulted to make a decision about which college to attend.

B. Briefly discuss the purpose and use of access options (print indexes, abstracts, CD-ROM databases, IO+ (locally mounted databases). Discuss tradeoffs.

OVERHEAD 5: "Format matters"

▶ Think-Pair-Share (6 Minutes)

IV. Generating Terms to Use for Subject Searches

OVERHEAD 6: "Trust Yourself"

Logistics: Distribute copies of 4 tabloid articles. Students at each table receive the same article. Instructions to class: Pretend that you want to find additional articles on the subject discussed in the tabloid article since your instructor says you cannot use *National Enquirer* material. Allow students 4 minutes to read article and write down terms they would try using in indexes/databases.

OVERHEAD 7: "Find the Second Right Answer"

When time is called, each person shares his/her headings with a partner. (1 minute each)

► Small Group Work (10 minutes)

V. Subject Searches Using Print Indexes

Logistics: Distribute print indexes to each table. Each student tries looking terms up in 4-5 different indexes (if they seem appropriate). Students record results. Allow 5 minutes for exploration. Librarian circulates and coaches.

A. Group Processing (5 minutes)
Allow different individuals to explain what happened as they used different terms/indexes

Summarize successful strategies on board. Some possibilities: moving from specific to broader heading; following "see" references; using synonyms; moving to an appropriate subject index.

VI. Summary and Preview of Second Session

A. Must think like an indexer when using print indexes/abstracts; other access tools more flexible.
B. Summarize useful strategies: using more than one index; moving from general (RG) to subject index; using specialty indexes for newspapers, book reviews, government documents.
C. Next session:
   1) Parts of a citation
   2) Strategies for coping with mutilation
   3) Hands-on work using databases

Second Session

I. Advantages of CD-ROM databases and IO+ for subject searching.

A. Explain keyword Boolean subject searching
B. Demonstrate live search in IBIS
C. Have students work in small groups to complete same worksheet used in the Contemporary Materials session.

II. Coping with mutilation/missing material (Slide show)

A. Microfiche/film (show examples)
B. Magazine collection
C. Other holdings
D. Interlibrary loan

III. Tour of UGL Periodical Unit

IV. Hands-on CD-ROM and IBIS searching practice. Students work in pairs to complete worksheet. Allow 30 minutes or more for this section. Depending on TA's preference and assignment, may concentrate on one or the other.

University of Illinois at Urbana-Champaign Undergraduate Library
Script for Research Skills Instruction: Contemporary Materials

▶ Purpose and Audience

- Contemporary materials sessions are offered by the Undergraduate Library to students in Rhetoric 105, 108, and Speech Communication 111 as part of a larger bibliographic instruction program. This session is designed to provide beginning researchers with an understanding of when contemporary information is needed, how it is organized, and how it is accessed both intellectually and physically. Specific objectives are outlined in "Contemporary Materials Session Objectives."

- Locally mounted databases are an increasingly important source of information for UIUC students and faculty. Research shows that there is increased use of magazine and journal literature in libraries. The OCAC Measurement and Evaluation Subcommittee has done preliminary analysis of data collected during the Spring 1992 semester which shows that users obtained 36% of their citations to periodical literature through IBIS vs. 15% from CD-ROM products vs. 26% from traditional print indexes and abstracts.

- Many users are either unaware of the sources which exist or do not fully understand what locally mounted databases can offer them in their research and how they relate to other access tools (CD-ROM databases/print indexes and abstracts). The purpose of these guidelines is to assist librarians and graduate students in providing students with appropriate information about access to contemporary materials in the UIUC library system.

Instructional Design
The instructional session is designed to teach students through: 1) mini-lecture augmented with slides; 2) small group exercise; 3) group processing via real-time IBIS searching using LCD projection technology; 4) small group hands-on searching guided by worksheets (optional); 5) physical orientation to the UGL periodical tools, services, collection; 6) supplementary handouts.

Evaluation
Workshops will be evaluated by students (as part of the Instructor Course Evaluation Survey form) and by the teaching assistants. Results will be distributed to UGL teaching staff in a timely manner.

Logistics
Sessions are taught by UGL librarians and graduate assistants. A weekly listing of scheduled sessions will be posted on the door of Room 289. Sessions are held in Room 289, UGL. The last 15-20 minutes of the session will be held in the Periodical Collection area. Room 289 will be set up with four tables and chairs seating 30. Supplementary instructional handouts will be available in trays on each table.

▶ Mini-Lecture with Slides (15 minutes)

I. Introduction and Welcome

    A. Introduce yourself (name, where you work, what you do)
    B. Explain structure session: mini-lecture/group work/real-time group processing/tour of periodical area.
    C. Length of session (50 minutes or 75 minutes)

    SLIDE 1: "Have you ever wished you were better informed?" (Caesar & Brutus)

    D. Purpose of session is to teach process of finding contemporary materials; introduce options available (traditional print indexes & abstracts; CD-ROM; IO+); demonstrate IBIS searching.

    E. Questions
       Tell audience if they should interrupt you with questions as you go along or hold them until the end.

II. What Are Contemporary Materials? (SLIDE 2: Student reading magazine)

    A. SLIDE 3: Airplane crash at Tenerife Airport, March 1977, *Paris Match*

       Explain that contemporary materials provide up-to-date/current information on a topic/issue because articles get into print sooner than monographs (books) which take longer to write and publish.

       SLIDE 4: "Your chances of being kidnapped are greater than dying in an airplane crash." (CLIO ad, 1977)

       This ad appeared in 1977 and reflects the widespread concern over terrorism, particularly skyjacking. Contemporary materials appear during or near the time an event or idea first occurs and present the viewpoint held at the time the event occurred.

SLIDE 5: Array of popular magazine issues

Contemporary materials take the form of journal, magazine or newspaper articles. Mention that UIUC Library subscribes to over 82,000 periodicals and UGL holds 320 titles. The next few slides will highlight the differences between contemporary materials.

B. SLIDE 6: Characteristics of magazines

Indicate that these sources are not inferior per se, just written for a general audience and have no bibliography

SLIDE 7: Characteristics of journals

May be difficult to read since they are written by experts/scholars working in a specialized field. Journals used by scholars to communicate new research, ideas, theories, etc. to colleagues. Bibliographies can help you to locate related articles on a topic.

Activity: Ask students to pick up any journal issue on table and count the references at end of any article.

SLIDE 8: Characteristics of newspapers

Excellent sources of contemporary information.

C. Handout: "Characteristics of Contemporary Materials" (on tables)

III. Process of Finding Contemporary Materials (SLIDE 9)

A. SLIDE 10: A pile of periodicals

One approach to finding articles on your topic is to flip through issues of magazines hoping to discover articles on your topic. This is a very labor-intensive approach to doing research.

However, you can use tools such as indexes and bibliographic databases to find information on your topic. We'd like to discuss these options and some of their unique features to give you a better idea of when each might be appropriate.

B. SLIDE 11: Three cereal boxes labeled with options

First step in process: choosing an access tool (or source) to look for articles on your subject. At UIUC you have 3 options for locating periodical literature: print indexes, CD-ROM databases, IBIS (16 locally mounted data-bases)

SLIDE 12: Shows info typically found in indexes/abstracts.

Mention that all access tools will provide info needed to locate article although the formats will vary somewhat. Citation info can be recycled to write bibliography entries/footnotes.

1. SLIDE 13: Option 1: Sample of print indexes in UGL

One traditional way to identify what magazine , journal, or newspaper articles have been written on a subject is to use a print index/abstract.

Activity: There are old issues of READERS' GUIDE on tables. Ask students to spend 1 minute looking up their topic. Question to class: Ask students to raise hands if they found listings for topic.

SLIDE 14: Sample print citation

Question: Did anyone notice that the periodical title was abbreviated?
Questions: Ask students to raise hands if no listings found.

Suggest reasons why this might have happened or ask students.

Slide 15: 300+ print indexes/abstracts held by UIUC Library
Be aware that library may not own all titles indexed by a particular index and you may have to travel to other departmental libraries to get article.

Slide 16: Summary of print index/abstract features

Point out that print indexes are valuable because they provide retrospective (go back further in time) coverage not offered by most electronic databases. Use student topic as example.

2. Slide 17: Option 2: CD-ROM databases.

Circa 1985, optical disc technology made it possible to store about 10 years of a print index on a single compact disc (looks just like an audio CD)

Slide 18: CD-ROM printout

Slide 19: Summary of CD-ROM characteristics

3. Slide 20: Option 3: IO Plus (IBIS) (Main menu screen)

What is IBIS?
Explain this is a recent development (Fall 1991) at UIUC and represents an effort to combine access to book and periodical literature.

Slide 21: Advantages of IBIS

Explain keyword Boolean subject searching using board or Christine's video.

4. Handout: "Access Tools: A Comparison Chart" (on table)

▶ IBIS Search Demonstration (10-15 Minutes)

Logistics
Using LCD projection of the IBIS interface, the presenter introduces participants to the interface using example from board or Christine's video. The librarian searches IBIS explaining search options (menu), format options, troubleshooting as search proceeds. In the course of performing search, presenter can discuss output options (maybe send results to her/his e-mail address), point out location information on record, and demonstrate use of call number search in Online Catalog to further determine holdings.

▶ Think-Pair-Share (6 Minutes)

Logistics
The room is set up with 6 seats around each of four tables. The participants will work in small groups as defined by the tables at which they sit. Each pair/triad is given a research problem (selected from topics submitted by the instructor or sample topics on 5x8 cards in podium), worksheet, and directed to formulate search using Boolean logic (concepts).

Each member of a pair spends 2 minutes thinking and writing an individual response. When time is called, each person has 1 minute to share his/her work with partner. Person indicates level of confidence/satisfaction with answer. Librarian calls time and circulates around classroom to help students.

Each member of the group should be prepared to present the group's results. Librarian processes group work using easel to depict search concepts (2 minutes). Instructor may wish to give entire class one of two problems so that all work can be processed.

▶ Tour of the Periodical Area/IO+ Terminals (10-20 minutes)

Logistics
Move class from Room 289 and tour them through the Periodical area, pointing out:

1. Current issues on display shelving (not all issues displayed)
2. Back issues (arranged in alphabetical order by title; can't be checked out)
3. Print index/abstract area
4. CD-ROM site
5. Photocopy machines
6. How to find articles once you have a printout/citation
   a. Show locator lists (in red binders)
   b. Explain title search on Online Catalog
   c. What to do if issue/article physically missing
      (1) Handout (review options with students)Appendix 13

      (1) Magazine Collection
      (2) Other microform holdings
      (3) Other libraries may have duplicate copy

7. Importance of getting additional assistance
   a. Term Paper Research Counseling
   b. Periodical Information Desk
   c. Reference Desk

8. Show students IO Plus terminals in front.

9. Point out copy card machine

10. Handout: Each student receives a checklist of suggested access tools based on his/her topic. Explain that you have identified some helpful indexes/databases to help each person get started. Additional assistance available at Reference/Periodical Desks. May want to indicate CD-ROM product list so that students can see what's available in departmental libraries.

▶ Wrap-Up

Summarize session and thank students for coming.

**University of Illinois at Urbana-Champaig Undergraduate Library
Online Catalog Workshop Script**

Purpose and Audience

Online Catalog Workshops (OCW) are offered by the Undergraduate Library as part of the larger bibliographic instruction program. OCWs are designed to provide students with an understanding of when retrospective material is needed and how it is structured, intellectually accessed, and physically accessed. Specific objectives are outlined in "Online Catalog Workshop Objectives". While graduate students, faculty, staff, and others are welcome to attend the workshops, undergraduate students are seen as the primary audience for these sessions.

Instructional Design

The workshops are designed to teach students through: 1) mini-lecture augmented with slides; 2) small group brainstorming; 3) group processing via real-time online catalog searching using LCD projection technology; 4) small group hands-on searching guided by worksheets; 5) group processing through answer sheets and peer review; and 6) supplementary handouts.

Logistics

Workshops are taught by UGL librarians, graduate assistants, and experienced volunteers. The workshops begin in Room 289 of the Undergraduate Library where the introductory material is covered; the group is then moved to the terminal bank north of the Reference Desk for hands-on work in teams of 2/3. Prior to the workshop, signs reserving the terminals are put out by designated staff. Attendance is limited to 30.

▶ Mini-Lecture with Slides (10 Minutes)

I. Introduction and Welcome
    A. Introduce yourself (name, where you work, what you are—GA, librarian)
    B. Purpose of session
        1. To teach process for finding books (retrospective material) on a subject.
        2. To give overview of the Online Catalog and its relationship to card catalogs.
        3. To discuss the file structure of the Online Catalog
        4. To tell audience how/where they can use the system
        5. To teach basics of most commonly used searches.
    C. Session will last one hour.
    D. Questions
        Tell audience if they should interrupt you with questions as you go along or hold them until the end.
    E. Fill out statistics sheet
        Take a show of hands to see what percentage of the class was required to attend a workshop by their instructor. Record this on statistics. Count faculty, undergraduate, staff attendance. Count men/women.

II. Locating Retrospective Materials (Books) (Slide show begins)
    A. Traditional way has been use of card catalogs.
    B. With advent of computer technology, an increasing number of libraries have developed online catalogs.
    C. In some libraries, the online catalog has completely replaced the card catalog; in others, online catalog is used in conjunction with card catalog (the case at UIUC).
    D. Five steps at UIUC
        1. Identify appropriate subject heading
            a. What is a subject heading?
                1) Terms under which materials on your topic are listed in the catalogs
                2) Subject headings are used to group books on the same or similar topic under one term..
                3) Provide controlled vocabulary

                Hold up can of Sprite. Give students 30 seconds to think of term they would use to describe object. Ask them to share with person next to them. Ask students how many people came up with same word. Share LC term for "Sprite".

                4) At UIUC we use Library of Congress Subject Headings — available in red volumes or in the Online Catalog (Authority File).
                5) LCSH: located throughout the library. In UGL, next to terminal clusters.
                6) SUBJECT HEADING HANDOUT (located in trays on table)

        2. Consult the catalogs.
            a. Once you've identified subject heading(s), look them up in the catalogs.
            b. UIUC uses both a card catalog and an online catalog. The card catalog lists materials by subject (from 1868-1975). Online Catalog lists material by subject only from 1975 to the present.

    c. Depending on topic, you may need to check both.
       1) Question to class: Where would you look to find book on 1980 Olympic Boycott?
       2) Question to class: Where would you look to find histories of the Civil War?
    d. Evaluate record for book: currency; length; index; bibliography? (Light blue handout)

  3. Check the circulation status
    a. Circulation status includes where book is physically located; whether or not it can be checked out, how many copies we have, whether or not book is available.
    b. Computerized circulation systems allows you to check books out via computer.
    c. Lists books in all 35 UIUC libraries by call number as well as books in 30 other academic libraries in Illinois.

  4. Find the book on the shelf
    a. Go to the appropriate library on campus.
    b. Locate the book on the shelf using the call number (Dewey or LC)
    c. Evaluate book further: preface; introduction; language (Light blue handout)

  5. Check the item out
    a. Take book to the circulation desk.
    b. No limit on number of books you check out.
    c. Your student ID is your library card.
    d. Renewals through Phone Center (333-8400)

III. Access to Online Catalog
  A. In the library, location of terminals:
    1. Each departmental library has at least one public terminal.
    2. Largest cluster of terminals: UGL and second floor of Main Library.

  B. Remote Access (Dark Blue Handout)
    1. If you have a computer terminal and modem and access to a phone line or the campus network, you can access the online catalog. Refer interested students to handout for full details.

  C. Telephone Center (333-8400)
    1. Library runs a special center to help you use the system by phone.
    2. Phone Center staff will:
      a. Renew, charge, save books for you
      b. Search the database.
      c. Provide information on the system (explain when/why it's down and when it will be up)
      d. Troubleshoot remote access problems.

▶ Small Group Work (5 minutes)

Logistics
The room is set up with 6 seats around each of four tables. The students will work in pairs/triads as defined by the tables at which they sit. Each person is given a research problem worksheet and asked to prepare individual answers to the questions. Time limit: 2 minutes. Then, each person shares his/her answers with the person sitting next to him/her. Time limit: 1.5 minutes per person. In addition to sharing answers, each person must also comment on how confident they feel about their answers. Each pair/triad will have one of two problems. Sheets are colored coded. Librarian circulates and coaches.

▶ Group Processing (5-10 minutes)

Logistics
Using a LCD panel to project the Online Catalog, the librarian introduces the students to the interface. One group spokesperson explains their strategy. The librarian searches the catalog, using the strategy suggested by the students, explaining and troubleshooting as the search proceeds. The librarian also asks for input from other groups which have worked on the same problem. If time permits, the librarian can demonstrate the second research problem.

▶ Hands-On Searching (25-30 minutes)

Logistics
Librarian passes out worksheets. Librarian explains that they will now move to the computer terminals and in small groups (2-3 students per terminal) work through the searches. Students are instructed to take turns keyboarding at the breaks indicated on the sheet. During the hands-on searching, librarian circulates among group and coaches as necessary.

▶ Group Processing

With five minutes left, the librarian distributes the answer sheets to each group for them to check their work and make appropriate changes on their sheets. The librarian answers any questions. Answer sheets are returned to librarian; students keep their worksheets which serve as their proof of attendance. The librarian thanks all for attending.

INSTRUCTIVE
SESSIONS

B.I. Instructional Design:
Applying Modes of Consciousness Theory

David W. Allan and Lisa A. Baures

Allan is coordinator of the Educational Resource Center, media librarian, and instructional developer and **Baures** is reference/cataloging librarian, Mankato State University, Mankato, Minnesota.

INTRODUCTION TO THEORY

David W. Allan

The pedagogical objective of any instructional session is to attempt to reach the information needs of the students, to elevate and optimize their level of information literacy, and to expose them to information that best meets individual modes of consciousness. According to Jana Varlejs, today's information-literate student must be able "to locate, evaluate, and use effectively the needed information."[1] Current instructional practices need to cover the spectrum of information literacy including an understanding of individual learning styles and styles of knowing. Although students may differ in many ways, they tend to use one of two modes of consciousness. The two modes of consciousness include the left-brain mode, which follows linear, analytical, verbal, abstract, deductive, temporal, and digital thinking activities; and the right-brain mode, which follows global, nonlinear, intuitive, impulsive, imaginative, associative, and subjective thinking activities. People do not process cognitive information wholly within any one cerebral hemisphere. Instead, they tend to prefer one hemisphere of thinking over another. Communication and the interchange of mental activity between each cerebral hemisphere is an ongoing condition.

The cerebral hemispheres are not relationally separate, stated Anthony Wilden, nor are they isolated, a dichotomy, in competition, or in contradiction to each other.[2] Communication between the two cerebral halves happens through a large tight bundle of nerve fibers called the corpus callosum. In *Grammatical Man*, information theorist Jeremy Campbell said, "The right side tends to use a 'top-down' strategy, processing information as a whole, perceiving its full meaning, rather than approaching it 'bottom-up,' using the parts to construct the whole, which is often more than the sum of its parts. In the case of language, the right hemisphere thinks in terms of entire sentences, rather than single words, and is sensitive to the way sentences fit into paragraphs."[3] The recognition of another human being, especially the functions of deciphering facial codes, falls into the realm of right-brain activity. Robert Finn wrote that "the right hemisphere is the brain's jack-of-all-trades, a generalist that addresses new problems without preconceptions and tries many solutions until it hits on one that works. The left hemisphere, in contrast, is a specialist, solving familiar problems quickly and efficiently by using established methods."[4]

When communicating via media, the left and right hemispheric functions play an important interactive role. Society gives more importance to the verbal, logical, and analytical—albeit, language, mathematics, science, and technology—as the driving forces behind this view. It is nevertheless important to give equal status to the nonlinear, global, and aesthetic kinds of thinking activities represented by right hemisphere brain activity. Perhaps all along the right hemisphere was doing a credible job without our really knowing it or understanding it. In Howard Gardner's text on creativity and cognition, Gardner summarized what current researchers have discovered: "The right hemisphere emerges as vital, perhaps even more important than the left hemisphere, in dealing with narratives, metaphors, jokes, morals, and other complex or subtle aspects of language."[5]

This has led us to believe that too often library instruction has favored those students who are dominantly left-brained. Today's television/pictorial culture relies on visual icons for communication. Early cave dwellers during the period of Cro-magnon man, some 12,000 years ago, initiated iconic communication with powerful and colorful paintings and drawings. Iconic visual communication attracts a wide contemporary audience. In order to meet the needs of our visually oriented students and to assist those students who have a preference for right-brained, nonlinear thinking, we decided to use a visual metaphor for teaching this part of bibliographic instruction.

Metaphor, as a figure of speech, implies a comparison and, unlike the simile with its explicitness, carries over meaning from one idea to another as explained by Aristotle in his seminal definition of metaphor. Words, derivations from their meaning, and word similarities help to separate figurative and literal meaning, according to Mark Johnson's reference to Aristotle's monumental work, *Poetics*.[6]

By using a visual metaphor, we expect some students to readily see the analogy between the common information storage and retrieval concepts of "real" file cabinets, groups of files, files, and records and the "conceptual" files, sub-files, and records of a typical computer database. People with strong preferences for graphic imagery in communication use pictorial imagery not only to prompt new information but also to illustrate a relational structure, a global relationship, or reinforce current information. In fact, pictures in many ways transmit information—summatively and symbolically—and many times in a more direct, clear, succinct manner than do words and sentences. Summative and symbolic information tends to be long lasting because of cognitive transfer and easily remembered iconic information.[7]

There is more to learning and thinking than just cerebral hemispheric preferences, personal repertoires of knowledge, and iconic language. There are learning modalities and perceptual elements, as well as many other factors that influence communication and learning. A number of different learning modalities, said Sandra Yee, have been identified and include "perceptual, cognitive, emotional, and social, as well as others."[8] The basic perceptual elements we are all familiar with include "print, aural, interactive, visual, haptic (touch), kinesthetic (movement), and olfactory (smell)."[9]

Artist and visual researcher Deborah Curtiss, in discussing how we think visually, said that two levels of thinking occur—one, external where extraneous, visual phenomena, consensual reality, and visuals occur; and two, internal where visualizations and perceptual-cognitive experiences take place.[10] Edward Tufte, statistician and renowned visual theorist, concluded that the mind envisions visual information beyond the "flatland" of flat pictures, graphs, charts, and maps. Cognitively, I believe, the human mind layers, separates, and shapes three-dimensional images in a global iconic manner. It takes small multiple segments of visual information and rearranges them for greater meaning within visualization schema and visual thinking patterns. Beyond the graphic/pictorial flatland, the mind imposes upon us a macro and a micro world of iconic experiences.[11]

The strength and power of visual information, visual literacy, and the combined use of aural and visual forms of communication have been long known to the business world. According to Lynn Oppenheim, et al., in a 1981 study made by the Wharton Applied Research Center (the Wharton School, University of Pennsylvania) on overhead transparencies, it was shown that overhead transparencies greatly influence decision making, give a more favorable perception of the presenter to the audience, shorten presentation time, and influence the speed with which a group—or a class—may reach consensus.[12] In a more recent baseline study, Douglas R. Vogel, et al., in 1986 prepared a study with the University of Minnesota and the 3M Corporation. In that study, they researched the persuasiveness of visual support in presentations. This rigorous, theory-based study concluded that a variety of visual support media, 35 mm slides and overhead transparencies, proved to be 43 percent more persuasive than presentations made with no visual support.[13] In a library instructional environment, universal communication and presentation requirements are similar to those found in a business and corporate setting.

APPLYING MODES OF CONSCIOUSNESS THEORY

Lisa A. Baures

Before presenting the instructional session developed to accommodate nonverbal learning styles, it is necessary to digress and explain how the instructional session evolved. Unlike the time period predating library automation, patrons entering a library could pull out a drawer of the card catalog, peruse the listings, and quickly obtain a rough idea of the materials available in a collection. Although patrons may not have been familiar with the organizational structure of the card catalog, the author, title, and subject guide cards provided patrons with a rudimentary means of determining the number and types of materials in the library. Unfortunately, existing online catalogs do not adhere to a standardized retrieval format. Oftentimes the mechanics for retrieving information from a database, as well as the indexing structure, differ from system to system. Consequently, patrons are unable to retrieve any information without some knowledge of a given system.

A point of further confusion for the patron is the fact that the card catalog was a discrete unit, whereas the online catalog is usually one of many component parts of an automated library system. Ironically, in the quest to improve the ease with which information can be retrieved, online catalogs have been linked to electronic indexes and abstracts, resulting in the development of highly sophisticated and complex systems that seem to bedevil the average patron. The clearly defined function of a library catalog and an index are no longer discernible to the patron. Distinctions between the catalog as providing a list of items in the library and their location and an index as providing a comprehensive listing of references to periodical literature, become blurred when information on library holdings is appended to the index citation entry. If this is not enough, add the following repertoire of library skills to the equation and the chance for confusion increases: Boolean searching, accessing other library catalogs and databases via the Internet, accessing electronic journals and bulletin boards, and document delivery.

The cumulative effect of these technological advancements renders many of the research processes developed for the print environment useless. As a result patrons are left without a conceptual framework within which to assimilate new research techniques and are severely handicapped because new library concepts and skills do not directly relate to their existing paradigm of research. In essence what bibliographic instruction librarians must do is develop instructional strategies to bridge the chasm between the old and new research paradigms.

After considering many different teaching techniques, a decision was made to explore the use of analogies to "bridge the chasm" created by technological advancements. Succinctly stated, an analogy is a comparison of two ideas or concepts which draws upon prior knowledge to expedite the assimilation of new information. There are two different types of analogies distinguishable by the different goals accomplished by each. Conceptual analogies involve the use of "separate individual analogies to help structure each concept within the content."[14] Conversely, comprehensive analogies involve the use of a single global analogy to

integrate the "known knowledge into an organized representation or model of the content."[15] A caveat to note when using an analogy is that it does not represent an exact definition or example. One must be aware of the potential for misunderstandings or distortions to arise when incorporating an analogy into an instructional session.

Focusing on database structure and the three Boolean operators (and, or, not), it was decided to construct a comprehensive analogy using a filing cabinet to represent the structure of a database and to illustrate the concepts of Boolean searching. The image of a filing cabinet was selected because it appears on many of the reference aids developed at Mankato State University for the ERIC and Information Access Company (IAC) databases. In addition, the terms "database" and "file" are often used interchangeably among the general populace familiar with personal computers and word processing programs. This tendency to interchange the two words signifies a conscious or unconscious use of the file analogy. And although the filing cabinet analogy lacks originality, it is one that most people can relate to and understand.

To maximize the teaching effectiveness of an analogy, the literature suggests that a combination verbal-pictorial format be employed.[16] The verbal-pictorial analogy to be presented is the result of a collaborative effort undertaken by Dr. Allan and myself. Comparing the organizational structure of a filing cabinet to a database, an analogy was constructed whereby filing cabinets, drawers of a filing cabinet, hanging file folders (representing groups of files), individual file folders, and records within the file folders were depicted to correspond respectively to databases, subfiles within the databases, indexes, search terms or phrases, and bibliographic records. By extrapolating this analogy, the functions of Boolean searching were also explained and illustrated (see figures 1-5). Please note that the appended copies of the transparencies are composites of the various cells or layers developed to represent specific concepts. Each cell or layer is numbered on each composite copy of the transparency to illustrate the sequence of revelation.

Facilitating the presentation of the analogy was the physical organization of the classroom. In the front of the classroom in each corner was an overhead projector and screen. One of the overhead projectors was connected to a liquid crystal display unit, which in turn was connected to a microcomputer. The microcomputer was connected to the PALS (Project for Automated Library Systems) and a CD-ROM player. This connectivity enabled the instructor to provide an interactive demonstation of the online catalog, the various reference files loaded onto the PALS, and the CD-ROM databases. The other overhead

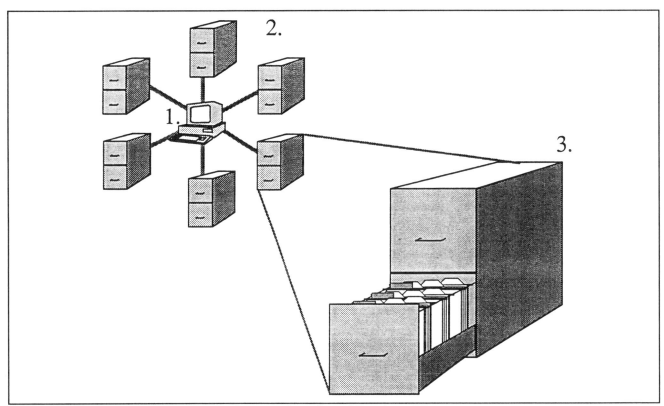

Figure 1: Overview of Database Files

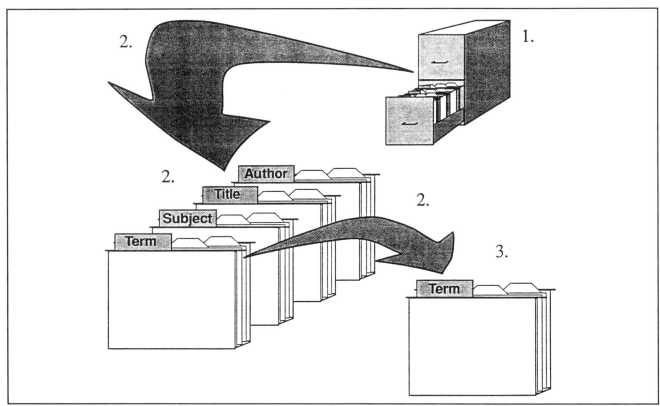

Figure 2: Overview of Database Structure

— DAVID W. ALLAN AND LISA A. BAURES —

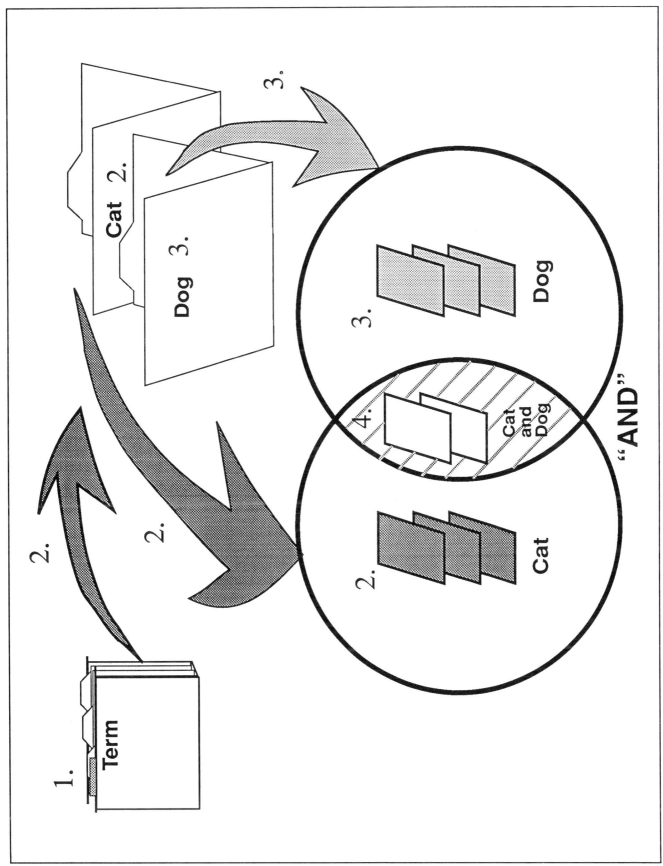

Figure 3: Boolean "AND" Search Strategy

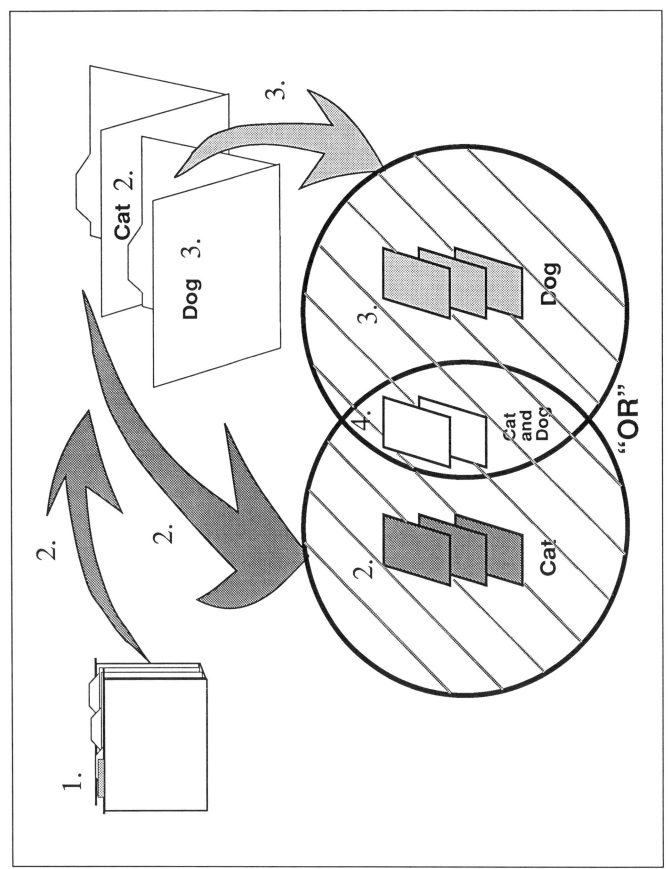

Figure 4: Boolean "OR" Search Strategy

— DAVID W. ALLAN AND LISA A. BAURES —

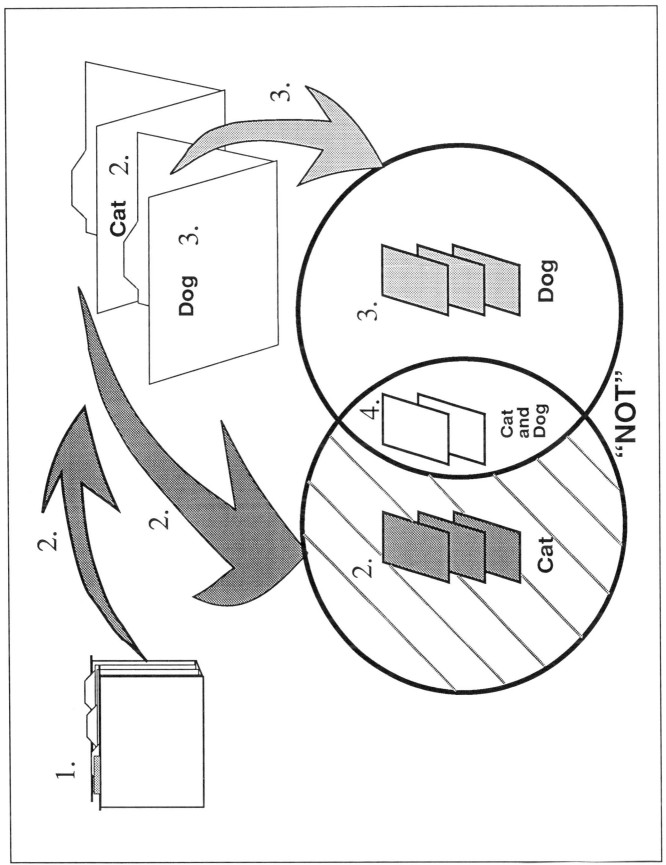

Figure 5: Boolean "NOT" Search Strategy

projector was used to display the transparencies developed to visually illustrate the analogy between a filing cabinet and a database. A three-dimensional representation of the analogy could be provided by integrating the use of manipulative props into the instructional session. A couple of filing boxes, hanging file folders, file folders, and sheets of papers are inexpensive, easy to obtain, and can be readily incorporated into the presentation.

The transparencies developed to illustrate the analogy are appended and represent the culmination of numerous efforts by the presenters to refine the visual depiction of the analogy to effectively communicate the concepts associated with database structure and Boolean searching. To date, the transparencies depicting the filing cabinet analogy remain a work in progress. Feel free to contact the presenters if you have any suggestions for improving the visual representation of the analogy.

NOTES

1. Jana Varlejs, ed., *Information Literacy—Learning How to Learn* (Jefferson, NC: McFarland & Company, 1991), 1.

2. Anthony Wilden, *The Rules Are No Game* (New York: Routledge & Kegan Paul, 1987), 239.

3. Jeremy Campbell, *Grammatical Man* (New York: Simon and Schuster, 1982), 239.

4. Robert Finn, "New Split Brain Research Divides Scientists," *Science Digest* 91:9 (1983): 54-55, 103.

5. Howard Gardner, *Art, Mind, and Brain* (New York: Basic Books, 1982), 311.

6. Mark Johnson, ed., *Philosophical Perspectives on Metaphor* (Minneapolis: University of Minnesota Press, 1981), 5.

7. David Winslow Allan, "Probing Motion Media Communication: Process, Message and the Iconic Phenomena Communication Model," Ph.D. diss., Union Institute, 1990, 196.

8. Sandra G. Yee, "Information Literacy Skills: How Students Learn Them and Why," in *Coping With Information Illiteracy: Bibliographic Instruction for the Information Age*, ed. by Glenn E. Mensching, Jr. and Teresa B. Mensching (Ann Arbor, MI: Pierian Press, 1989), 45.

9. Yee, 45.

10. Deborah Curtiss, "Visual Thinking: How Do We Define, Identify, and Facilitate It?" in *Investigating Visual Literacy*, ed. by Darrell G. Beauchamp, Judy Clark-Baca, and Robert A. Braden (Bloomington/Normal, IL: The International Visual Literacy Association, 1991), 345.

11. Edward R. Tufte, *Envisioning Information* (Cheshire, CT: Graphics Press, 1990), 12.

12. Oppenheim, Lynn, et al., *A Study of the Effects of the Use of Overhead Transparencies on Business Meetings* (State College, PA: Wharton School, University of Pennsylvania, 1981), 28.

13. Douglas Vogel, Gary W. Dickson, and John A. Lehman, *Persuasion and the Role of Visual Presentation Support: the UM/3M Study*, Working Paper Series #MISRC-WP-86-11 (Minneapolis: School of Management, University of Minnesota, 1986), 5.

14. Donald A. Stepich and Timothy J. Newby, "Analogical Instruction within the Information Processing Paradigm: Effective Means to Facilitate Learning," *Instructional Science* 17 (1988): 134.

15. Stepich and Newby, 135.

16. Stepich and Newby, 140.

— DAVID W. ALLAN AND LISA A. BAURES —

"Striking It Rich with the Internet": An Interactive Workshop for Teaching Faculty the Internet

Donna L. Miller and Michael C. Zeigler

As more institutions gain access to the Internet, the training of faculty and staff on Internet services will be critical. "Striking It Rich with the Internet: 'There's Gold in Them Thar' Networks'" was an interactive workshop designed to teach the faculty and staff of Lebanon Valley College of Pennsylvania (LVC) about Internet resources.

The workshop, co-developed by Donna Miller, readers' services librarian at LVC, and Michael Zeigler, LVC's director of user services and workshops, was designed for the novice Internet user. Subsequently, portions of the workshop were also presented at an Association of College Libraries of Central Pennsylvania workshop.

"Striking It Rich with the Internet" was a day-long workshop that covered the various Internet navigational tools and information sources. Navigational tools were defined as applications used to gain access to information at remote computer sites and included electronic mail, remote login/telnet, and file transfer protocol (ftp). The information "accessors" were called travel agents and included such applications as Gopher, Archie, Veronica, Wide Area Information Server (WAIS), and World Wide Web (WWW).

Miller is readers' services librarian and *Zeigler* is director of user services and computer workshops at Lebanon Valley College of Pennsylvania, Anniville, Pennsylvania.

The format of the workshop was to 1) explain the various utilities, 2) demonstrate the features, and 3) have the participants practice the features on the Internet. At the conclusion of the workshop, participants were able to send Internet electronic mail, subscribe to a list service, and access information on the Internet by using the LIBS program, a simple, menu-driven interface from Sonoma State University. The workshop was introductory in nature and required the participants to practice and explore using the information they received in the workshop. All participants were also provided with a resource manual that contained several Internet guides, lists of available services, notes relating to information presented in the workshop, and practice exercises. The resource manual is available by contacting Donna Miller at LVC.

Our LOEX presentation was based on the process that we followed while developing the "Striking It Rich..." workshop. Following is a summary of our actual LOEX presentation and examples of exercises included in the resource guide (see appendixes 1-10).

We hope you find this information useful and look forward to discussing any questions. We can be reached via the Internet at miller@acad.lvc.edu and zeigler@admin.lvc.edu.

The Presentation

The following is a summary of the presentation made at the 21st LOEX Conference in Racine, Wisconsin, 14-15 May 1993. The session was co-presented by Donna Miller and Michael Zeigler, both members of the administrative staff at Lebanon Valley College (LVC).

Participant Survey

We started with an informal survey of our session attendees. From the survey, we determined that the majority of attendees had less than two years' experience on Internet resources. Most participants were, however, responsible for teaching the Internet to their respective campus staffs, and a few had already trained faculty on Internet use.

Session Outline

Our presentation followed this outline:
Introductions
Campus support of Internet services
Review of the workshop goals and objectives
Workshop development process
Workshop organization
Resource manual
Presentation logistics (equipment, supplies)
Critical evaluation
Presentation excerpts

Campuswide Support for the Internet at Lebanon Valley College

Lebanon Valley College is a small liberal arts college in central Pennsylvania. Full-time enrollment is approximately 900 students, with a student population of slightly over 1,200.

In 1990 central computer accounts were issued to all incoming freshmen. As a result of this policy, by 1992 over 80 percent of LVC's current students had accounts on the central systems. During the same period we also expanded access to desktop computers for our faculty. Currently, over 80 percent of the faculty have desktop units. Both students and faculty have access to the Internet through the college's membership in the Pennsylvania Research and Economic Partnership Network (PREPnet), which we joined in the summer of 1991.

By late 1991, with a growing number of users having both the ability and a desire to use the Internet, we felt it was critical to provide quality support. We developed an approach which provided for the support of Internet services through the combined efforts of

the library and the computer services department. The library provides the "what, where and how" support, while computer services provides technical support and maintains our connection to PREPnet. Thus, the two departments complement each other: while the library helps users find and access information available on the Internet, computer services assures that the connection is working properly, assists users in interpreting addresses and maintains the campuswide information system (CWIS).

Based on feedback from our LOEX sessions, shared support of the Internet appears to be a unique approach but one that has proven to be very successful.

LVC Internet Workshop Goals and Objectives

There were several objectives and tasks that we wanted the workshop participants to accomplish by the conclusion of our training. These were to

- Perform the following basic Internet activities: send/receive Internet mail messages, subscribe to a list, access information sources through the LIBS system on our CWIS; and

- Obtain an awareness and basic understanding of navigational tools and travel agents: email, telnet, ftp, LIBS; and WAIS, W3, Archie, Gopher, Veronica.

Two-Step Process

We decided to introduce faculty to the Internet in two steps over the course of a year. We began shortly after our connection to PREPnet was completed. These initial sessions in 1992 involved a brief introduction to the Internet, an explanation of the differences between BITNET and the Internet, and a short electronic mail demonstration and training session. Throughout the year, we explained additional services upon request (e.g., accessing library catalogs and subscribing to list services).

In 1993 we began the second step: to teach the Internet in-depth. We provided day-long workshops of explanation, demonstration, and hands-on practice. In order to meet an unexpectedly high demand, we conducted three sessions of our "Striking It Rich..." workshop.

Success?

In considering whether our approach was successful, we looked at both the pros and cons of the workshops.

Pros

On the positive side, our two-step approach accomplished much. It gradually familiarized the faculty with the Internet, allowed the presenters to developed their expertise, whetted the faculty's appetite for more information on the Internet, and introduced items slowly through expansion of our CWIS.

By introducing Internet resources over the course of the year, we allowed the faculty to start using some of the basic resources (e-mail, telnet) of the Internet before moving on to the more advanced (ftp, WAIS) features. As individuals asked about more advanced features, they were instructed one-on-one by the library and computer services staff.

We also felt that by introducing resources slowly and allowing the faculty to familiarize themselves with the Internet, we would arouse their curiosity for more information. Because of the daunting amount of information and features available on the Internet, we felt a slow, purposeful introduction of features was more appropriate than an overwhelming deluge of information, which would likely cause information overload.

Also at this time, we were in the process of developing our campuswide information system (CWIS). In 1991, the only campus information available on our central systems was student and staff directories. In 1992, we started the process of defining, implementing, and expanding the LVC CWIS. Although our CWIS system started slowly, it has expanded in its power and features through cooperative efforts of several departments on campus, mainly library services, registrar's office and computer services. Computer services continues to maintain the CWIS software but relies on other departments to maintain the information it contains.

Several items show the evolution process that the CWIS has taken at LVC. As mentioned above, while users could initially access student and staff directory information, an early version of the CWIS provided menu access to this information. Currently student, staff, and electronic mail address directories are available. In addition to these directories, individual student schedules and class rosters are also available to faculty and staff. The academic calendar, sports, and lab schedules are also available through a menu choice on the CWIS. One of our most recent additions to the CWIS has been a closed course list. Faculty have found this very helpful in advising students during the pre- and post-registration process.

In addition to LVC information, we have also made available for campuswide use the LIBS Internet Access Software developed by Mark Resmer at Sonoma State University. LIBS, a menu-driven Internet access system, was added to our CWIS shortly after our connection to the Internet was complete. We have found this program to be easy to use due to its menu driven interface and widespread coverage of Internet resources.

Another item on our CWIS that demonstrates its dynamic nature is the weather option. Initially the weather option was used to display the local weather report as reported in a local newspaper. (The process involved the library staff copying the local weather report and hand carrying it to the computer services department, where it was then manually entered into the central system. This process worked but was obviously tedious and inefficient.) Users now connect directly to the University of Michigan Weather Underground to obtain the latest U.S. Weather Service report for any city throughout the United States including the extended forecast for the region.

Cons

On the negative side, several problems reduced the workshop's effectiveness. These problems included the day-long length of the workshop, the low experience level of some participants, and a too high expectation by some participants of what the Internet had to offer.

Based on participant evaluations and our teaching experience, we felt the day-long workshop was too long. As we will discuss later, two half-day workshops would permit better pacing of instruction and assimilation of the information by the participants.

The only prerequisites we placed on participants were that they had an account on a central system, had logged in, and received electronic mail training from computer services. Unfortunately, not all participants met these prerequisites prior to coming to the workshop; thus their Internet knowledge level was not high enough for the material presented. Often these participants were confused by basic terminology and procedures for computer connections.

In some cases the participants' expectations of Internet services and their ease of use were unrealistic. We also stressed the varying quality of information located via the Internet. Since there is currently no "governing" body verifying and validating information, Internet users must be aware that they will have to sort through information critically to determine what is acceptable and what is not.

WORKSHOP DEVELOPMENT PROCESS

The development process for the workshop began more than three months prior to the first session. Donna and Mike met weekly to co-develop the workshop. Initially these meetings were to determine exactly what we wanted participants to be able to do upon completing the training.

In the beginning of the planning process, we also reviewed several Internet training books. These books included *Crossing the Internet Threshold: An Instructional Handbook* by Roy Tennant, et al., *Internexus*, a workbook used at The Pennsylvania State University for Internet training, Ed Krol's *The Whole Internet User's Guide and Catalog*, Brendan Kehoe's *Zen and the Art of the Internet*, and Tracy LaQuey's *The Internet Companion: A Beginner's Guide to Global Networking*. We also retrieved several request for comment (rfc) documents through ftp. Several of these rfc's were subsequently included in the reference manual that was provided to each participant. Two that we found very helpful included "The Network Neophyte" by Martin Raish and "There's Gold in Them Thar' Networks" by J. Martin.

In addition to reviewing guides, we also subscribed to several list services. One of the lists we found helpful was NETTRAIN (NETTRAIN@UBVM.CC.-BUFFALO.EDU). This list was useful for finding guides and receiving notification of rfc updates.

After identifying workshop topics and reviewing numerous Internet guides, we began to learn the various features that we wanted to teach. We divided the topics using the dual support approach explained earlier. Mike (computer services) taught himself Internet technicalities and Internet navigational tools, or file transfer protocal (ftp), e-mail, telnet (remote login). These navigational tools are used to access remote computers over the Internet. They are also the tools that are the foundation for the LIBS program that we use on campus as our Internet access point. In the meantime, Donna (library) was experimenting with the various travel agents—Veronica, WAIS, and W3. Donna also needed to use the navigational tools to access and retrieve Internet resource guides. In the course of developing this workshop, we ftp'd more than 110 documents/guides on Internet services.

Relatively early in the planning process, we met with our two co-presenters, Rob Paustian, director of libraries, and Bob Riley, executive director of computing and telecommunications. Rob and Bob would become instrumental in the development and presentation of the workshop. Ideas and products were shown to them for review and input. They also began developing their own expertise on campuswide information systems, electronic bulletin-boards, archives, and Gopher.

About one month into the planning process, we began establishing deadlines for the completion of the resource manual, the distribution of a brochure an-nouncing the workshop and the registration procedures, and the logistics of scheduling rooms and lunch.

After distributing the brochure and receiving an overwhelming response, we realized there was no turning back. The presenters started pulling together their presentation materials. As all four presenters started outlining their material, the information was entered in *Lotus Freelance Graphics for Windows*. *Freelance* permitted us to produce professional presentation overhead slides, presentation notes, and speaker notes. Early in the development process we decided that we would include duplicates of our overhead slides in the resource manual. These duplicates of the overhead slides, or presentation notes, reduced participants' need to take notes. They also allowed them to retain the entire presentation for reference at a later time. The use of this presentation software was critical: it provided a professional look to the workshop. Another advantage of *Freelance* was the simplicity of making modifications. At one point we made corrections to our presentation minutes before the workshop began.

After the manual was sent to the printer, we began practicing. In each of the several practice sessions, a presenter would present and demonstrate the assigned information and the others would critique the presentation. It was from these practice sessions that we obtained a feel for working with both the *Freelance* overhead slide program and the Internet connection.

Since we conducted three sessions of our workshop we were able to incorporate participants' suggestions in subsequent presentations. In the second presentation we were more aware of what participants found difficult to understand and slightly modified our presentation. In the third workshop, we modified the exercises, correcting several minor errors, and chose to restrict access to Internet services that were more "user-friendly" and would guarantee success.

Workshop Organization

Our Internet workshops were day-long sessions. Basically, the full-day session was broken into two halves—a morning session and an afternoon session. In the morning session, a broad overview of Internet was presented. We discussed how connections were made, that is, how modems connected personal computers to one of the LVC central systems, how the central systems accessed PREPnet and through PREPnet, the Internet.

We spent approximately an hour on the topic of "what is on the Internet." CWISs, bulletin board services (BBS), supercomputers, databases, and library catalogs, and list servs were several of the items discussed. List servs were covered extensively, especially the subscription process. Faculty were taught how to subscribe to a list without announcing that they were novice Internet users to thousands of other subscribers.

After the broad overview of "what is the Internet" and "what is on the Internet," we next presented brief sessions on what we considered to be Internet navigational tools: e-mail, ftp, and telnet. Navigational tools were presented as those utilities needed to get to the information on the Internet. E-mail was not covered in detail since all of the workshop participants were required to have accounts and to have sent electronic mail prior to coming to the Internet workshop.

Telnet and ftp were briefly explained and demonstrated. Around 11:00 we broke for an hour of hands-on exercises. Participants worked through "cookbook-like" exercises on topics covered in the morning session: list serv subscriptions, telnet, ftp, and LIBS.

In the afternoon session, we covered the Internet travel agents: Gopher, Archie, Veronica, WAIS, and WWW, or W3. These travel agents were presented as "middle-man services" that take the hassle out of finding information on the Internet. We spent about ten minutes describing the advantages and disadvantages of each of these services offered and did a live demonstration of each service. Once again, an hour and a half of hands-on practice followed the description and demonstration.

"STRIKING IT RICH WITH THE INTERNET" RESOURCE MANUAL

Each workshop participant received a "Striking It Rich with the Internet" (SIRWI) resource manual. The manual was divided into eight main sections, with the sections color-coded, and dividers and title pages separating the sections as well.

A detailed outline of the contents of the SIRWI manual follows:

I. Contents page
II. Introduction
    A. Diana Oblinger, *Understanding the Internet*
    B. Presentation Notes - Handouts of all presentation overhead slides developed in *Freelance*.
III. Internet Services - documents retrieved or compiled from resources on the Internet. Hunt results were included to show how other users approach information access and retrieval.
    A. *December List*
    B. *Yanoff List*
    C. Electronic Conferences
    D. Internet Databases
    E. Electronic Journals
    F. *Internet Hunt Results*

IV. Questions & Answers/Resources & Guides - guides for new users, covering terminology and questions often asked.
    A. *Frequently Asked Questions of New Internet Users*
    B. *"There's Gold in Them Thar' Networks!"*
    C. *Network Knowledge for the Neophyte*
    D. LISTSERV Command Summary
V. PREPnet - information on our regional network (Pennsylvania Research Economic Partnership)
VI. Lebanon Valley College Resources - resources and guides on reserve in the library; mail and file transfer guides developed by LVC Computer Services.
    A. ftp'd Internet Guides/documents on reserve
    B. Electronic Mail Guides
    C. KERMIT File transfer procedures
VII.   Glossary/Bibliography
VIII.   Exercises
    A. E-mail/LISTSERV Subscription
    B. ftp/telnet
    C. LIBS
    D. WWW, WAIS, Gopher, Archie, Veronica

PRESENTATION TOOLS

During the workshops, we used two computers, one for the presentation (overhead slides) and one for an Internet connection. We also used two LCD panels, two overhead projectors, and two projection screens. For our hands-on times (approximately three hours worth during the day-long session), we had 12 PCs with Internet connections. Three of the fifteen participants in each session "leaned over shoulders" to watch others work through the exercises.

As mentioned earlier, our overhead panels were created using the software presentation application *Lotus Freelance Graphics*. This allowed us to put our workshop outline into professional-looking panels, which could be projected on a large screen via an overhead projector.

Since we had a "live" connection to the Internet, we were able to demonstrate a number of features and resources. We preferred the live connection because of the rapidly evolving Internet services, and because of user expectations of Internet speed. Problems with the "live" Internet demonstrations were slowness of response, rapidly changing sources, and an inability to connect to a specific source. While these were drawbacks, it was useful for the users to see the presenters encounter "real-time" problems. Participants were thus made aware of some of the problems they would encounter while using the Internet. Presenters should be prepared for these difficulties and we would recommend the availability of several jokes to pass the time while waiting for a connection. (In other words, be aware that demonstrating live Internet connections incurs high levels of stress upon the presenters.)

PROCESSING THE WORKSHOP
(Critical review/debriefing)

We completed a "debriefing" to incorporate presenters' feelings and suggestions for areas needing improvement and revision. Following the three workshops, all four of the presenters met and reviewed the workshop evaluations, critiqued the presentations, and discussed those areas we would improve.

What Would We Change?

The length of the workshop received the most negative comments on our evaluations. Several attendees asked for half-day sessions, and for our next few Internet workshops we decided that we would try two half-day sessions.

Interestingly enough, though several participants left before their hands-on practice was completed, a number of comments were received asking for more hands-on time. Three hours of hands-on practice was built into the workshop, yet participants seemed to want more. We resolved to increase this time in our next workshops.

The first set of exercises that we provided to the participants caused them, and us, some grief. In the first workshop, we gave them a great number of telnet and ftp choices. Several participants became trapped in one university library's catalog. For our last two sessions, we narrowed the participants' telnet/ftp choices, and focused upon sites which were "friendly." We also enhanced the exercises—we bolded commands that they needed to type in and tried to choose sources used in the exercises that would guarantee success, especially since this was their first taste of the Internet.

Next to Dos

In the upcoming academic year ('93-94) we plan to produce discipline specific mini-workshops, or half-day Internet workshops, which focus on a specific topic (i.e., psychology, biology, sociology). It is also our intent to offer Internet workshops to the students, either in the fall of '93 or spring of '94.

If possible, the library and computer services would like to encourage the incorporation of Internet into curriculum. This was done in one of the journalism classes in the spring of '93, though as a first attempt it did not run very smoothly.

CONCLUSION

"Striking It Rich with the Internet: 'There's Gold in Them Thar' Networks!'" was a workshop that reached approximately fifty percent of the faculty, as well as a number of administrative staff members. Based upon the comments received from the workshop participants, the workshop was very well received by the campus community.

We believe our success depended on a number of factors. Most importantly, our supervisors supported us from the very beginning, with both funds and words of encouragement. We are especially grateful to Rob Paustian, director of libraries, and Bob Riley, executive director of computing and telecommunications, for their support and understanding. LVC administration was also supportive: the dean of the faculty, Bill McGill, provided us with the funds needed to cover the costs of the workshops.

Our timing was also crucial. We scheduled the workshop during the "down-time" between semesters. We also gave the faculty members a great deal of advance notice—pamphlets were mailed in October to announce the January workshops.

The "SIRWTI" pamphlet, which was composed on *WordPerfect*, printed on a laser printer, and run off on specially designed, attractive, tan and green-colored pamphlet paper, caught the eye of many faculty members. Also crucial were the resource manual, the overhead slides produced from *Freelance*, and the hands-on time given to the attendees during the workshop.

Last, but by far the most important key to our success, is the relationship that exists between the library and the computer services department staffs. We've been working together now since October of '92, and it has been an extremely enjoyable and productive working relationship.

BIBLIOGRAPHY

Kehoe, Brendan. *Zen and the Art of the Internet: A Beginner's Guide*. Englewood Cliffs, NJ: Prentice Hall, 1992.

Krol, Ed. *The Whole Internet User's Guide and Catalog*. Sebastopol, CA: O'Reilly, 1992.

LaQuey, Tracy, and Jeanne C. Ryder. *The Internet Companion: A Beginner's Guide to Global Networking*. New York: Addison-Wesley, 1992.

Martin, J. *There's Gold in Them Thar' Networks!*. Ohio State University, 1991, ftp'd document.

— DONNA L. MILLER AND MICHAEL C. ZEIGLER —

Polly, Jean Armour. "Surfing the Internet: An Introduction." *Wilson Library Bulletin* 66 (June 1992): 38-42,155.

Raish, Martin. *Network Knowledge for the Neophyte: Stuff You Need to Know to Navigate the Electronic Village*. Binghamton University, 1993, ftp'd document.

Tennant, Roy. *Crossing the Internet Threshold: An Instructional Handbook*. San Carlos, CA: Library Solutions Press, 1993.

Electronic Mail Exercise

"Electronic mail is quickly becoming a vital communications medium... It is perhaps the most popular application of the Internet because it extends and enhances our ability to communicate with others." (Tennant, 39)

Some "netiquette" to remember when using email:
--   Access your mail regularly
--   Stop your mail when you go on vacation (set nomail)
--   Be careful when using the reply command (r)
--   Do not use all caps. IT HAS THE EFFECT OF SHOUTING.
--   Avoid flaming. Beware of strong, emotional, angry, or sarcastic comments.
--   Always include a meaningful subject line
--   Think before you forward (f)
--   Use :-) ;-) :-(smilies to indicate emotion.
--   Use > before someone else's email message that you are replying/referring to

- To start the mail software, at the system prompt $, type: **mail**
- To send mail, type **s** at the **Mail>** prompt
- In the **TO:** line, type: **smtp%"miller@acad.lvc.edu"**
- At the **CC:** line press <ENTER>
- At the **SUBJECT:** prompt type: **Internet test** press <ENTER>
- In the body of the message type: **This is a test message**
- Press <CTRL> **Z** to end your message
- To send the message, type: **exit** at the **Mail>** prompt
- To leave mail, type: **exit** press <ENTER>

- To reply to a message, you must have the message you'd like to reply to on the screen. (NOTE: replying to a list message OFTEN goes to the WHOLE list...KNOW to whom you are replying)
- To reply, type: **R** at the **Mail>** prompt,
- At the **TO:** prompt the sender's address will automatically be filled in. (Make sure it is not the List Name)
- At the **CC:** prompt (carbon copy), either press <ENTER> to bypass it, or type an email address of a person you'd like to carbon copy the message to.
- The **Subject:** is automatically filled in, press <ENTER>
- You will be presented with the message to be replied to, you can mark the comments you are replying to with a > in front of each line. You may edit the comments for brevity by using the delete or backspace key. Type your reply after the original comments
- Press <CTRL> **Z** to end your message
- To send the message, type: **exit** at the **Mail>** prompt
- To leave mail, type: **exit** at the $ prompt and press <ENTER>

Electronic Discussion
List Subscription Exercise

Electronic discussion groups permit people with similar interests to discuss current issues, and share information via the Internet. It is a one-to-many type of electronic communication.

There are two addresses to electronic discussion groups. We'll use the reference librarian electronic list as the example. The list address for the reference librarian list is libref-l@kentvm. Messages sent to this address will be sent to ALL 4,000 subscribers of the libref-l@kentvm list. The listserv address is listserv@kentvm. Mail sent to this address goes to the software responsible for subscriptions, storing files and setting NOMAIL.

Find an electronic discussion group that interests you in the <u>Striking it Rich</u> guide. Write down the list address. To convert the list address to a listserv address, merely drop whatever is before the @, and replace it with the word **listserv**.

Remember:

1. ALWAYS subscribe to the listserv address
2. Because you are dealing with a BITNET address (no periods=BITNET), you need to "translate" the BITNET address "into" an internet address. (See e-mail handout on BITNET address conversion.)

- To start the mail software, at the system prompt $, type: **mail**
- To send mail, type **S** at the **Mail>** prompt
- In the **TO:** line, type: **smtp%"listserv%kentvm@bitnet.cc.cmu.edu"**
- At the **CC:** line press <ENTER>
- At the **SUBJECT:** line press <ENTER>
- The screen will clear and you will be in the editor
- In the body of the message type: **subscribe libref-l firstname lastname** (subscribe for subscribe, the list name, then your name)
- Press <CTRL> **Z** to end your message
- To send the message, type: **exit** at the **Mail>** prompt
- To leave mail, type: **exit** at the $ prompt and press <ENTER>

If you were successful, within a few minutes you should receive a subscription letter.

File Transfer Protocol
FTP

FTP allows you to transfer files from one computer to another. In other words, with FTP, you could connect to a computer in California, for example, and transfer files to the college computer you are working in. Almost all of the Internet documentation on LVC's reserve was ftp'd.

There are a several ftp commands you'll want to remember:

--	ftp <host.computer.name>	[connects you to the host computer]
--	user anonymous	[lets you login without an account]
--	password: guest	[bypasses the password--you may also use your internet address here]
--	cd <directory name>	[Places you in the proper directory]
--	get <filename>	[retrieves the file]
--	quit	[exits the host computer, puts you back to your system prompt]

Whenever you want to FTP something, you MUST have the following information:

ftp Host:	csd4.csd.uwm.edu
Directory:	/pub
File:	inet.services.txt

You CANNOT ftp without the host address, the directory name, and the file name. These three pieces of information are crucial. Using the information given in the paragraph above, we're going to ftp Scott Yanoff's list of Internet services.

* Initiate a connection to the ftp host with: **ftp csd4.csd.uwm.edu** <ENTER>
* When connected to ftp host, type: **user anonymous** <ENTER>
* At the password prompt, type: **your internet address** <ENTER>
* At the host computer prompt, type: **cd /pub** <ENTER>
* You should see the computer respond with "*CWD command successful*"
* At the host computer prompt, type: **get inet.services.txt** (in lower case) <ENTER>
* At the **Local file:** prompt, type: **yanoff.txt** <ENTER>
* To close the connection after the transfer, type: **quit** <ENTER>

---

* Back at the $ prompt, to check for the file you just transferred, type: **dir**
* To print the file you just transferred, at the $ prompt, type: **pport yanoff.txt**

— DONNA L. MILLER AND MICHAEL C. ZEIGLER —

Telnet Exercises

Telnet allows you to connect to a remote computer and use that computer as if you were directly attached to the remote system. "For this reason, [telnet] is sometimes called [an] interactive connection." (Tennant, 61) Through the use of Telnet you can connect to library catalogs across the world, to DIALOG, RLIN, and OCLC, to ERIC, to campus-wide information systems (CWIS), and to many other remote databases and information sources.

There are two Telnet commands you'll want to remember:

--   Telnet <internet address>   [connects you to the remote site]

--   <control>] or <control>^ q   [Telnet escape sequence--if all else fails when trying to quit]

Telnet to full-text Shakespeare plays and sonnets, the Bible:

- At the $ prompt, type: **telnet lib.dartmouth.edu**
- Choose the file: **select file bible** or **select file shakespeare plays**.
- Follow screen instructions.

Telnet to full-text **CHOICE** book reviews:

- At the $ prompt, type: **telnet pac.carl.org**
- Choose: **5 - VT100** <ENTER> <ENTER> <ENTER>
- Choose: **3**   <ENTER>
- Choose **60**
- Follow screen instructions.
- //exit <ENTER> to quit

Telnet to **Reference Works**, which includes a full-text dictionary, thesaurus, and The CIA World Factbook:

- At the $ prompt, type: **telnet info.rutgers.edu**
- Choose **Library**
- Choose **Reference**
- Follow screen instructions.

LIBS Exercise

LIBS is software for VAX/VMS or UNIX systems. It is a menu-driven gateway to many Internet services: in other words, it painlessly connects you to a variety of Internet resources. LIBS will greatly simplify Internet connections, but ONLY if you read and note the screen instructions carefully before connecting.

The main command you'll want to remember with LIBS is <control> c q <ENTER>. This key sequence will "break" out of any Internet connections you may have become "stuck" in, and will bring you back to the LIBS software.

To try LIBS software, if it is not mounted on your college computer, telnet to vax.sonoma.edu and login as LIBS (...this site should only be used to test/evaluate LIBS). LVC has installed LIBS, so for this exercise, we'll go to the LVC campus-wide information system (CWIS) to access LIBS.

- At the $ prompt, type: **info** **<ENTER>**
- Choose: **I** **<ENTER>** **L LIBS**
- Choose: **4** **<ENTER>**
- Choose: **8** **<ENTER>**
- Choose: **1** **<ENTER>**
- Read screen instructions carefully **BEFORE** connecting.

- On your own, using the screen instructions, explore LIBS.

- When finished with LIBS, to return to the $ prompt, keep pressing the **<ENTER>** key.

— DONNA L. MILLER AND MICHAEL C. ZEIGLER —

Appendix 6

WWW or W3 (WorldWideWeb)
Exercises

WWW was developed at CERN, a European Particle Physics Lab in Geneva. W3 provides access to Internet documents and data through the use of hypertext, or links. W3 also accesses telnet, ftp and WAIS.

With hypertext, "selected words in the text can be 'expanded' at any time to provide other information about the word. That is, these words are links to other documents." (Krol, 228).

Access to WWW is provided through LIBS or via telnet. WWW Telnet addresses: info.cern.ch or eies2.njit.edu or vms.huji.ac.il or info.funet.fi.

WWW Commands (which will be appear at the bottom of the screen) you'll want to remember:
-- find <keywords>   [searches for keywords]
-- 1-37   [select referenced documents]
-- <ENTER>   [move down a page w/in a document]
-- quit   [leaves WWW]
-- Back   [back to last document]
-- Up   [up one page w/in a document]
-- home   [return to start of WWW]
-- help   [displays help screen]

For the WWW exercise, we'll access W3 through LIBS.

● At the $ prompt, type: **info** <ENTER>
● Type: I (Internet) <ENTER>
● Type: L (LIBS) <ENTER>
● Choose - **5** Wide-area information services <ENTER>
● Choose - **5** WorldWideWeb <ENTER>
● Follow screen instructions to connect
● To search by subject, type: **1** <ENTER>
● To search the CIA World Factbook, choose the number shown after CIA World Factbook.
● Type: **find somalia** <ENTER>
● Type: **3** <ENTER>
● Menu commands are at bottom of screen
● To go back to the beginning screen, type: **home**

_____

● Using search by subject, find Roget's Thesaurus and search for the word diligent.

_____

● Explore WWW information on a topic of your choice.

WAIS Exercises

WAIS, or Wide Area Information Servers, "allow you to find and access Internet resources without regard for where they really reside". In other words, you don't need to know WHERE the information is located: just WHAT you are looking for. WAIS searches "indexes", and generally every word in a document is indexed. WAIS also rates the relevancy of the documents/data it retrieves, with 1000 being the highest rating.

Access to WAIS is through LIBS, or by telneting to: quake.think.com or nnsc.nsf.net or wais.funet.fi or sunsite.unc.edu. Login as wais or swais.

WAIS commands (which will appear at the bottom of the screen) to remember:

\<space bar\>	selects/deselects sources
w	keyword search
up/down arrows	scroll through list
\<ENTER\>	executes keyword search
q	backs out of documents; leaves WAIS

- At $ prompt type **info** \<ENTER\>
- Type: **I** (Internet) \<ENTER\> \<ENTER\>
- Type: **L** (LIBS) \<ENTER\>
- Choose Wide Area Information Services
- Choose WAIS
- Read and note screen instructions carefully before connecting
- When in WAIS, ALWAYS begin with the directory-of-servers. This is an "index" to over 300 sources. Find the directory-of-servers by either scrolling down with your down arrow key, or by "guessing" the swais number. A good guess would be 123. Type in **123** \<ENTER\> .
- Using the arrow keys, highlight the **directory-of-servers**. Next, press the \<space bar\>. Notice that an asterisk appears to the right of the **directory-of-servers** wais number. The asterisk tells the computer to "search this source".
- For a keyword search of the **directory-of-servers**, type: **w**. Next, you'll type in your BROAD keywords. We'll be searching for journalism, so type in: **journalism**. Hit the \<ENTER\> to begin the search. Write down, or remember, the source file rated 1000 (journalism.Periodicals). Type: **s**.
- Go back to the **directory-of-servers** and \<space bar\> on the **directory-of-servers** to remove the asterisk. Locate **journalism.Periodicals** by using the arrow keys, or by guessing with swais number. A good guess here would be 190. Type in **190** \<ENTER\>. Highlight **journalism.Periodicals** by using the arrow keys. \<Space bar\> on **journalism.Periodicals**. For a keyword search in this source, type the letter **w**. CAREFULLY backspace to remove journalism. Type in: **gulf war** \<ENTER\> to begin the search.
- Hit the \<space bar\> to view a highlighted document. Remember that once you are in a document, **q** will back you out.
- Use WAIS to locate information on a topic of interest to you.

Veronica Exercises

VERONICA, or Very Easy Rodent Oriented Net-wide Index to Computerized Archives, allows one to search over 300 gopher-server menus by keyword to locate information on the Internet. Veronica will connect you directly to the data, and will mail the information that you find to your internet address. Bear in mind that Veronica searches words in the TITLES of the documents only.

Veronica commands (which will appear at the bottom of the screen) you may wish to remember:

--	?	[for help]
--	q	[to quit]
--	u	[to go up a menu]
--	**<ENTER>**	[to continue]
--	**<m>**	[to mail the document to yourself]

- $ prompt type: **info**
- Choose **I** (Internet) <ENTER>
- Type: **L** (LIBS) <ENTER>
- Choose **Wide Area Information Services** <ENTER>
- Choose **Gopher Server** <ENTER>
- Connect to **gopher** (follow instructions on screen)
- Choose **9** **<ENTER>** To select other gophers
- Choose **2 -gopherspace using veronica** <ENTER>
- Choose **2 -search many titles in gopherspace using veronica** <ENTER>
- Choose either **search gopherspace by _single keyword_ veronica** OR
- Choose **search gopherspace by_partial boolean_ veronica**
- Type in your keyword <ENTER>
- Once your search has been executed, up/down arrows scroll, <ENTER> on item retrieves the document/data.

- Find the molecular weight of the **element** Boron.

- Find the national **unemployment** rate, and mail this document to yourself.

- Locate information on **alcoholism**.

- Locate information on a topic that interests you. (May be slow...)

Archie Exercises

"...originally began as a searchable database of the files available at several hundred Internet anonymous FTP archive sites. ...Besides this service, archie now includes a "whatis" database. This is a database of descriptions of over 3,500 public domain software packages, data sets and informational documents." (Tennant, 87).

Archie may be accessed via the LIBS software, or by telneting to: archie.rutgers.edu or archie.unl.edu or archie.ans.net. Login as archie.

A few Archie commands you may wish to remember:

--	prog <filename>	[searches for files]
--	whatis <keyword>	[searches whatis database]
--	quit	[leaves Archie]
--	bye	[leaves Archie]
--	help	[provides help]
--	mail <your Internet address>	[mails most recent search results to you]
--	about	[describes Archie]

- At the $ prompt, type: **telnet archie.rutgers.edu**
- At the login prompt, type: **archie**
- Search for a citation on internet information by Tracey LaQuey.
  Type: **whatis laquey**
- Mail these results to yourself.
  Type: **mail <your internet address>** (e.g. mail miller@acad.lvc.edu)

- Try searching for information on homebrew. Use both the **whatis** and **prog** commands.
  (i.e. type: **whatis homebrew**, then **prog homebrew**).
  Which command was successful?
  What is the difference between the two commands?

- Search for a topic of interest to you. Try both **whatis** and **prog**.

— DONNA L. MILLER AND MICHAEL C. ZEIGLER —

Appendix 10

Gopher Exercises

"Gopher is an application that organizes access to Internet resources using a uniform interface that's simple to understand and easy to use. It provides smooth passage into other computers, allowing you to browse and search documents, and links you to resources and databases... So while you're "sniffing" around "Gopher-space", you may not know it, but you're actually doing things like transferring files, changing directories, telneting to computers, and querying servers (including archie and WAIS) all over the world...." (LaQuey, 106-107)

Some of the more interesting things Gopher accesses include: popular ftp sites, fun and games, and libraries (includes keyword searching of electronic books on Internet; electronic journals; U.S Gov't information; Library of Congress records; newspapers, magazines, and newsletters; reference works). You'll want to look at all of the information available through the root gopher server before trying "other gopher and information servers".

Gopher may be accessed through LIBS, or by telneting to consultant.micro.umn.edu or gopher uiuc.edu or gopher.uwp.edu or panda.uiowa.edu. Login as gopher.

Gopher commands to remember (all appear across the bottom of the screen):
- -- 1-999 <ENTER> [typing a document number & hitting <ENTER> takes you directly to the document]
- -- u [moves you up a menu]
- -- ? [provides help]
- -- q [quits]
- -- <space bar> [used to continue when viewing a document]
- -- <m> [mails the document you are viewing to your internet address]
- -- <ENTER> [used to continue--at end of document you are viewing]
- -- up/down arrows [scroll through document titles]

- At the $ prompt, type: **info**
- Type I <ENTER>
- Choose **LIBS** LIBS Libraries, etc.
- **5 - Wide Area Information Servers**
- Choose **Gopher Server**
- Read screen instructions to logon
- Choose **5 - Libraries**
- Choose **1 - Electronic Books**
- Search for <u>Alice in Wonderland</u>. Mail a chapter of the book to your Internet address. To do this, you'll need to space bar to the end of the document/chapter, and when the screen says **<ENTER> to continue, <m> to mail**, type: **m**. Follow screen instructions.

- Back at the main gopher root directory (press the u key until back at main menu)
- Choose **5 - Libraries**
- Choose **2 - Electronic Journals**. Follow screen instructions to locate a journal of interest to you.

- From the main gopher root directory, **Choose 5 - Libraries; Choose 7 - Reference works, Choose 7 Periodic Table; Choose 8 Boron**. What is the molecular weight of Boron?

Teaching the Teachers in an Electronic Environment

Sandra Duling and Patrick Max

Introduction

Sandra Duling and Patrick Max will be speaking about "Teaching the Teachers in a Electronic Environment," although much of what I have to say falls under the conference's more general rubric, "The Impact of Technology on Library Instruction."

Sandy and I both work at Castleton State College, a small public liberal arts college in central Vermont. Between the two of us we have about 20 years experience in bibliographic instruction, 15 years teaching experience in elementary and secondary education, and several years teaching experience in community college, college, university, and graduate school. We have written and spoken on the topic of library instruction in the past. Ms. Duling's focus today will be on her current bibliographic instruction classes, particularly as they relate to school restructuring, the implementation of site-based management, research-based learning, and the new technology. My job, on the other hand, is to meander through those "meta-issues" (the truly amorphous "stuff," if you will) that are the milieu in which librarians and teachers work. I get to speak with you about the nature of librarianship, the general positive and negative effects of technology on the profession (or of the profession on technology), reading, and so on. I also intend to regale you with anecdotes, poetry, and film. [I began with the by now notorious "Pig-with-the-Wooden-Leg" story, using it

to illustrate the point that our society has a tendency to identify beneficial resources and then to use such resources (often inappropriately) as a panacea for an ever-growing number of social problems. I will not repeat the pig story here. Suffice it to say, people found it hilarious. Those present laughed until they cried.]

Ambivalence and Technology

Although in many ways, it is clear that one ought to be quite ambivalent regarding technology and libraries, there is no question that technology has had an enormously salutary effect upon library service.

[Here I showed a very brief clip from the film "Witness." The clip, a few seconds long, depicts an Amish horse and buggy moving from screen left to screen right through a lovely bucolic scene. As it reaches screen right, the sound of a large engine gearing down is heard. The next few frames show the buggy again moving from left to right, but behind the buggy we now see a semi and a lengthy line of cars.]

This clip from this film directed by Peter Weir illustrates Weir's great ambivalence regarding "progress" by contrasting an agrarian society (technology), if you will, with modern society. The horse and buggy and the semi become metaphors for a cultural argument—on one side are simplicity, elegance, the past; on the other side are power, speed, pollution, the future. In reality there is little choice for the Luddite or the techie. While the agrarian past is powerfully engaging, the powerful future is decisive. Although I will speak of technology critically, the semi, however problematic, represents real human progress. As I have

Duling is head of reference and bibliographic instruction and *Max* is library director at Castleton State College, Castleton, Vermont.

said elsewhere, the new technology does merit our faith and hopes, and it does merit our considered professional attention because it provides a new way to think about library service and issues and/or provides new solutions to longstanding problems. I cannot imagine a library in the latter half of the 20th century not having overhead projectors, film, videodisc and tapes, video projectors, fax machines, computer systems, online access to networks (Internet and NREN), and so on. I do believe that I am unequivocally "for" such technology. I believe that it is "good" technology (i.e., it provides real benefits for patrons). Libraries that do not explore the ways in which these technologies respond to patrons' needs will be left behind (horse and buggy) because they have such a limited view of their role in regard to information, learning, and human development. Those who shrug the Internet off as someone else's responsibility will eventually find themselves without meaningful work.

Frequently when librarians are discussing "the new technology," they are really discussing computers. Therefore, it may be useful to focus on computing for a few moments. The computer has made possible substantial progress in data storage manipulation and integration and permits remote access to databases. It has enabled us to share in enormous databases that were previously unavailable (by remote log-in, if preferable); it has given us the ability to search in ways never possible (including very effective means of formulating inquires); it has changed our professional relationships in significant ways. All of this is to say that the computer has powerfully influenced the real infrastructure of the library.

But . . .

[Here I showed a clip from Spielberg's "Empire of the Sun." The clip shows a young abandoned English boy in a Japanese internment camp in China during World War II. The young boy is enchanted by airplanes. His attraction reaches a feverish pitch when the camp is attacked by U.S. planes. The boy rushes to the upper level of a tower, and, placing himself in harms way, runs about hysterically shouting, "Mustang P51, Cadillac of the skies." Rushing to his rescue, the camp doctor is finally able to calm the boy by grabbing him and telling him to "stop thinking." The boy immediately calms down and in tears says that he cannot remember the color of his mother's hair, but then proceeds to recall several intimate experiences with his mother.]

Like children in an electronic arcade, our enthusiasm for things technological has reached the level of (destructive) hysteria—what really matters is that we review the contributions technology has made (i.e., evaluate results after the dust has cleared). We should remember that we are human beings with human needs,

understandings, and goals. There is no quick electronic fix for many of our problems. For example, during the last presidential election, I became passingly interested in the then-current fascination with a resurrected Jerry Brown. I tuned in to a televised interview and heard a question and answer or two. Then, the interviewer asked Jerry how he would solve the problems of public education in the U.S. Jerry had a one-word answer; "computers." I could not get the remote control "off" button pushed fast enough (and they say electronic devices don't contribute enough to our daily lives!). At any rate, we must use the same critical facilities to judge technology as we use to judge toothpaste, used cars, films, Madonna, and the problems in the former Yugoslavia.

There is "good" technology (useful technological products) and "bad" technology. Bad technology generally falls into one of two categories:

1. the electric knife/can opener/toothbrush syndrome: the technology "works" but performs no new real service;

2. the electric hand dryer syndrome: the technology neither performs a useful service nor works. (Pertinent here is the universally hand-interpolated final step, "4. Wipe hands on pants.")

Why do we purchase, tolerate, and/or defend library technologies that do not work:

1. OCLC's complicating cumbersome searching ("4, 3, 2"; "4, 4") (not, of course, its prodigious database-building efforts);

2. "Help" screens that trap you without commands or menus that indicate the next step;

3. search products that have no (or sloppy) keyword/Boolean facilities, and so on.

However, what I find most disingenuous about the computerization of the profession is the lowering of priorities on all issues not amenable to quantification. Even more disturbing are library articles "produced" (*not* written) by individuals whose approach to significant problems is to pass raw quantitative data through an axiomatic, jargon-replete process that resembles nothing so much as data spewed out by a malfunctioning Commodore 20. We have replaced complex human reflection and evaluation with a hi-tech thought process that badly imitates the most mundane computer processes. If you are not sure what I am getting at here, simply look at the latest issue of many library journals.

We cannot make technological progress without knowing what services we perform for society, the implications of technology for those services, and any new social role that may be permitted by use of the new technology. Without such reflection a powerful tool for the intellectual organization and distribution of human knowledge will be reduced to shoddy hardware that incorporates poorly designed software in support of irrelevant databases.

At any rate, the old wisdoms of the profession appear to provide us with a reasonably useful structure for discussing library service. We select, acquire, preserve, caretake, make accessible this collective storehouse of human knowledge, and we create a free, open, democratic environment for sharing this information. This work implies that we take an active role in preserving and making available the record of human knowledge. This includes the great variety of formats and processes that contribute to this record (*including* the real contribution made by a *variety* of new technologies). We have a special responsibility for free and open access to this human record. Fair access to information along with freedom of speech and the right to an education are the backbone of the democratic process. The new technologies have forced us to broaden our perspective in this regard. For example, what role do we have in ensuring fair access to a wide variety of telecommunications services? Thus, to be able to deal with the new technology and to successfully teach the "teachers" we need to think about these things and to come to some understanding of the work of teachers.

Roles: Teachers, Technicians, Libraries

What does a teacher do? I am not sure that I am competent to deal with such a daunting question. So I am going to refer you to a poem by Stephen Spender [Here I read Spender's "An Elementary School Classroom in a Slum" and discussed the way in which teachers provide an opportunity for children to share in the collective wisdom of humankind.] I would suggest, however, that although there is much shared territory among libraries and teachers, especially in the area of bibliographic instruction, the two are not identical social functions, and we ought not to treat them as such.

Perhaps the best way to illustrate the relevant use of library technology in teaching the teacher is to talk about the ways in which teachers, librarians, and technical specialists come together around some specific topic—for example, reading. In the beginning, I think it might be helpful to "just say no" to the "skills" perception of reading. I would say that writing "skills" as they are most frequently discussed are not skills;

reading "skills" are not skills, nor are library "skills" necessarily skills in the narrowest sense of that term. This is so unless, for example, we are willing to call the Constitution and Bill of Rights mere training manuals. Like most library/teaching/ technology issues, if we take the short view (i.e., we are training for a skill) then we misrepresent the very nature of the experience and cannot respond to our most important challenges. Bruno Bettelheim in *On Learning to Read* says, "literature in the form of religion and other myths was one of man's greatest achievements since in them he explored for the first time his existence and the order of the world. Learning to read, then, appeals to the highest and the most primordial aspects of the mind."[1]

In *Myths, Dreams*, and *Mysteries*, Mircea Eliade says that reading is the magical way in which a culture creates a new vision of itself in order to meet new and different challenges. He says, "reading replaces not only the oral folk traditions, such as still survive in rural communities of Europe, but also the recital of the myths in the archaic societies. Now, reading, perhaps even more than visual entertainment, gives one a break in duration, and at the same time an 'escape from time.' Whether we are 'killing time' with a detective story, or entering into another temporal universe as we do in reading any kind of novel, we are taken out of our own duration to move in other rhythms, to live in a different history."[2] Speaking directly of the teaching process in relation to reading Bettelheim says, "to the modern educator, who views learning to read as the acquisition of a particularly important cognitive skill, it may seem a far-fetched idea that this can be mastered well only if initially and for some time to come reading is experienced subconsciously by the child as a magic art, which potentially confers great and in some ways unknown powers." So, it is only when the librarian, teacher, and technical specialist understand this issue that meaningful work can take place. All must make major commitments with this sort of understanding.

So librarians must provide, protect and make available a book stock that fairly represents our inherited collective wisdom. Librarians fail, for example, when they allow the stock to be plundered by censors, or when they do not use technology to support more sophisticated access for patrons. The teacher fails when she or he substitutes a mechanical training process for the profoundly deeply moving experience of reading literature of significance. Technical specialists fail when they create texts solely based on the principle of "readability" (a euphemism for "it's-easy-but-who-would-ever-find-it-even-vaguely-interesting") or when they design ineffective or unnecessarily complicated electronic databases.

Obviously, this sort of discussion might be extended to other library/information issues: fair access to telecommunication systems; the right to privacy, and many others. These are the important issues that should drive technology and our professional relationships. Without such reflection we cannot reasonably meet our own social responsibility, let alone "teach the teachers."

TEACHING THE TEACHERS

Sandra Duling

If we are committed to the broad concept of information literacy, then education students are the most significant group with whom we work. These are the people who will have the strongest voice in how libraries are, and are not, used in the nation's schools. They will shape the role of libraries and librarians and will have an impact on the distribution of information in our society.

Academic librarians have not traditionally thought of future teachers in this way. We have tended to think of them as "those students who need ERIC to write their papers" and have viewed our job as helping them learn the mechanics of the compact disc. On some campuses, education departments are looked upon by other departments as lacking in academic rigor—an easy major, a quasi-professional program with a soft foundation of knowledge. It shouldn't be that way. Preparing the next generation to be literate, responsible members of our society may be the most important of all professions.

The current school restructuring movement provides academic librarians with an unprecedented opportunity to help education students become information literate, and to enlist their aid in assuring that libraries, books, and information systems evolve as vital aspects of the school curriculum and of students' lives.

"School restructuring" is a movement that began in the 1980s, has grown, and will probably gain momentum in the nineties. Like the educational reforms of the fifties which resulted from concern over Soviet superiority in space, the current movement stems from alarm over a perceived U.S. inability to compete in a global economy. Schools are seen as failing in their mission to educate. The hope is that if we restructure schools, their rates of success will improve. The restructuring movement has proposed numerous options—some are quick fixes; others involve broad based changes. Three of the salient features of the restructuring movement are:

- a trend toward site-based management;
- an emphasis on resource-based learning;
- a quest for incorporation of new technologies.

I will take each of these three "salient features" and make some suggestions concerning implications for our work with education students. I will include examples from our work at Castleton State College. Like many state colleges, Castleton was formerly a teachers' college and continues to have a large undergraduate education department, as well as a modest graduate education program.

Trend toward Site-Based Management

The first of these salient features, the trend toward site-, or school-, based management, parallels the trend in business toward participatory management. Many see it as a trend toward the "professionalization" of teaching—teachers being asked to make decisions, which were previously made by administrators.

The trend has implications for our work with education students. In order for site-based management to succeed, teachers *must* develop research skills, critical habits of thought, and skill in communicating findings. They must be prepared to update their understanding of issues by career-long referral to, and participation in, the conversation which characterizes a professional literature. Of course, these attitudes and abilities have always been desirable. But if site-based management is to work, they are now indispensable.

I begin every BI session for education students by reminding them of their need to be acquainted with their professional literature, and of their career-long need to use it. It is always good practice to define the objectives of instruction. I remind them of this at the beginning of a session, indicating that my immediate (although secondary) objective for this class is to help them get through the assignment at hand. My more important objective is helping them learn to deal with future professional issues and problems. I refer to teachers' status as professionals, a topic they discuss in foundations classes. I might mention the medical and legal professions—how unlikely, even unethical, it would be for an institution to graduate medical or legal professionals who did not have a sound understanding of their professional literature, and how the same should be the case with teachers. I give examples of situations where teachers might do research to solve a problem. For instance, the elementary teacher who is presenting the school board with a recommendation for reducing class size, and wants to cite research showing a correlation between class size and reading achievement. Or the teacher who is preparing a K-12 environmental education curriculum and needs an overview of issues or model curriculum guides.

Many BI librarians are reluctant to spend class time like this. There are all those nuances of the OPAC which should be covered, and students need to know how to use the periodical holdings list. I am convinced, however, that time spent discussing the concept of a professional literature, and a teacher's role in using it, takes precedence. It is clearly a new concept to a majority of education students. It is a new idea to some of their instructors as well. The discussion establishes the rationale for everything else we do with these students. From the introduction on, all examples I use with education classes are working situations, not class assignments or term paper topics. For instance, if I am using ability grouping as a sample topic, I don't talk about a student working on a paper on ability grouping. Rather, I talk about a teacher who is on a committee to establish school policy on ability grouping. I am convinced that the distinction, although seemingly superficial, is significant. It gives a more serious and professional tone to the class and to students' subsequent work in the library.

Education faculty may not think of library instruction as preparing their students for an important aspect of their careers. Most faculty bring classes for BI because students are unfamiliar with ERIC, and faculty hope for better papers if students get some instruction. Faculty also often need to be educated concerning the role of information literacy for teachers.

We have all lent a sympathetic ear to faculty who despair over the quality of student papers. Many of us know faculty who experiment with alternatives to the traditional paper, have discussed the merits of those alternatives, and have offered suggestions. Particularly in what are sometimes referred to as professional programs (including education), I have worked with faculty on successful assignments whose goals are to investigate simulated work problems or issues. (Appendix 1 is a handout which suggests a few such assignments for education students.) Again, there is little difference between the subject matter of these assignments and traditional term paper topics. My experience indicates, however (and is corroborated by faculty), that the alternative format generates more enthusiasm, a more serious research strategy, and better results.

Optimally, we should see education students for formal instruction a number of times:

- Foundations class—perhaps for an introduction to the OPAC, for an introduction to the concept of professional and trade journals, and to use *Education Index*;

- Curriculum class—which might be an opportunity for a 75-minute session on ERIC;

- Tests and measurements class—for help in identifying and critiquing tests;

- Special education class—perhaps for an introduction to sources on education law, or for a review of controlled versus free-text searching (it's hard to find a field which changes its jargon more often than special education);

- Whole language or content area reading class—for tools which identify materials on specific subjects, at particular ability levels.

All of this presupposes a solid working relationship with the education department. And we all know it isn't easy to build a working relationship with an entire department. Most of us have a few faculty with whom we work closely, and others with whom we have little contact. Establishing a BI program which is entrenched in several areas of the curriculum is particularly difficult when a department has a high turnover rate, or when an academic program is in a state of flux, as many education departments are. (As a result of the school reform movement some institutions are dropping education as a major, requiring education students to major in a liberal arts subject with education as a minor, or are promoting education as a fifth year or master's degree.) However, if we are persistent, confident, and creative, that state of flux can be an advantage—an opportunity to participate in change and to shape the kind of BI program we would like to offer.

Emphasis on Resource-Based Learning

"Resource-based learning," the second salient feature of the school restructuring movement, implies a departure from textbook-based instruction. It emphasizes higher order thinking as opposed to memorization, and stresses use of a variety of resources rather than a single textbook series. Examples of the trend include the whole language approach in reading, the abandoning of social studies and science textbooks in favor of an assortment of learning resources, and an emphasis on teaching of reading and writing in content areas, not just in language arts classes.

This trend means that school libraries and librarians should be taking an increasingly active role in curriculum and planning as well as in identifying, procuring, and organizing materials in support of the curriculum. If there is to be a successful alternative to a textbook-based curriculum, then teachers need access to other materials that are well suited to the needs and abilities of their students. The obvious resource for getting these materials is the school library. I would venture to guess, however, that only a small percentage of the courses offered in whole language, in reading in the content areas, in science and social studies methods even mention the role of a library or librarian. We can help change that.

Following is an example of a recent effort along these lines at Castleton. We can't extrapolate nationally, but I suspect many can recognize the situation. The professor in my example is energetic, dedicated, and popular. We learned, via reference questions, that she had assigned two reading-related classes to develop unit plans. Students were asked to identify a range of materials (books, poetry, films, plays) which relate to a chosen theme. As far as I could tell, librarians had not been mentioned, and although students occasionally asked for a location, they were generally relying on the library's OPAC, their own memories, and suggestions from friends. I found, as I'm sure most of us have, students sitting on the floor in the juvenile section, browsing for titles that might relate to robots, or trees, or the Civil War. These people needed two things: 1) an awareness of bibliographic finding tools that would help them identify useful materials, and 2) the knowledge that a librarian could be a valuable partner in developing a successful unit.

I was persistent in contacting the professor, finally managing to speak with her at a faculty assembly meeting. She agreed to have me compile a set of suggested resources and to spend part of a class explaining a few of them.

I began the class session by talking about school libraries. As we were discussing the resources on their handout, I made frequent reference to the role of the librarian, interlibrary loan, and electronic access. This session accomplished at least three things: 1) it helped students produce better unit plans because they were able to find a wider variety of materials; 2) with a wider, sometimes overwhelming variety of materials, they were forced to compare and evaluate much more than when they were simply taking anything they could find; 3) they had one more opportunity to practice using the library themselves and, in many instances, to incorporate library use into lesson plans for their students.

Quest for Incorporation of New Technologies

I have chosen to use the word "quest" in describing the third salient feature of the school restructuring movement. I am aware of the connotations associated with the word (the holy grail, Don Quixote) and am satisfied that they apply. The most naive of the school

restructuring literature holds up educational technology as the long sought answer to the country's economic and educational woes. If only students were all "computer literate," if only there was a fax machine in every classroom, all would be well. (Appendix 2 is a bibliography of selected readings on "teaching the teachers." A couple of the items on it contain some elements of this theme of technology as a quick salvation. I have included them because it is important for us to be aware of the flavor of discussion in the popular media.)

Technology does have a crucial role to play in the future of American education. Thoughtful and creative teachers are experimenting with applications of a range of technologies. But money and energy are also being spent on short-sighted, even silly applications, by people with fine intentions but little grasp of the issues involved in a technological future, or of sensible ways of preparing children for such a future. Our job is to assist education faculty in ensuring that future teachers with whom we work don't fall into this latter category. We also need to do what we can to ensure that school libraries and librarians (people with sound training and a solid grasp of the issues of an information age) play a strong supporting role in the development of technologies in education. If the literature of school restructuring is an accurate indicator, this is not happening.

What can we do? An obvious step is to teach education students to use technologies—computer databases, telecommunication systems, audio and video formats, as well as printed materials. They must understand these technologies in order to incorporate them in their teaching, and to prepare their students for an age when information is available in many ways. But we must do more than teach system mechanics, for the mechanics we teach today will be obsolete tomorrow. We need to help education students understand the difference between *data* and *information* and *knowledge*, and help them assess technology's role in storing and transmitting each. We must ensure that they think about technology—that they analyze and compare, becoming capable of informed decisions about uses of technology in their work.

I began this discussion by suggesting we need to do more with education students than teaching them to use the ERIC CD. This is not to say that we don't need to teach them to use ERIC. All education students need at least one full class session devoted to understanding the ERIC database, in conjunction with assignments which require fairly sophisticated use. I don't necessarily recommend teaching undergraduate foundations (first-year) students use of the electronic ERIC. They are generally better served by instruction and practice in using the OPAC and *Education Index*. For undergraduates, an education class such as a curriculum or a methods course can be a likely opportunity to introduce ERIC.

A great deal has been written on teaching the ERIC database. At Castleton, we have tried several approaches: online tutorials, workbooks, lectures, transparencies. I am most satisfied with a modestly enhanced, traditional lecture method, when an assignment requiring use of the database is pending. I take the CD equipment and an LCD to a classroom so the lecture can include many examples. I tell students to take notes, and if they don't seem to be writing down crucial concepts or details, I tell them what to write. I also make certain they know how to get help while searching (online, help sheets, and so on).

In introducing the ERIC database, it's useful to demonstrate a simple search right away, with little initial explanation, and to have students look carefully at a couple of records. I ask students to picture themselves as ERIC indexers, or at least to think of an ERIC indexer as someone like themselves, with a document in hand to be entered in the database. This approach does a couple of things: 1) it personalizes the process, helping them establish a mental link between placement of information in a record and retrieval of that information, 2) it's a good introduction to the *Thesaurus* and to the idea of a controlled vocabulary (they picture the indexer thumbing through the *Thesaurus* looking for the 10 to 12 terms which best describe the article). Finally, this approach emphasizes that the database is created by people and is subject to inaccuracies and a degree of subjectivity.

I begin *any* instruction in database searching for education students by telling them that as teachers they will have to do what I'm doing now—teaching people to interact with electronic systems. I ask them to think about how I am presenting the material, to analyze my teaching methods, and to think about how those methods might apply to their own situations. When illustrating a search strategy, a problem or pitfall, I often do it in terms of problems they may encounter or techniques they might use in teaching electronic systems. For example:

- I mention the difficulty children (and adults) have in understanding that "it's a dumb machine," which doesn't know to look for synonyms, alternative spellings, or suffixes. The concept of "teenagers" is a good example—there are many alternative words and phrases.

- I mention research that indicates it may be best to give people a "mental model" of an electronic system since otherwise most people will devise their own, which may be less accurate than one you give them. Use analogies: tell them they

might "think of it as (a card file, a scroll, shuffling forms into piles...)."

- I mention that there is some evidence that students learning computer systems in pairs or small groups are more successful than those learning alone. (Education students are generally familiar with the current literature on cooperative learning.) I suggest they make their first attempt at ERIC with a partner and that they think about groupings when they teach electronic systems.

- I discuss the complexity of our use of language in describing concepts and the difficulties this creates in using electronic systems. The *ERIC Thesaurus* is a good way of illustrating the hierarchical nature of subject terms. I talk about the difficulty of helping children understand this concept and give examples such as teaching the telephone book's yellow pages in elementary classrooms (if a narrow term doesn't work, try a broader one—i.e., if there's nothing under canoes, try boats). I remind them that all of this is tough. It presupposes an understanding of the subject area in question, as well as a level of cognitive development able to understand hierarchical classification.

- I give examples of ways I have tried to teach Boolean logic and discuss my successes and failures. I remind students that learning style may have a lot to do with how they, and their students, best understand a technology, and that they should try to teach to a variety of learning styles. The following outline is an illustration of how one might attempt to address variations in learning style when teaching Boolean logic:

(Step 1) Without an initial explanation of Boolean operators, demonstrate a sample online search which uses "and" and "or."

(Step 2) Explain the Boolean operators, using both common language and mathematical terminology, a blackboard, and Venn diagrams. For those who learn best with abstract models, this is the ticket.

(Step 3) Give an unrelated example of the logic of the Boolean "and" (some people learn best with analogies). An example I've borrowed from a colleague is the apartment-hunting scenario: you go to a real estate agent, looking for an apartment which fulfills certain criteria (it is within one mile of the college AND it allows pets AND it has space for a garden).

(Step 4) Do another sample search, having a student do the keyboarding, again illustrating "and" and "or," reviewing the search logic as the student enters it.

(Step 5) Present a research problem, and have the group suggest search terms and strategy.

(Step 6) Present another problem, or ask a student to suggest one, and ask each student (or pairs of students) to write down a search strategy. Try a few of their suggestions.

During each of these steps I encourage students to take notes. Although we have handouts, I prefer to make them available after class. Taking notes ensures a degree of active as opposed to passive attention.

I spend little time teaching students the mechanics of the ERIC system. I explain that we have limited time, and that I am confident they can use documentation and help screens to learn how to show, mark, print, and so on. What is important, in our limited time, is that I help them understand what the database includes, how it is constructed, and how a search logic can enable them to identify useful material.

I have used ERIC as an example of teaching education students about electronic databases. Many of these suggestions are equally applicable to teaching other electronic systems. And education students should be exposed to as many systems as possible. (There is an unfortunate tendency for education students to do all of their research in ERIC, bypassing both print and electronic sources that might be more appropriate, and that would broaden their horizons).

In conclusion, BI librarians should think seriously about the education students with whom we work. We *can* have an impact on how they think about libraries and research; and more important, we can have an impact on what they teach their students about research, libraries, and information systems. We need to be persistent in establishing a working relationship with education faculty. We must make it clear that we are interested in their work and that we have a role to play in helping prepare students to be successful professionals.

If the literature on school restructuring is an accurate indicator, teachers will have a powerful voice in how schools are run. Teachers who value literature, libraries, and research will balk at budget cuts that target library services. Teachers who have been taught to value independent thought and research will foster those values in the next generation. Conversely, teachers who have *not* been taught to think independently and to use library and other information sources to solve difficult problems will not foster those values in their students and will not protect and promote libraries. When budgets must be cut, they will not see a need to preserve library resources.

Future teachers are an important group. We owe it to them, to our profession, and to our children to help them prepare to be thoughtful users of information age resources.

NOTES

1. Bruno Bettelheim and Karen Zelan, *On Learning to Read: The Child's Fascination with Meaning* (Aldred A. Knopf: New York, 1982), 50.

2. Mircea Eliade, *Myths, Dreams and Mysteries: The Encounter between Contemporary Faiths and Archaic Realities* (Harper & Brothers: New York, 1960), 36.

APPENDIX 1: TEACHERS DOING RESEARCH: SOME ALTERNATIVES TO THE TERM PAPER FOR EDUCATION STUDENTS

The importance of learning to write a traditional academic research paper is beyond doubt. A carefully researched and well-written paper is evidence of mastery of subject matter, of skill in communicating facts and ideas, and of advanced analytical and critical thought processes. However, there are some education courses, and certainly some segments of such courses, for which other assignments may be equally appropriate vehicles for this type of learning.

Research assignments that are presented in terms of real cases, problems, and professional responsibilities are sometimes a useful alternative to those presented in the format of the standard academic research paper.

Alternative assignments can further serve to reinforce the concept that teachers are professionals—people who consult a body of professional literature in the course of carrying out their regular duties. Most teachers must be prepared to take on assignments that are similar to the following examples:

1) You are on a committee charged with investigating the advantages and disadvantages of ability grouping in your junior high school. The school is considering a switch from homogeneous to heterogeneous grouping. Your committee must submit a report that outlines current professional

thought on this subject and must also make a recommendation for your school.

2) You've been asked by the PTO to present a panel discussion on learning disabilities. Parents seem particularly concerned with integration of learning-disabled children in the regular classroom.

3) You are on a committee charged with devising a set of districtwide textbook selection policies and procedures. Your final report should include your findings concerning the salient issues along with a proposed set of guidelines and procedures.

4) Your committee has been asked to draft a K-12 drug and alcohol education program. Your proposal must be in compliance with state guidelines and must include an estimation of impact on budget and staffing

5) The school board would like to clarify and formalize its faculty hiring procedures. It has asked your faculty committee to propose a set of guidelines for hiring of classroom teachers.

6) A group of parents have raised the issue of gender equity in your school system. The administration has asked your committee to prepare a K-12 faculty in-service workshop. The workshop should aim to heighten staff awareness of the scope and nature of the issue and of ways of dealing with questions of gender equity at all levels.

7) Your district is interested in responding to the community need for after-school child care. You have been asked to investigate programs in existence in other districts, as well as issues, problems, potential solutions to problems, and so on associated with such programs. You must make a proposal based upon your findings.

8) You are among a group of teachers who are dissatisfied with your school's current use of standardized testing in the area of language arts. You propose a switch from standardized testing to a system of portfolio assessment. You have been asked to make a presentation, both written and verbal, in order to argue your case and to answer questions.

9) Following an evening news item concerning school liability for athletic injuries, your faculty athletics advisory committee has been asked to research and report on rate of risk (to athletes and to schools) of various sports. Yours is a large school district and currently offers a wide array of elementary, middle, and high school athletic activities. Which, if any, are likely to be cause for concern? Why, and to what degree?

10) A few years ago the primary grades in your school switched from a basal reading series to a whole language reading program. Standardized test scores have not improved, and teacher opinions are divided over whether the whole language program should be continued, or if a basal series should be reinstituted. You are part of a committee assembled to investigate the current professional thinking on the issue and to make a recommendation.

APPENDIX 2: TEACHING THE TEACHERS: A SELECTION OF READINGS

American Association of Colleges for Teacher Education. *A Call for Change in Teacher Education.* Washington, DC: American Association of Colleges for Teacher Education, 1985. (ERIC Document Reproduction Service No. ED 252 525).

American Association of School Librarians and Association for Educational Communications and Technology. *Information Power: Guidelines for School Library Media Programs.* Chicago: American Library Association, 1988.

Beyer, L.E., W. Feinberg, J.A. Pagano, and J.A. Whitson. *Preparing Teachers as Professionals: The Role of Educational Studies and Other Liberal Disciplines.* New York: Teachers College Press, 1989.

Bibliographic Instruction for Educators Committee, ACRL's Education and Behavioral Sciences Section. "Information Retrieval and Evaluation Skills for Education Students." *College and Research Libraries News* 53:9 (1992): 583-588.

Bodi, S. "Critical Thinking and Bibliographic Instruction: The Relationship." *Journal of Academic Librarianship* 14:3 (1988): 150-153.

Borgman, C.L. "Mental Models: Ways of Looking at a System." *ASIS Bulletin* 9 (December 1982): 38-39.

Breivik, P.S. "A Signal for the Need to Restructure the Learning Process." *NASSP Bulletin* 75:535 (1991): 1-7.

Carnegie Task Force on Teaching as a Profession. *A Nation Prepared: Teachers for the 21st Century*. New York: Carnegie Corporation, 1986.

Carr, J.A. "Academic Libraries and Teacher Education Reform: The Education of the Professional Teacher." In *Libraries and the Search for Academic Excellence*. Metuchen, NJ: Scarecrow Press, 1988.

Carrier, C.A. and G.C. Sales. "Pair Versus Individual Work on the Acquisition of Concepts in a Computer-Based Instructional Lesson." *Journal of Computer-Based Instruction* 14:1 (1987): 11-17.

Collins, A. "The Role of Computer Technology in Restructuring Schools." *Phi Delta Kappan*, 73:1 (1991): 28-36.

Dill, D.D., ed. *What Teachers Need to Know: the Knowledge, Skills, and Values Essential to Good Teaching*. San Francisco: Jossey-Bass, 1990.

Foster, W. "Restructuring Schools." In M.C. Alkin, ed., *Encyclopedia of Educational Research*, 6th ed., 1,108-1,114. New York: Macmillan, 1992.

Frick, E. "Theories of Learning and Their Impact on OPAC Instruction." *Research Strategies* 7:2 (1989): 67-78.

Goodlad, J.I. *Teachers for Our Nation's Schools*. San Francisco: Jossey-Bass, 1990.

Haycock, C.A. Resource-Based Learning: A Shift in the Roles of Teacher, Learner. *NASSP Bulletin* 75:535 (1991): 15-22.

Haycock, K. *The School Library Program in the Curriculum*. Englewood, CO: Libraries Unlimited, 1990.

Higgins, J.J. "Electronic Schools and American Competitiveness." *Business Week* (10 December 1990): 8ED-10ED.

Holmes Group. *Tomorrow's Teachers*. East Lansing, MI: The Holmes Group, Michigan State University, School of Education, 1986.

Keegan, B., and T. Westerbert. "Restructuring and the School Library: Partners in an Information Age." *NASSP Bulletin*, 75:535 (1991): 9-14.

McClintock, R.O., ed. *Computing and Education: The Second Frontier*. New York: Teachers College Press, 1988.

National Commission on Excellence in Education. *A Nation at Risk: The Imperative for Educational Reform*. Washington, DC: U.S. Government Printing Office, 1983.

O'Hanlon, N. "Library Skills, Critical Thinking, and the Teacher-Training Curriculum." *College and Research Libraries* 48:1 (1987): 17-26.

O'Hanlon, N. "The Role of Library Research Instruction in Developing Teachers' Problem Solving Skills." *Journal of Teacher Education* 39:6 (1988): 44-49.

Pickert, S.M., and A.B. Chwalek. "Integrating Bibliographic Research Skills into a Graduate Program in Education." *Catholic Library World* 55:9 (1984): 392-394.

Sein, M.K., and D. Robey. "Learning Style and the Efficacy of Computer Training Methods." *Perceptual and Motor Skills* 72:1 (1991): 243-248.

Shulman, J.H., ed. *Case Methods in Teacher Education*. New York: Teachers College Press, 1992.

Soltis, J.F., ed. *Reforming Teacher Education: The Impact of the Holmes Group Report*. New York: Teachers College Press, 1987.

Thompson, J.C. "Resource-Based Learning Can Be the Backbone of Reform, Improvement." *NASSP Bulletin* 75:535 (1991): 24-28.

United States Department of Education. *Alliance For Excellence: Librarians Respond to A Nation At Risk*. Washington, DC: United States Government Printing Office, 1984.

Tierno, M.J., and J.H. Lee. "Developing and Evaluating Library Research Skills in Education: A Model for Course-Integrated Bibliographic Instruction." *RQ* 22:3 (1983): 284-291.

Ward, A. The Electronic School [special supplement]. *American School Board Journal* 178:10 (1991).

Wirth, A.G. *Education and Work for the Year 2000: Choices We Face*. San Francisco: Jossey-Bass, 1992.

— SANDRA DULING AND PATRICK MAX —

THE CORE CURRICULUM AT ADELPHI AND AN APPROACH TO LIBRARY INSTRUCTION

Valerie Jackson Feinman

INTRODUCTION

We have seen bibliographic instruction change drastically, from small groups learning how to use bibliographic tools and produce bibliographies to enhance and accompany their papers, to full-blown classroom sessions in using all library resources.

This change, in which we have seen BI flower from being an adjunct to reference services into being the heart of reference work, is one result of the ever-widening use of technologies within our libraries. We all contribute to OCLC, which allows access to many resources nationwide. Mediated searching, using hundreds of databases, increased the work of librarians. Then we developed OPACs, which made searching our own databases easier—and forced us to spend more time teaching relational concepts. Next we added CD-ROMs—and we librarians no longer perform the searches, but teach our users how to do so.

The impact of CD-ROMs on reference and BI has been well chronicled. We must teach the user how to select the appropriate database, develop a search strategy, understand the indexing process, and evaluate search results. Questions were raised concerning limiting of searches to in-house periodicals, whether search needs are being met, and the best methods for what has become document delivery.

Feinman is coordinator of library instruction, Adelphi University, Garden City, New York.

In all this the focus of reference work has changed more toward user education, and indeed some would say that reference work now *is* user education.

These new technolgies have greatly changed the BI lecture, as we need more time within the lecture format to talk about search strategies vis-a-vis our available technologies, and those of us with multimedia facilities are able to perform demonstrations. Because these reactions to technological developments require time during our lectures, we at Adelphi sought a means to remove the necessary orientation or general introduction to the library from the BI lecture and introduce it at an earlier point in the semester. We believe that this method introduces a teachable moment at an appropriate time and provides the first step in a continuum of instruction throughout the students' college careers.

ALTERNATIVES TO THE LIBRARY WORKBOOK

Background

Ever since Miriam Dudley created her workbook in the late sixties, the use of workbooks has been deemed more or less a panacea for overworked librarians. Workbooks, as a method of teaching and assessing the introduction of library resources to incoming freshmen, became very popular in the seventies. Most were based on the Dudley model—several chapters, each introducing a research or resources concept and followed by questions to be answered and turned in for grading. Dudley[1] wanted to provide incoming students with BI beyond the simple orientation and was motivated by the need to provide effective BI to 3,500 freshmen each year.

During the seventies many workbooks were produced. Shelley Phipps[2] wrote a funny and thoughtful article in 1980 called "Why Use Workbooks? or Why Do Chickens Cross the Road? And Other Metaphors, Mixed," in which the purpose of workbooks is defined as "to give practice in using a large academic library, and by doing so learn to do just that." She noted that disorganization is more apparent than order to students newly viewing the library, that the student must actually come into the library in order to follow the workbook, and that the workbook may be viewed as a scavenger hunt with clues, riddles, and rewards.

In 1981 Donald White[3] wrote a review article chronicling the advantages of using workbooks. He noted that the printed vehicle ensured that information is uniform in quality and quality and allows inclusion of charts and diagrams.

That same year Carolyn Kirkendall[4] questioned the use of workbooks, noting that they have been accepted as *panaceas*, but are at best pedagogically unsound, or, an experience in futility. Her respondents answered severally that workbooks are not/should not be panaceas, but can be essential elements of an instructional program.

> **panacea**—from the Greek panakeia, all-healing; a remedy for all ills or difficulties, a universal remedy.

Farber[5] added to the workbook discussion in 1982, noting that the major disadvantage of workbooks is that they are uniform and must be aimed at a common denominator so that variations are quite limited. They are most successful when large numbers of students must be taught, and other teaching methods *should* also be used.

Marsha Markman[6], in 1987, noted that we must analyze student attitudes before making decisions about BI methods (this was the year *we* began to develop a workbook) She found that students considered workbooks frustrating, stupid, useless, time-wasters, and irrelevant.

Certainly by this time many BI people had realized that students only saw a value in workbooks if the topics covered pertained directly to course work being done. Studies were done to question how and whether workbooks could be improved (and made more palatable).

By 1989, when Teresa Mensching[7] published her article on trends in BI comparing data from 1987 and 1979, we saw some firm data. In 1987, 8 percent of reporting units had required workbooks, and the use of workbooks had increased from 11 percent to 26 percent. Course-related exercises were used by 31 percent. There were big increases in the use of printed guides, from 49 to 73 percent; bibliographies, from 56 to 75 percent; and pathfinders, from 40 to 51 percent. Use of printed handbooks decreased from 55 percent to 38 percent. As technology began to change rapidly, more of us relied on easily revised one- or two-page handouts!

Recent articles have noted that BI and/or workbooks must also be available to transfer students, foreign students, and physically challenged students. And in 1992, Feinberg and King[8] described a study in which they changed their program, from self-paced workbooks alone to a program of workshops and practicum and workbooks, to ensure learning rather than rote response.

We may conclude that workbooks have been both lauded and panned, that some reasons for using them still apply, and that there are new reasons for using them *in conjunction with* other elements in a well-formulated BI program. And we note that many writers proclaim that the *preferred* BI mode is still one-on-one.

Circumstances have changed since that era of growth in freshman classes and in budgets:

- Technologies have encroached on our teaching time, as ever-more automated tools must be taught, such as CD-ROMs.

- Libraries have fewer dollars to produce workbooks.

- Students have fewer dollars with which to purchase workbooks.

- Libraries have insufficient staff—then because enrollments mushroomed and now because budgets are being cut.

- Students are now less willing to read anything, are more used to soundbites, would rather play with terminals, and just might read a pathfinder if necessary.

- Instant gratification era wants instant answers.

- Easy revision prompts use of brief data sheets.

And so I move on to what I decided to do about workbooks, and why, after I became coordinator of BI in 1987.

About Adelphi

Our library has long had an active program of BI-on-demand, with sessions timed to coincide with assignments which require use of library resources. Sessions related to freshman English ceased a decade ago. English faculty members deemed that they taught reading and writing skills using primary materials and did not require the teaching of secondary source usage. Attempts to persuade them to include small library-related projects had failed. They provide examples of citations for their students to use when citing a primary source. Farber has frequently noted that one shouldn't "waste time beating one's head against walls" when a particular professor or department was not interested in BI, because there are usually more productive ways to achieve one's ends. Our concentration was on course-related instruction for faculty who indeed requested it.

Our BI sessions for the past several years have been held in a mediated classroom in the library building, and consist of the following:

1) An animated hypertext introduction to the library building and its floor plans, with breakouts to special areas. For each area one then discusses its importance to the course being treated;

2) Discussion of the research process, geared to the literature of that course or discipline;

3) Use of the OPAC, demonstrated from the LAN and seen on the wide screen above, using course examples;

4) Use of indexes and abstracting services relative to the course content, by use of transparencies or with CD-ROMs demonstrated from the LAN to the screen;

5) Question-and-answer session, or problem solving;

6) Handouts from our collection of pathfinders and other guides; and

7) Prearranged CD-ROM practice sessions.

Our OPAC is INNOPAC, and thus very easy to use. It is named *ALICAT*, for the *A*delphi *Li*brary *Cat*alog. The panther is the sports symbol for Adelphi, and we bar-coded a panther to be our ALICAT.

The Core Curriculum

The advent of a new core curriculum, a common set of courses required of all freshmen and transfer students, provided the opportunity for the library faculty to interact more directly with teaching faculty in the development of course-related library instruction. A librarian was appointed to the core curriculum committee (CCC), which developed courses for the program. The BI coordinator worked independently, using the CCC librarian as conduit.

The backbone of the core curriculum was to be a two-semester freshman course chronicling western civilization in the 20th century, entitled Modern Condition, and called thereafter ModCon. It was supplemented by an origins course and followed by sophomore level modes and versions courses and a senior seminar. Because every student was required to take ModCon (and many transfer students were not required to take freshman English), it was decided to target ModCon for the tie-in with BI. ModCon would require several papers, some of which would use library resources. All students were following the same curriculum, although individual faculty varied it with their particular subject expertise.

The freshman class was divided into three sections by ability grouping based on GPA and SAT. There were three classes in the Honors program, twenty-one classes in the regular program, and six classes of general studies or "experimental admits." Of the twenty-one "regular" classes, seven were made up of transfer students just entering the core and now taking ModCon courses. We wished to reach all of the students, but feared we'd have less success reaching the transfer students who would already have some familiarity with a college or university library.

Library Planning for the Core Curriculum

The library faculty appointed an orientation committee to produce a plan—not for orientation only, but for development of BI throughout the core curriculum. The committee began its work more than one year before implementation of the core in the fall of '91, and would have the opportunity for a trial period in the fall of '90 when several classes were to try out the ModCon courses. This committee considered using a library workbook that had been developed by an earlier committee.

This workbook was in the mode of Dudley's, with 18 chapters each introducing and explaining a library concept or resource, and followed by two or three questions, which were based on CC ModCon readings. We did not make the error of using irrelevant exercises. Students would work through the book, completing chapters one at a time, and turn in the completed workbook, or question pages, for grading. Chapters included an overview, how to use ALICAT, encyclopedias, journal indexes, and so on.

Reality check, please. The workbooks were meant to be purchased for $7. Only half of the trial class students made the purchase. No one wanted to do the exercises—there was no tangible incentive. Faculty said students had enough work to do without the workbook exercises and did not encourage its use. Conscientious students found that when their first assignment was given, they had not yet reached the needed chapters. The testing period proved that the workbook concept was unworkable at this time and place, and in this manner.

We needed commitment from faculty teaching in the core, rather than the core planning group, to work cooperatively. We needed an exercise that was meaningful and did not take so much freshman time. We needed something earlier in the semester that started things off right. We now had the spring semester in which to develop a useable "product" for fall '91.

BI Philosophy for the Core Curriculum

The orientation committee rethought its philosophy. After much discussion and research they decided that the goals of the "product" were these:

1. to encourage freshmen to actually enter the library building at the beginning of the semester, rather than later;

2. to encourage exploration of the library building and the location of its resources;

3. to allow freshmen to meet library faculty in a non-threatening setting (i.e., before reference help is needed);

4. to introduce ALICAT and encourage its use;

5. to encourage teaching faculty to request full BI sessions in our mediated classroom at the point when papers were assigned; and

6. to provide an incentive for completion of some library-related activity.

We went to the CCC with an analysis of the problems related to the workbook concept and described this new philosophy. Those faculty who usually requested BI for their classes were queried as to what they believed students should learn about the library even before BI was provided. All were asked what the

core program would demand from its students. Teaching faculty were very receptive to this contribution from the library faculty, and told us to go ahead. They realized that "library literacy" was an important component of the core experience. They also suggested that the exercise had more likelihood of being completed if students were given an incentive, and suggested that a part of the final ModCon grade be reserved for this. All in all, these discussions with the core faculty were most helpful in airing problems faced by both teaching and library faculty, and in building relationships between the two.

BI Product for the Core Curriculum

We decided to produce a booklet, which would be given to each student at the compulsory freshman orientation program in August of 1991. A library faculty member would make a presentation during the program and would introduce the booklet. This booklet would contain all the most important information about the library and its resources, a self-guided library tour, a test, a statement on plagiarism, forms to be used in researching a paper, and a glossary of library terminology. The self-guided walking tour of the library building was color coded and keyed to large bright numbers put up in all major resource areas. The 20-item test was based on reading and walking through the tour.

After the CCC had approved both the booklet contents and its cost, a letter and a copy of the booklet were sent to all core faculty. The letter explained the intent of the exercise, noted that the CCC mandated 5 percent of the student's final grade for successful completion of the exercise, and invited requests for classroom BI at the appropriate time.

The self-guided tour had been carefully vetted by all the library faculty and some staff, so we were content that it was reasonable. The tour test, which had been similarly tested, contained such questions as

• What is ALICAT?

• Use ALICAT to find the location of a book on Ancient History.

• Who is the reference librarian on duty while you are taking this test?

• Where will you find the latest issue of the magazine *Time*, and who/what is on its cover?

• We encouraged group discussion and group effort.

August came, orientation took place, and the booklets were distributed. By early September, we saw throngs of students wandering around in the library. Surprisingly our hard work in preparation reaped its due reward. The always-busy reference desk was not overwhelmed—as most students were indeed able to proceed independently. We did note that one or two of the tour questions seemed ambiguous and should be reworded in later editions. Some teaching faculty made the test obligatory. One English faculty insisted on a near-perfect score. At least one core faculty pooh-poohed the whole exercise. This all was to be expected. We found peer pressure at work: "Has your whole class completed the tour-test? Ours has." Teaching faculty called to ask for names of students who had not yet handed in their tests, and chided students for late entries. The library faculty member who watches OPAC transaction logs reported heavy traffic.

The library packet was included in the package of orientation materials, and students were told this at orientation. Of course several students simply tossed all the materials handed out at that time. Other students had not been present: for example, the soccer team was playing a demo game during orientation. Extra copies of the tour and test were available at the reference desk.

Grading Process

Tests were returned to the test box and were removed at intervals for grading, so that all 600 would not need to be graded at once. We were also eager to see the results! One person did all the grading, for consistency, and it was not an onerous task. After the first week it was seen that half-points would be needed for some questions, and all papers received by that time were regraded. At this time we restructured the master grading sheet and its correct/acceptable answers.

We also saw which questions were causing problems, and why. Reference librarians agreed to provide certain clues when needed. For example, students seeking location of items were referred to the location chart mounted on the wall above the ALICAT terminals. This had seemed obvious to us, but the tour directions did not mention the chart. The question requiring students to name the on-duty reference librarian meant that each student met at least one of us in a nonthreatening situation—we wore name tags, but these were small and required a close look. This resulted in many laughs and some casual conversation, and resembled an autographing session.

The question requiring students to list their personal barcode number, an item required to turn their ID cards into library cards, caused the most problems.

We wanted them to sign up for barcodes during orientation to get all the associated paper work done early in the semester. At this point in time, students did not yet have their permanent IDs and did not realize that they should enroll for the barcodes anyway, as we would code their temporary IDs. Many students simply ignored the question and forfeited the point. This marked a needed change in the next edition of the tour description.

Grading Techniques

Once the tests were marked, grades were entered on class lists for each course. Copies of the course list and grades would be sent to the classroom faculty later. All tests were then filed in one alphabetical arrangement, to allow analysis independent of class. We did not plan to return the papers to the students, even after all had been received. When I mentioned this to many students, they seemed only interested in their grades. A few did ask to look at their papers, and one requested the return of his when I had finished. This method was consistent with our purpose of attracting students to the library, rather than testing their research abilities.

Grading was done by hand. We had considered using some sort of computer-graded test, but decided that we preferred subjective answers rather than multiple choice or true/false. This decision might be quite different were the freshman class much larger.

Grades were reported to teaching faculty after two weeks. Faculty spoke to their classes, and a flurry of tests came in. Grades were again reported after the third week. Most students met the deadline of 29 September. We planned to publish the correct answers to the test on a library bulletin board and in the student newspaper.

But by late September several core faculty were ready to assign papers and had requested BI sessions. They requested that we also answer questions about the test during the session and allow late papers to be handed in. In fact, one transfer class suddenly woke up and desired to begin the process of tour and test. This caused several problems: 1) I couldn't publish answers until all results were in, and ended up not publishing them. In the next test period, we will be firmer about deadlines; 2) Some tests would be handed in by students in classes which had also received BI before the test deadline. Had I dated the papers upon receipt, this would not have been a problem. As it was, I could not separate pre- and post-BI papers and could not analyze whether the BI session improved the test results. This became another topic for analysis in the Fall 1992 session.

Grading Results

The result most easily seen was this: those students who were in classes that received BI returned more test papers and received higher grades than students in other classes. There may have been a halo effect, with faculty who requested BI being those who more strongly encouraged tour-and-test participation. Some classes had 100 percent return.

A second and perhaps obvious result was that honors students were better overall at the exercise than regular students. Is this a surprise? No. And the lower ability-level students had lower overall grades than either the "regular" or "honor" students. Again no surprises.

The third result was that when students were reminded about the 5 percent, many came in to ask whether it was too late to take part.

In the honors group, 97 percent returned their tests. One class had 100 percent participation. One of the three classes requested BI. Grades were very high, with all students receiving 18.5 out of 20 or higher. In the regular classes, we saw the division of transfer and non-transfer, with the former group less participatory. For the 20 freshmen classes, 69 percent returned the test, and grades ranged from a perfect 20 down to 16, with most around 18. Of the same 20 freshman classes, 15 requested BI. The experimental group decided to postpone the exercise until the spring semester.

When some students saw their grades, they came in voluntarily to retake the test. All bettered their grades. Some other students who obviously "failed" the test, were sent in by their professors. All seven of them were given appointments and received personal instruction, particularly in the areas they didn't understand. They improved their grades, and the new grades were reported back to the professors. Remember this: the actual grade was not as important as the process of becoming familiar with the use of the library and its resources, and the "grading" was actually pass/fail, with "pass" the preferred result.

No, we did not reach every student, even with the mandatory grade agreement. Some students simply forfeited that incentive. I talked to several of these students later in the semester, when I became acquainted with them for one reason or another, and they had various reasons. One said she knew her way around the libraries and had better things to do. Three members of the soccer team were upset that they had not done the exercise, and after some basic instruction suggested that I chase down the team next year for special coaching. (Yes!) Others said they didn't have time, and we pointed out that the time they were wasting in November was more valuable than the time they hadn't used in September.

Analysis of Grading Procedures and Process

At the end of the exercise, the correct answer sheet was made available to students at the reference desk. We considered posting it in the student newspaper but did not follow through on this because of late returns. In future years we plan to do so, as a reminder of the importance of the exercise.

Questions were studied to determine which were ambiguous and which received the most wrong or unsatisfactory answers. The core curriculum committee has requested a regular, annual library orientation tour-and-test, so that they may tally the results into their longitudinal studies. For reasons of consistency, they would prefer us not to make major changes from year to year. Thus we could not drastically change the test, even if we had wanted to do so. The tour-and-test as prepared for the entering fall '92 class was very similar but not identical. We added a few phrases to the tour where ambiguities existed or when library areas had changed. (For example, we added a copy center and an additional CD-ROM station.) Test questions are now less ambiguous and arranged in a more logical progression.

The CCC manual given to each faculty member teaching in the core now includes a stronger statement about the purpose, usefulness, and grading mandate for the tour-and-test. It also contains a statement about classroom library instruction sessions, and an invitation to request these at the appropriate time (i.e., when a research paper is assigned).

GOALS ACHIEVEMENT

Did we achieve our goals? Yes! Students came in to the library in September in numbers never before seen; our turnstile count was higher than in any prior September. Most of the freshmen received their barcodes before the end of the month. Great numbers seemed to be working on the tour-and-test. 72 percent of the newly enrolled students completed the test-and-tour, and each one of these spoke to at least one of the reference librarians. Of the core teaching faculty, 40 percent requested BI at the appropriate time. Those not requesting BI were, for the most part, not assigning research papers during this semester.

Reference librarians who had feared an overwhelming burden at the reference desk found that most students easily mastered the ALICAT and were not afraid to use it. Questions asked at the desk were not "Do you have...?," but "Where else might I look...?"

Students were comfortable asking questions during orientation, and still comfortable when they were working on class assignments. Some bonding had occurred. This is a qualitative judgment, but we also have some quantitative data which I'll reach soon.

Ease of the use of the OPAC led to ease of use of CD-ROMs later, when classroom instruction was given in search strategy. There was obviously some carryover, from known to unknown.

Qualitative Results

Students are flocking to the library earlier in the semester and in greater numbers and are gaining familiarity with the extent and location of library resources. They are meeting reference librarians in a nonthreatening situation, and are comfortable about asking questions later. Classroom faculty see that the library faculty have made a positive contribution to the core program through the development of the tour-and-test, the availability of BI, and the analysis of results. Library faculty see the tour-and-test as a grand introduction to resources, which makes later reference interviews more sophisticated.

Students are already familiar with the building and with our OPAC when we provide regular BI sessions, and these sessions are now more geared to the philosophy of searching subject-related resources and to specific CD-ROMs to be used in the assignment at hand. Students who have completed the test more easily use the OPAC and our reference guides and are both more receptive to librarian intervention and more willing to try to use CD-ROMs, and are more successful at using them.

Quantitative Results

We can't attribute all these reults to the core BI program, or to the core curriculum itself, but our statistics for the fall of 1991 were amazing. From September 1990 to September 1991, we saw the following:

- turnstile count increased by 33 percent;

- circulation increased by 42.4 percent;

- ILL increased by 27.4 percent;

- CD-ROM use increased by 142 percent;

- ALICAT use was up to 50,000 transactions per month;

- BI classes increased by 45 percent; and

- number of students in BI classes increased by 82 percent.

We saw more freshmen and more students generally. This was to be expected with a new program, but the results went far beyond expectation. There was obviously a heightened awareness of library usage on the part of students and faculty. Faculty who taught both in ModCon and within their discipline saw the value of BI and requested sessions for their other classes. Several English faculty requested BI for advanced English classes. New faculty were contacted to be told of our willingness to help. When unprepared students from one class arrived, we called their professor to offer classes.

Unexpected Results

The success of BI within the core made the program more visible across campus. Several schools realized that we had something to offer them and began discussing mandatory BI for graduate and some undergraduate programs. The school of social work specialist had long offered a two-hour session on social work resources, several times at the beginning of each semester. These became mandatory for all SW students. The school of nursing developed a new curriculum and added compulsory BI. The school of business is also revising its curriculum, and will include compulsory BI as a theme within their required communications course. The school of education felt left out and is now negotiating the inclusion of BI at the point when students declare their major. The psychology department has tied BI in the use of Psyclit to its compulsory lab for all new majors. Our effort to make the library and library faculty an important element within the core is paying off in unexpected ways. Because the library faculty reached out to the teaching faculty and offered excellent service, teaching faculty are responding by insisting on library resources instruction.

- I am known: I can't walk anywhere in the building or on campus without being accosted by someone saying: "I was in your.....class, and I need help with...."

- Faculty who had shunned BI realized that their students do benefit from it, and indeed now request BI.

- Library literacy—or information literacy—became a mandated part of the core, a goal, along with numeracy and computer literacy. I was invited to speak at the annual faculty forum, when the topic was literacy, and at several core workshops.

- Upper level core courses requested more, and more specific BI.

- The senior seminar courses built in a BI assignment.

- There is a heightened awareness across campus of the need to request and use BI as an adjunct to almost any course.

The harder I work, the harder I have to work. One semester I received many fewer BI requests. I queried one of my regulars and was told: "But you didn't send out letters soliciting classes this semester, so we assumed you were too busy."

Never Assume! I had assumed that they would contact me, and they assumed that I was too busy. Did I really *need* more BI sessions? Yes, of course I did. Students always need reminders of how to use the library efficiently and effectively. My statistics were now depressed for the semester, at a time when statistics are needed as libraries fight for funds. I *should* have ensured that classes were invited.

WHAT HAPPENS NEXT?

The process was repeated in the fall of 1992, and will be repeated each fall. In January 1992, we decided to repeat the test for new transfer students. Students who had not performed the exercise in the fall clamored to earn their 5 percent in January. Analysis and improvement continue.

Exercises are being developed for second and upper level courses, and for non-core courses.

We plan to develop an assessment tool to measure growth in our students' knowledge of library usage. The tour-and-test is not really a pre-test of knowledge, but some questions are suitable for demonstrating knowledge acquisition.

SUMMARY

The use of a workbook was tried and evolved into a self-guided tour-and-test. In the method chronicled, it became a necessary, important, and practical adjunct to our BI program, providing both a logical introduction and other more tangible results. We have faced the problems raised by the increasing use of technologies, and the demands made upon us to teach these, and have produced an introductory program which both introduces the student to the library and begins the continuum of BI-throughout-the-core-curriculum.

NOTES

1. Miriam Dudley, "The Self-Paced Library Skills Program at UCLA's College Library," in *Educating the Library User*, ed. by John Lubans, Jr. (New York: Bowker, 1974), 330-335.

2. Donald J. White, "Workbooks for Basic Library Instruction," *Canadian Library Journal* 38:4 (August 1981): 213-219.

3. Carolyn Kirkendall, "Library Instruction: Column...," *Journal of Academic Librarianship* 6:6 (January 1981): 346-347.

4. Shelley E. Phipps, "Why Use Workbooks? Or Why Do the Chickens Cross the Road? And Other Metaphors, Mixed," *Drexel Library Quarterly* 16:1 (January 1980): 41-53.

5. Evan Ira Farber, "Teaching the Use of the Library: Part II: Implementation," *Library Issues* 2:3 (January 1982): 3-4.

6. Marsha C. Markman and Gordon B. Leighton, "Exploring Freshman Composition Students' Attitudes about Library Instruction Sessions and Workbooks: Two Studies," *Research Strategies* 5:3 (Summer 1987): 126-134.

7. Teresa B. Mensching, "Trends in Bibliographic Instruction in the 1980s: A Comparison of Data from Two Surveys," *Research Strategies* 7:1 (Winter 1989): 4-13.

ADDITIONAL READINGS

Berge, Patricia A., and Judith Pryor. "Applying Educational Theory to Workbook Instruction." In *Theories of Bibliographic Education*. Ed. by Cerise Oberman and Katina Strauch, 91-110. New York: Bowker, 1982.

Cox, Jennifer, and Ralph Johnston. "Transfer Students in the Library: The Forgotten Population." *Research Strategies* 10:21 (Spring 1992): 88-91.

Dudley, Miriam. "The State of Library Instruction Credit Courses and the State of the Use of Library Skills Workbooks. In *Library Instruction in the Seventies: Papers presented at the Sixth Annual LOEX Conference, May 13-14, 1976*. Ed. by Hannelore Rader, 79-84. Ann Arbor, MI: Pierian Press, 1977.

Dusenbury, Carolyn, et al. *Read This First: An Owner's Guide to the New Model Statement of Objectives*

— VALERIE JACKSON FEINMAN —

for Academic Bibliographic Instruction. Chicago, IL: BIS, ACRL, ALA 1991.

Graves, Gail T., and Barbara Adams. "Bibliographic Instruction Workbooks: Assessing Two Models Used in a Freshman English Program." *Research Strategies*, 6:1 (1988): 18-24.

Holt, Joan S., and Steven Falk. "Evaluation of Workbooks in a Community College Setting." *Reference Librarian* 11 (Fall/Winter 1984): 321-334.

Kirkendall, Carolyn. *Academic Library Skills Workbook Listing.* Ypsilanti, MI: Project LOEX, 1979.

Mellon, Constance A. "Library Anxiety: A Grounded Theory and Its Development." *College & Research Libraries* 47:2 (March 1986): 160-165.

Nash, Vivien. "Workbooks in Library Skills—Palliative, Panacea, or Placebo?" In *Third International Conference on Library User Education, 1983.* Lough-borough, England: Loughborough University of Technology, INFUSE Publications, 1983.

Parsch, Janet H. "Using a Mainframe to Generate Question Sets to Enhance Traditional Library Resource Assignments." *Research Strategies* 5:3 (Summer 1987): 108-120.

Poirier, Gayle. "The Cassette Tour: An Effective, Efficient Orientation." *Research Strategies* 10:3 (Summer 1992): 143-144.

Sugranes, Maria P., and James A. Neal. "Evaluation of a Self-Paced Bibliographic Instruction Course. *College & Research Libraries* 44:6 (November 1983): 444-457.

Ware, Susan A. "A Competency-Based Approach to Assessing Workbook Effectiveness." *Research Strategies* 4:1 (Winter 1986): 4-10.

Ware, Susan A. "A Statistical Evaluation of Basic Library Skills Instruction." *Research Strategies* 1:3 (Summer 1983): 118-124.

A LIBRARY INSTRUCTION COURSE VIA THE COMMUNITY LEARNING NETWORK

Bill Orme

Indiana University-Purdue University at Indianapolis (IUPUI) is a large urban campus offering both graduate and undergraduate programs. A significant number of our 28,000 students are "New Majority" students—adults returning to school. Additionally, the university actively seeks to serve those potential students who, for various reasons, find it difficult or impossible to pursue the baccalaureate degree.

In pursuit of this goal, IUPUI sent a proposal to the Annenberg/CPB Project to be included in their "New Pathways to a Degree" initiative. The Annenberg program was designed to "help colleges use technologies to develop academic programs that are accessible to the New Majority of learners."[1] The New Pathways initiative wished to test the proposition that colleges could offer new kinds of academic programs made possible by technologies—new programs that were "accessible, supportive, academically rich, and rigorous."[2]

IUPUI proposed the formation of a "Community Learning Network." This proposal embraced three key ideas:

- putting classes and meetings at community sites easy for students to reach and that provide support to students;

- building on the pioneering work of Uri Treisman at Berkeley, who has been successful in helping minority students succeed in difficult subjects by working with them to form supportive study groups that use peer tutoring as well as active involvement of the faculty; and

- using technologies—including television and computers—to bring the courses to learners and enable students and faculty to work closely together even when they are physically separated.

To realize this goal, IUPUI proposed the establishment of community learning sites. These sites, building on existing community-based organizations, would be electronically linked to the campus and to each other. Courses would be broadcast to learners' homes via cable television. Courses would also be videotaped and copies of the tape made available at the community sites. Additionally, each learning center would have computers connected to the IUPUI campus and library, a television set with cable access, a videocassette player, a fax machine, a telephone with voice mail capability, and a library of information resources including textbooks and required readings.

The Annenberg/CPB Project received over two hundred proposals for the New Pathways initiative. The Community Learning Network was one of seven that were funded.

IUPUI proposed that five courses be developed to launch the Community Learning Network.

Orme is bibliographic instruction coordinator, Indiana University-Purdue University at Indianapolis, Indianapolis, Indiana.

Chemistry, Appreciation of Literature, and Finite Mathematics were existing courses that were re-tooled to fit the CLN concept. A history course and a course entitled "Information Resources and Student Research" were to be developed specifically for CLN.

As bibliographic instruction coordinator at University Library, I was asked to develop the student research course. University Library is preparing to move into a new facility with enhanced technological capabilities. The chance to develop a course concerning information resources and student research offered several opportunities—to break beyond the barriers of the traditional fifty-minute "one shot" BI session as well as the opportunity to address new technologies and, even more importantly, to address questions of critical thinking and what has come to be known as "information literacy."

When it is completed, "Information Resources and Student Research" will comprise fifteen fifty-five-minute lectures. These lectures are being videotaped in a studio, without an audience. Students enrolling in the course will be provided with a handbook including the course's objectives, a syllabus, a list of exercises and assignments, details on how grading will be accomplished, and a profile of the instructor. The course is scheduled to be offered as a one-credit course through the Indiana University School of Library and Information Science beginning in spring of 1994.

In developing the course, numerous issues had to be resolved. Issues of pedagogy, technology, and administration all had to be addressed.

The first issue concerned the basic notion of course development. Since my prior experience had been confined to single-session BI presentations, developing a course was a new experience. On the positive side, developing a semester-length course afforded me the opportunity to seriously examine what I considered the important issues and to focus on what I thought students should learn about information and research. The campus provided an instructional designer whose expertise has been indispensable. She has provided guidance on developing course objectives, has helped me shape the course (starting with parameters and resulting with lecture sequences), has accomplished technical tasks such as digitizing print material so that images could be stored and recalled from a computer hard drive, and has critiqued graphics used in the lectures. Additionally, she acts as floor manager during lecture tapings.

Additionally, I did not have an existing textbook from which to work, so the tasks of gathering, assimilating, and writing have been extremely time-consuming. Fortunately, I have been granted release time from my customary duties to focus on course development. A colleague has taken over the bulk of my BI responsi-

bilities and I have been released from reference desk duty until the course lectures have been produced.

The distance education aspect of this effort presented its own issues and difficulties. While interactivity has been provided for electronically, taping lectures in an empty room to a video camera is obviously not the same as speaking to a roomful of people. It is simply not possible to gauge an audience's reactions and adjust to them. On a more mundane level, when I am speaking to a roomful of people, I prefer to move about. On television this becomes disconcerting. Since our camera is immobile, if I move too far, I leave the screen. On the plus side, however, I was able to expand beyond traditional classroom walls and bring in other people at will through the use of video-taped, edited interviews.

Distance education also presents technological problems. There is a tendency to "report" rather than communicate. Lecture scripts had to be written in a way that maximized eye contact and minimized reading. All of the lectures we have taped so far have gone through multiple drafts. Some of the lectures have been shot more than once. "Re-dos" can be the result of aesthetic problems (not enough eye contact, for instance), timing problems (too long or too short), or technical glitches.

Administratively, as I mentioned above, we had to find a home for the course. This was not an easy task to accomplish. Academic departments find it difficult to accommodate into their curriculum a course that they did not develop and that does not fit directly into their field. I was fortunate that this course is part of a larger initiative. I have not had to monitor the budget. Production deadlines, of course, are an ongoing concern and the cause of frequent distress (which miraculously dissipates once deadlines are met).

The videotape I am showing in this session consists of edited portions of the introductory lecture, several minutes of a subsequent lecture in which an information source intended for a popular audience is contrasted with one prepared for a scholarly audience, and finally a brief segment demonstrating the difficulties of reproducing computer screens on television.

The first lecture of the course accomplishes a seemingly simple task—defining information. This lecture begins with edited portions of "man on the street" interviews conducted on-campus. During these interviews students were asked to define information. Their responses were edited to provide a progression from very halting and hesitant efforts to very precise and confident responses. Additionally, responses were grouped, so that numerous responses concerning notions of "usefulness," for instance, appear together. In this way, similar responses were grouped together and followed by complementary or contrasting groupings.

The ability to select significant portions of interviews for inclusion in a lecture is one illustration of a distinct advantage of the taped telecourse approach. In a lecture hall, live interviews of this sort might be haphazard or unproductive. Utilizing taped interviews, however, provides an ability to "shape" the interviews to help illustrate specific points.

After these interviews, a graphic is shown which re-iterates some of the students' responses. Graphics of this sort, in these lectures, have been used in the same way a blackboard would be used in a classroom.

As a companion piece to the student interviews, I interviewed four professionals whose views on information I thought might prove interesting. The professionals I chose were a mechanical engineer, a business systems consultant, a library science lecturer, and a professional musician (and distinguished professor of jazz). In the same way that I was able to focus the student responses, I was able to select meaningful elements of these interviews to illustrate various perspectives on the nature of information.

The bulk of the course's first lecture consists of a survey of definitions of information. Most of this material was adapted from John Christopher Fox's book *Information and Misinformation*.[3]

The segment concerning popular and scholarly information sources comes from the course's fourth lecture and was chosen for inclusion here to illustrate the ability to digitize print material and offer it on videotape. Legibility is not an issue in course presentation, since the intent is not to have students read the article at hand, but rather to offer the article as an illustration. Sections of articles are shown to emphasize certain features (such as the abstract at the front of a scholarly article, research conclusions, and the list of references included in the article). The ability to show real-life examples allows the lecture to have a more visual component while grounding the lecture content in a context most students are familiar with (news magazines, for instance).

The segment containing the introductory screen of our online catalog comes from the thirteenth lecture in the course and illustrates the difficulty of realizing computer screen images on a television monitor. We are not satisfied with our current results, but we have devised a strategy of "boxing" sections of the screen and then "blowing up" the contents of that box so that they are legible. Computer screen instruction will focus primarily on screen conventions such as the location of command menus, command language/function keys, and how results are displayed.

The development of a course, particularly a distance education course, is extremely time-consuming and is full of frustrations. The opportunity to reach new audiences, though, is an opportunity not to be missed. I think it is important to note that the utility of this effort goes beyond the campus and the students we will enroll. These lectures, broadcast to the community, provide a communication link we have not had before. Even those community members who do not enroll in the course can watch our lectures. I am hopeful that this type of exposure will induce a measure of critical thinking in the public at large. The potential educational impact on the community at large is a significant byproduct and may ultimately prove more beneficial than our stated aims.

NOTES

1. "New Pathways to a Degree." Washington, DC: Annenberg/CPB Project, n.d.

2. "New Pathways to a Degree."

3. John Christopher Fox, *Information and Misinformation: An Investigation of the Notions of Information, Misinformation, Informing, and Misinforming.* Westport, CT: Greenwood Press, 1983.

THE ELECTRONIC LIBRARY:
LIBRARY SKILLS FOR OFF-CAMPUS STUDENTS,
PROGRAM AND EVALUATION

Carole J. Kabel, Rose P. Novil, and Jack Fritts

EVALUATING THE IMPACT OF
BIBLIOGRAPHIC INSTRUCTION

Carole J. Kabel

INTRODUCTION

National-Louis University (NLU), a private institution founded in 1886, offers 13 degrees extending to the doctoral level and certificate programs across its three colleges and over 30 academic programs. The university serves more than 16,000 students annually from its three Chicago-area campuses and at academic centers throughout the United States and Europe.

HISTORY

In 1978 a field-based model of instruction was adopted, attracting adult learners facing time and travel restrictions and family and professional obligations that made it difficult to return to a college campus for traditional programs.

The library instruction program is an integral part of the NLU field programs. The librarian spends one four-hour session with the students giving them biblio-

---

Novil and *Fritts* are librarians at National-Louis University, Main Campus, Evanston, Illinois. *Kabel* is librarian at the Chicago campus of National-Louis University.

graphic instruction and hands-on experience using library resources and materials and computerized searching. NLU librarians have been giving library instruction to the field program students since 1978. Throughout the years since then, the library program and its manual have been changed, edited, revised, and updated to reflect modern technology. This has been done with input from the librarians who do the instructions and from the faculty who teach in the field programs. However, since the implementation of the library program fifteen years ago, there has not been any formal feedback whatsoever from students.

Did they need this instruction? Did they learn about the library and its resources? What was their attitude towards the library and the instruction? Did the library instruction help them with their thesis or project?

METHOD

To help answer these questions I developed a two-page survey (see figure 1) in 1992 and mailed it out to former National-Louis University students who successfully completed and graduated from the Masters of Science in Management field program during the years 1989 to 1991. The classes these students attended were all located in the Chicago metropolitan area. A total of 189 questionnaires were mailed; 2 were returned from the post office, address unknown. Of the 187 delivered questionnaires, 115 (62 percent) were returned to me. Eight were not completed because the student was absent on the library instruction night. A final total of 107 completed instruments was used (57 percent).

SECTION I.

Directions: For each statement, please circle the number which most accurately describes how strongly you agree or disagree with the statement.

	Strongly agree (5)	Agree (4)	Undecided (3)	Disagree (2)	Strongly disagree (1)
1. The library night helped me with the following:					
A. How to use an index.	5	4	3	2	1
B. How to locate journal articles.	5	4	3	2	1
C. How to find books in a library.	5	4	3	2	1
D. How to find information relevant to my topic.	5	4	3	2	1
E. Explained computerized database searching.	5	4	3	2	1
2. The library night made me aware of the various resources available.	5	4	3	2	1
3. The library instruction night was not necessary.	5	4	3	2	1
4. The library instruction helped me complete my thesis.	5	4	3	2	1
5. The library manual I received was useful.	5	4	3	2	1
6. The information presented at the library night was helpful.	5	4	3	2	1
7. The library night session was time well spent.	5	4	3	2	1
8. Because of the library night I now feel more comfortable using a library.	5	4	3	2	1
9. The library instruction increased my knowledge and expertise.	5	4	3	2	1

Figure 1: Library Instruction Questionnaire

SECTION II.

1. Please evaluate the scheduling of the library night in the program.

   Too early _____
   Just right _____
   Too late _____

2. Please evaluate the level of content presented.

   Too simple _____
   Appropriate _____
   Too advanced _____

SECTION III.

Please respond to the following questions.

1. What helped you the most from the library night instruction.

2. Looking back at the library night, what changes would you make?

3. Regarding the library night, is there anything you would have liked to have spent more time on?

4. Is there anything you would have liked to have spent less time on?

5. What year did you receive your undergraduate degree?

6. Any additional comments, questions, or suggestions that you may have are appreciated.

RESULTS

Based on the results of the survey, it appears that the library night instruction is a relevant and needed component in the field program of NLU. Some general findings follow:

- An overwhelming number of subjects either strongly agreed or agreed that the library night helped them use an index, locate journal articles, find books, find information on their topic, and understand computerized database searching.

- The library night instruction made 94 percent of the subjects aware of the various resources available.

- 81 percent disagreed with the statement that the library night was not necessary.

- A majority of students felt that the instruction helped them complete their theses, and that the manuals they received were useful.

- It was encouraging to note that approximately 85 percent strongly agreed or agreed that the information presented was helpful, and that the library night session was time well spent.

- 52 percent, or over half, now feel more comfortable using a library, and for 66 percent, the library instruction increased their knowledge and expertise.

- The scheduling of the library night in the program was just right for 77 percent, and 83 percent thought the level of content presented was appropriate.

- What helped the students the most from the library night instruction was 1) learning about database searching, and 2) learning about indexes and locating journal articles.

- They would have liked to spend more time on computer searching.

- They would like to have spent less time on 1) going through the manual, 2) lecture, and 3) basic library "stuff."

- The majority received their undergraduate degree in the 1980s or 1970s.

- The students suggested more "hands-on" time and more help with individual topics.

RECOMMENDATIONS

After going through the survey results and the comments offered by the respondents, I would recommend the following:

- The field program at National-Louis University should continue to include a library night instruction.

- The instruction should continue to include some basic library "stuff" like how to use an index, how to locate journal articles, how to find books (on an online catalog), how to find information on a topic (subject searching), and an explanation of computerized database searching.

- Students should continue to receive the manual, but it should be updated more frequently using timely examples. Also, library faculty when doing the instruction should refer to the manual but not "go through it."

- Instruction librarians should allow as much time as possible for hands-on computer searching. This is difficult if the class is meeting at a site where there is only one computer station available. The librarian must encourage the students to return to the library at another time for additional help and computer time.

- There must be better communication with field program faculty so that the students are better prepared for their library instruction (know their topic and understand that the library night session is an introduction to the library's resources—they might have to spend additional time on their own in the library).

- It must be stressed throughout the library night session that the students can call us any time for individual help (we hand out our business cards at the beginning of each session).

The library night instruction is a valuable session for our field program students. It serves as an introduction to the library and its resources and to the librarian. Hopefully the students walk away with a positive understanding and attitude towards both—I believe the survey proved this to be true.

THE ELECTRONIC LIBRARY: LIBRARY SKILLS FOR OFF-CAMPUS STUDENTS (Overview)

Rose P. Novil

HISTORY

National-Louis University (NLU, formerly National College of Education) is a coeducational private institution granting baccalaureate through doctoral degrees. NLU offers programs in areas including business, education, performing arts, human services, allied health, and computer information systems. The institution serves over 16,000 students annually at its three Chicago-area campuses, several extension sites within Illinois, and at academic centers located in Wisconsin, Missouri, Georgia, Florida, Virginia, and Germany.

Our three Chicago-area campuses each have library collections and a variety of compact disc databases available for student, faculty, and staff use. NLU's main campus, in Evanston, Illinois, is the base from which all library services are coordinated. We have a coordinator of off-campus services who supervises and works with our academic center librarians and oversees the instructional component of our services at all locations. Each of our academic centers has been equipped with a PC-based workstation to provide dial access to our online catalog (ILLINET Online) and with CD-ROM databases appropriate to the curricular offerings at the site.

How did NLU get involved with these off-campus field programs to educate the nontraditional adult student—the often full-time employed student whose time is extremely limited?

By the mid-1970s the handwriting was on the wall. Serious declines in undergraduate college enrollments, particularly for small private single mission colleges like NCE, were causing such institutions to take a hard look at their survival.

The high demand for elementary educators declined, and so did the revenues associated with training these educators. By 1976, the college knew they needed to look at an alternative to the traditional on-campus single program curriculum.[1] Therefore, in 1978 National-Louis University started delivering educational programs to nontraditional adult students.

Our philosophy since 1978 has been that our out-of-state academic centers' students and faculty are entitled to the same quality library services as our on-campus students and faculty. Classes sometimes met at one of NLU's area campuses, but most met at public schools, hospitals, churches, community centers, and businesses throughout the metropolitan Chicago area. Because the classes were off-campus, students did not have easy or direct access to the university library, and because the field program included a very substantial research project component, the University Library has been an integral part of the curriculum in every program.

At the time, computer-based bibliographies were seen as a quick and efficient way to support off-campus research. The DIALOG online system was chosen because of the large number of databases that were available and the extended hours of operation that were needed to serve the evening classes. At the beginning, two librarians visited each group twice. The first visit was to provide a bibliographic instruction session and the second was to perform online database searches via DIALOG over public telephone lines using a Texas Instruments portable terminal and producing a printout in the form of a specialized bibliography for each student.[2]

LIBRARY BIBLIOGRAPHIC INSTRUCTION TODAY

As the programs offered in the field model expanded, the library's role evolved. With the increasing number of programs and students, now we can no longer manage to send even one librarian to meet with each group twice. Every program continues to have a strong library presence, but the format has changed over the years. Each program offered has a specific library component built in. This part falls at different times as determined by the individual program requirements, but it is consistent within each program.

The library piece of the curriculum now is a combination of lecture and laboratory experience in which the students are presented with a theoretical grounding in the place of research in their field along with a hands-on session during which the online catalog and the various CD-ROM databases available at each location are introduced.

The library session is fairly evenly split between the lecture and the lab portions. The University Library faculty have developed a text for the lecture portion, which undergoes regular revision and updating. This text, *Literature Review and Library Research Manual*, which is in the ERIC database, covers the basic information needed to assist our students with their research projects and major papers. It includes examples of the types of resources available, hints for conducting successful research, examples from the APA style manual to help the students with the writing of the text and the bibliography for their papers, and examples of correct citations to avoid plagiarism.

During the hands-on session each individual is given a chance to get a feel for the computer and the information available. Students with home or office computers with modems can also dial into our online catalog. Dial access permits direct borrowing from the NLU collections and from the collections of about forty other Illinois academic libraries. This direct borrowing access speeds up the entire research process since the requested materials are in transit almost as soon as the students transmit their requests.

We distribute a series of handouts including journal, book, Eric Document request forms, and computer database search request forms. Also included in our handouts is information on how to connect to our OPAC-IO, our 800 telephone number, plus our fax number. We encourage them to call us or fax us. We also renew ILL books and our own books via telephone.

An important component to our BI sessions is our personal interaction with the students. Since many of the students we serve never see the mother institution, the Evanston NLU campus, they are often operating out of a vacuum. We are representatives from the university they may never see and we are aware of the impact we can make.

Many times we teach in a classroom setting along with one lone computer to support our teaching the electronic resources. The students come from many walks of life but share a common thread: they are terrified—this may be a strong word; let's say highly anxious—about doing any library research and are equally anxious about entering a library that reflects all the new technological changes (i.e., no card catalogs, just computers).

Each librarian who does BI is extremely sensitive to these adult returning students and many times our role is broadened from that of a librarian to a hand-holder, networker (i.e., what person in this vast organization is the proper one to get answers to their financial aid). We are attuned to creating a learning climate by nurturing the students through the library research process emphasizing that this is a process in critical thinking. The students can experiment with their ideas, they can take risks trying to locate data to support their hypotheses, and ultimately realize that they have gone through a discovery process—from the embryo of an idea to actualizing their studies. We encourage them to change their topics if they do not find what they are seeking and emphasize that all of them will find information. Our goal is to empower the student so he or she can be comfortable doing research in any library.

Another positive part of our BI is that we sometimes perform a team teaching role where we work with the class faculty member and share our common knowledge about doing library research. This portion is not formally part of the curriculum but is a welcome addition and adds a lively component to the class.

Yes, we continue to do individualized database searches for our off-campus students using both CD-ROM databases and DIALOG online databases providing comprehensive coverage of their topics. We mail them their own tailor-made personalized bibliographies and they love it! There is a 7-10 day turnaround time.

THE "ELECTRONIC LIBRARIES"

What does the off-campus academic library look like? Each off-campus academic center has an area set aside for the library which is nontraditional in its appearance. There are one or two PCs with modems which offer students access to IO, and stand-alone CD-ROM databases. The academic centers are not housing book collections, but are "electronic libraries." The PCs are accessed to the parent NLU central office at Evanston and provide library resources in a timely manner to students and faculty at off-campus sites. We also support our off-campus students by giving them the option to use local libraries and we reimburse them for guest library cards if they request them.

How many BI librarians and paraprofessionals are available to staff and support our on- and off-campus programs? Currently we have 5 1/2 FTE library faculty and 2 1/4 FTE professional staff doing BI.

At our off-campus academic centers, we have a variety of schedules for our librarians. At our Northern Virginia/Washington, DC centers, we have one full-time librarian, at our Atlanta center the librarian is hired for approximately ten percent of a FTE position, and at each of our St. Louis and Tampa academic centers, the librarians work at a 25 percent FTE equivalent.

TRENDS

The trends over the years with the advent of CD-ROMs and our "electronic library" have changed the way we serve our students. When we first started doing computer searches for our off-campus students, we were doing as many as 200 per month,[3] but now we are doing approximately 50 per month. We attribute this decline in computer searches we perform for students to the CD-ROM technology. The students are now doing their own searches with one of us usually training them initially.

The library is the hub for many of the adjunct faculty and students who are far away from the actual university. We are proud to connect the students with their resources for their research and to also represent the university as a helping hand in their entire educational process.

To sum up the University Library's impact on the university community, since we started external degree programs, the library has gained more status and recognition within the university. Our librarians have become more regularly involved with students, faculty, and administrators at all levels. We have high visibility on campus and in the field as information specialists, educators, and as representatives of National-Louis University.[4]

NOTES

1.   D. Strasser and G. Weinstein, "National College of Education's Extended Campus Library Services: A Model Program," in *Off-Campus Library Services Conference Proceedings, St. Louis, Missouri, October 14-15, 1982*, ed. by Barton M. Lessin (Mt. Pleasant, MI: Central Michigan University Press, 1983), 138-145.

2.   C. Kabel, *Evaluating the Impact of Bibliographic Instruction*. Unpublished master's thesis. National-Louis University. Evanston, IL (in progress).

3.   J. Ream and N. Weston, "The Effects of Innovative Extended Library Services on Total Library Operations," in *Off-Campus Library Services Conference Proceedings*, 129-137.

4.   Ream and Weston.

— CAROLE J. KABEL, ROSE P. NOVIL, AND JACK FRITTS —

THE ELECTRONIC LIBRARY:
LIBRARY SKILLS FOR OFF-CAMPUS STUDENTS
(Electronic Resources)

Jack Fritts

A major component of each of our bibliographic instruction sessions is a hands-on segment designed to introduce the students to some of the available resources. Each academic center has at least one dedicated student-accessible workstation onsite. These systems provide dial access to our online catalog/circulation system (ILLINET ONLINE) and at least one CD-ROM product appropriate to the local curriculum. Every location has the ERIC database on CD-ROM, and all centers outside of Wisconsin also are provided with ABI/INFORM and Periodical Abstracts from UMI. Our Northern Virginia/Washington, DC Center also has Business Dateline, which is a full-text regional business publications database.

Through dial access our students can connect to our online catalog from the academic centers or from their own computers. ILLINET Online provides access to our entire collection, as well as the collections of 40+ other academic libraries in the state of Illinois. This system gives our students direct borrowing privileges to collections consisting of over 19 million volumes. Another benefit of IO is that it also allows the user to browse the holdings of approximately 800 other libraries in Illinois. This will allow the patron to identify materials that might not be held by the 40+ direct members, but that can be requested through interlibrary loan.

ILLINET Online also provides two additional resources—IBIS and CARL Uncover. IBIS stands for the Illinois Bibliographic Information System. This system currently consists of ERIC and five H.W. Wilson databases (Reader's Guide Abstracts, Business Periodicals Index, Social Sciences Index, General Science Index, and Humanities Index). Additional databases are being added to this system on a regular basis. By the Fall 1993 term there should be seven Wilson databases available to IO patrons. CARL Uncover is a current contents database that indexes the contents of those journals held by Illinois libraries that belong to SILO, which stands for Serials in Illinois Libraries Online.

Our Chicago and West Suburban campuses each have a selection of standalone workstations that provide ERIC, ABI/Inform, Periodical Abstracts, and PsycLit (Lombard). The Evanston Campus library has a CD-ROM LAN, which currently holds ten database

selections. The LAN is available on six public access stations, at the reference desk, and at additional staff terminals. The Baker Demonstration School Library (which is also one of our branch libraries) has one PC with access to the LAN.

As you can imagine, a great deal of our time is spent in training students on the use of the various electronic resources available. About half of each bibliographic instruction session is devoted to hands-on use of the various databases. One aspect of this training involves helping the students to develop an appropriate search strategy. One part of our mission is to develop in our patrons the skills necessary to become lifelong learners. It is not enough to point them to the computer and tell them to search their topics. Learning how to use the equipment is only a part of the process of becoming a lifelong learner. In order to be successful users, our students need to develop an understanding of how to construct a search, how to identify the appropriate terms to search, and how to focus the search on the most specific resources. For example, a student will come to the library looking for resources to write a paper on the topic of child development with no focus beyond the general subject area. We try to help that student focus on some particular aspect of child development rather than just trying to make some sense out of the thousands of citations that single term will identify. Occasionally it will turn out that the student's topic is actually something quite different from the initial request. In such cases, where we are able to help the user refine the initial question in order to find exactly what is desired, we feel the time we spend counseling our students on approach and technique is more than justified.

We also counsel students over the telephone on proper access to ILLINET Online. Anyone who has a computer with a modem can access our catalog and the other services available through ILLINET Online. We provide a handout from the Illinois Library Computer Systems Office (ILCSO), which we have slightly modified, that includes instructions on connecting directly to us. Computers being what they are, we still get calls asking why the connection doesn't work. At that point one of our reference staff can usually resolve the problem or refer the student to someone who can.

Our future plans call for expansion of the electronic resources available to our students. We have been discussing the possibility of placing full-text databases at each of our academic centers to speed up turnaround time. As a related issue, we are also investigating the possibility of supplementing our instruction librarians at each location with full-time paraprofessionals to maintain equipment and materials and to assist the students with their research needs. We have also been working toward better linkages between the Evanston

Campus Library and the other locations. The computer services department of National-Louis works cooperatively with the University Library in the development and enhancement of technology. Currently computer services is testing a LAN connection between Evanston and McLean, Virginia. At this point, the two locations are linked for most institutional support services and e-mail, and the library connection to this LAN is waiting for the installation of upgraded equipment at Evanston. In test mode the connection does work, so when the Evanston Campus Library file server upgrade is completed the McLean patrons will have access to all the databases available to Evanston patrons.

We are in the construction phase right now for our new West Suburban Campus location. We will be moving from our current location in Lombard, Illinois, into the former DuPage County Courthouse complex in Wheaton, Illinois, by September 1993. This facility will give the West Suburban Campus Library some much needed space for expansion. The plans have been designed so that network connections will be in place on opening day, providing this campus direct access to the Evanston-based LAN as well. By the end of the 1993-94 academic year, the Chicago campus and the other three academic centers in the U.S. should be linked into this developing institutional network, providing increased access to databases and other resources to all of our students, faculty, and staff.

Once the technology is in place and the instruction has been completed, the logical question is how to get the information to the students. The question of timely delivery has taken on added significance over the past two years as the various programs have been revised and reorganized. Some programs no longer require the major projects that provided closure to the students'

work over a period of about fifteen months. Instead, the students are now expected to plan, research, and write a series of shorter, more focused papers over the length of their programs.

These revised curricula and expectations put a great deal of pressure on both the student and the library, since neither has the time available to allow traditional interlibrary loan approaches to work. Some of the ways we have addressed this issue include making extensive use of the fax machine for processing requests, providing direct borrowing access through the use of ILLINET Online, utilizing overnight delivery services, counseling students regarding local resources, and purchasing guest cards at local libraries. Interlibrary loan/document delivery services at NLU are based at the Evanston campus. As is the case with most institutions, the growing availability of CD-ROM-based resources has resulted in extensive growth in demand for ILL services. At NLU the number of requests processed grew from about 5,000 in 1988 to over 20,000 in 1992. In order to meet this demand for service, the public services departments at NLU have developed a cooperative approach which utilizes a variety of resources to ensure that our patrons' needs are met in a timely manner.

Although the technology has become an important part of our daily operations at National-Louis University, we have not lost sight of our primary purpose. Our goal is to meet the students' needs by assisting them in the process of becoming lifelong learners. We achieve this goal through our bibliographic instruction program, through our individual counseling and training sessions, through our institutional communications network, and through our dedication to the principles of good service.

— CAROLE J. KABEL, ROSE P. NOVIL, AND JACK FRITTS —

THE ELECTRONIC LIBRARY: TEACHING STUDENTS AT A DISTANCE

Sharon M. West and Diane Ruess

BACKGROUND

Many of us work in institutions that have distance learning programs. These may be traditional correspondence classes, videoconferenced, computer conferenced, or audioconferenced, but in all cases the learner is not on campus. Distance education was developed by colleges and universities to meet the educational needs of a diverse population who can't come to "The Campus."[1]

Since a prime target population for distance education has been rural students, providing library and information services to off-campus learners has, by default, meant providing these services to rural populations. Far more students than we perhaps wish to admit have little or no access to a local library, public or otherwise. In 1989, over eight million people lived in communities of less than 5,000 people. While these communities had about 3,900 libraries in them, 46 percent of them reported collection sizes of less than 10,000 volumes.[2] Libraries of this size cannot meet the needs of a student in higher education.

For this reason, most universities with distance education programs have extended or off-campus library services. The Rasmuson Library at the University of Alaska Fairbanks is no exception. However, in Alaska, "rural" takes on a new meaning. In many states in the lower 48, rural means a town of less than 2,500 people—in Alaska, "rural" means a village or town

West is head of reference and instructional services and *Ruess* is head, IMPACT department, Rasmuson Library, University of Alaska Fairbanks.

without road access. Since there are only 5,679 miles of road in a state with over 500,000 square miles, we have, by definition, a large rural area to serve.

PROBLEM DEFINITION

Off-campus students at the University of Alaska Fairbanks (UAF) take almost all courses by teleconference. In establishing a new core curriculum in 1990, UAF committed itself to providing rural students with the ability to attain a baccalaureate degree via distance education. This commitment caused the Elmer E. Rasmuson Library, the library system for UAF, to face a triple dilemma:

1. One of the requirements of the core curriculum was that all students demonstrate a library and information literacy proficiency.[3] This requirement was strongly supported by the faculty outside the library, and the library faculty were able to establish a Library and Information Research course as the course to meet this requirement. This course was designed to be delivered only on-campus. This left the rural students with no opportunity to meet their library proficiency requirement.

2. Many of our rural students live where no library exists. In all of northern Alaska, there are only four university-affiliated libraries—in Bethel, Nome, Kotzebue, and Barrow. The remainder of UAF students, who can be spread from Petersburg to Little

Diomede (a distance over 2,000 miles), may have little or no personal experience with libraries.

3. Most of UAF's distance delivery students are native Americans. For example, the Chukchi campus in Kotzebue serves a population of 6,000 people of whom 88 percent are Inupiaq Eskimos and other Alaska native groups. The Kuskokwim campus serves approximately 4,000 people, many of whom speak Yup'ik Eskimo as their primary language and who retain their traditional cultural values.

One advantageous factor was the presence of computers in rural Alaska. Schools had Apple computers heavily integrated into their program; University of Alaska Rural Education Centers had personal computers available to their students. Unlike the early 1970s, when there was perhaps only one telephone in a village (usually in the village store), most individuals now had telephones in their homes. And, unlike the early 1970s, when data communications was expensive and unreliable, Alascom, the major telephone carrier in Alaska, had established AlaskaNet, a packet switching network with local telephone access for 45 communities statewide.

In the meantime, the Rasmuson Library had been developing, as part of a long-term strategy, an electronic library without walls. We had purchased, installed, and brought up an online catalog (called *Gnosis*), which was used by all university units statewide. On *Gnosis*, we had also developed and installed a periodical indexing database called the *Bibliography of Alaska and Polar Regions*, which contained over 75,000 citations relevant to the Arctic. We were in the process of developing a CD-ROM local area network, (*ElmerNet*) that would have remote access to it as well. *ElmerNet* would ultimately have over 20 different databases on it.

To solve the triple problem facing the library, it was decided to marry the electronic library, with its telecommunications capability, to the idea of teaching library research as a *process* and not necessarily as a place.

This may not appear to be a departure from many previous attempts to teach the library research process, but the profession has customarily taught the process as one that must take place in a library. In this case, the attempt would be to teach the process as though it could take place outside a library. This represented a shift in defining "access" as being solely electronic rather than being, at least partially, physical.

COURSE DESIGN AND DEVELOPMENT

To accomplish this goal, the authors designed and developed a course, a syllabus, and a textbook for a class that came to be known as Library and Information Strategies (LS 100). The underlying principles were: 1) most students would not be familiar with the library as a concept or a place; 2) they would have access to a computer and modem but would probably have minimal computing skills; and 3) they would have the same or similar information needs as on-campus students.

These principles led to the conceptual outline, which included seven major concepts:

1. Information
    a. Nature of Information
    b. Structure of Information
    c. Organization of Information

2. The Library
    a. Brief History of Books and Libraries
    b. How Libraries Organize Information
    c. Computers and Libraries
    d. The Electronic Library

3. The Library and Its Services
    a. The Reference Librarian
    b. Online Searching and Databases
    c. Interlibrary Loan and Document Delivery

4. The Library and Its Resources
    a. The Online Catalog
    b. Arrangement of Materials in Libraries

5. Types of Information Available in Libraries
    a. CD-ROM Databases and Periodical Literature
    b. Indexes
    c. The Reference Collection

6. Electronic Access to Libraries
    a. Online Mail Systems
    b. Telefacsimile
    c. Telecommunications

7. Understanding the Library Research Process
    a. Defining the Research Topic
    b. Using Appropriate Information Strategies to Research the Topic
    c. Synthesizing and Summary

The original conceptual layout of the course, which included the learning objectives for each concept, was logical and organized. The reality of writing the textbook that covered these concepts was more difficult. Like most birthings, it was a messy, painful, and ultimately creative process.

TEXTBOOK DESIGN AND DEVELOPMENT

It proved to be sufficiently difficult that the delivery of the course was delayed an academic year while West grappled with how individuals who had not seen or used a real library could learn the basic concepts of the library research process. After a great deal of thought and discussion with colleagues and faculty who taught in rural areas, the textbook organization differed somewhat from the conceptual design.[4]

Unit 1:   Information and Knowledge
Unit 2:   Computers, Libraries and Information
Unit 3:   The Library Catalog
Unit 4:   Gnosis: Author and Title Searching
Unit 5:   Gnosis: Subject and Keyword Searches
Unit 6:   Classification and Call Numbers
Unit 7:   Extended Campus Services and Interlibrary Loan
Unit 8:   Finding Periodicals: Using a Print Index
Unit 9:   Finding Periodicals: Using an Online Index
Unit 10: Using Reference Sources and Services
Unit 11: The Library Research Process

LIBRARY AND INFORMATION STRATEGIES
TEXTBOOK ORGANIZATION

It has been theorized by sociolinguists that Native Americans have an aversion to the written record because it places a barrier between experience and truth.[5] In using this theory to guide design of the textbook, an attempt was made to use "real" examples wherever possible, thus using experience to guide

learning from the written document. For example, when the nature of information was discussed, the "bit" of information that was analyzed to see what the parts of information are was the fact that John, a young man, had gone to fish camp. Most students in rural Alaska, native and non-native, will immediately recognize the informational context of fish camps.

This was the pattern followed throughout the development of the textbook. It was deemed vital that situations and contexts familiar to the students be used to teach processes, tools, and vocabulary unfamiliar to students. As will be explained in more detail later in this article, this same technique was used in the teaching of the course.

COURSE DELIVERY

Once the basic premise of the class had been developed and the textbook written, teaching methods and techniques appropriate for an audioconference setting had to be considered. Three major concerns became readily apparent: 1) teaching library research skills at a distance via technology; 2) teaching the use of current library applications of technology; and 3) teaching library research via technology to those who may never have used a library before.

Yet, before assessing these most important concerns, an obvious higher priority had to be considered: What was the nature of the student population? The comparison of on- and off-campus students provided insight into our potential audience, which in turn influenced daily classroom decisions. Table 1 is a comparison of the general qualities of on-campus and off-campus students.

In preparation for the first class meeting and in an effort to gain some understanding of individual situations, the type of library access each student had, if any, was determined and as a visual reference point

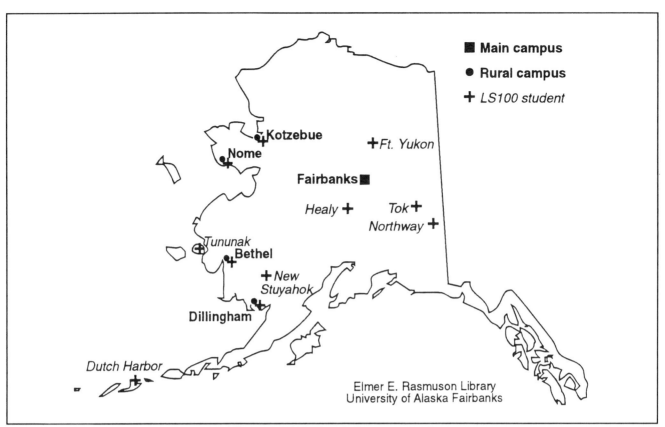

**Figure 1: UAF Rural Campuses and
Locations of LS 100 Students**

their communities were located on a map (see figure 1). Students were scattered around the entire state and in Alaska this means vast distances. Our experience from the two classes taught shows roughly 40 percent of our students had local library access. The significance of rural student difficulties becomes very clear upon visiting rural communities.

For example, Bristol Bay Campus is a typical rural site and serves 32 villages in an area of approximately 55,000 square miles. It is located in Dillingham, a fishing community on the south coast of Alaska. The campus library consists of three to four shelving sections of mostly out-of-date textbooks and a few reference books, generally inadequate to serve the needs of college students.

There is no ongoing library program or budget to serve faculty, staff, or students nor to buy new materials. Dillingham is one of the small number of rural communities which has a public library well supported by the community, and could benefit potential distance students. Unfortunately, the librarian would not allow use of public library facilities by university students or functions. One LS 100 student told the story of surreptitiously using the public library to complete class work. This is one example of a variety of obsta-

cles rural students face in completing college courses taken by audioconference.

Therefore, one of the more important concepts taught in this class was that a library is not the only option for locating information. Since a significant number of distance students live in communities with no library access, the textbook was designed to nudge students out into their communities to find examples of other sources of information (e.g., the local health center, post office, cooperative extension, hardware store, gas station).

ALASKA TELECONFERENCE NETWORK

For the period, Fall 1988 through Spring 1990, there were 15,548 distance students enrolled in audio-conferenced courses in Alaska. These students were pursuing degrees at all levels—associate, baccalaureate, and masters. All of these students gain access to their audioconference classes through the Alaska Teleconference Network, administered by the University of Alaska.

Instructors and students dial in using a toll-free number, and network operators make the necessary connections. A great many audioconference classes are taught at night for adult students who work during the day, in addition to the fact that the telephone rates drop considerably after 5:00 p.m.

TEACHING VIA TECHNOLOGY

Audioconference technology isn't itself revolutionary and has been around for quite some time, being used widely to teach distance courses. Its only requirements are a telephone, a telephone line, and a convener kit, which is a speaker with telephone and microphone connections. In Alaska, the more significant problems with teaching by audioconference relate to statewide telephone utilities. Long distance telephone connections to the lower 48 or even Europe are sharper than those in-state.

At times students may fade in and out of class because of a bad connection, bad phone lines, or bad weather. In fact, two students couldn't complete the course on time because of poor local telephone lines. One answer to these kinds of technical difficulties was to make an audio recording of lectures and mail them to students who missed class. Another solution was to call each student at least once a week, or more if he or she was having problems. This was easily accomplished with our small class enrollment but would be more difficult with larger classes.

Teaching classes by audioconference is quite obviously different from the normal classroom situation. Prior teaching experience is very important but doesn't prepare you to teach students you can't see. One of the first things to realize is that if you feel funny sitting in a room alone talking to a microphone, your students probably feel the same. The option of using visual aids or dial-in demonstrations is not an option. With no means of presenting information visually, you must rely on other methods of involving your students in class and make contact with individuals a priority.

AUDIOCONFERENCE TECHNIQUES

Polling class members at the beginning of each class worked very well. The first class meeting was not only an introduction to class requirements, but an opportunity to determine each student's local library access and the quality of his or her computing access, equipment, and experience. One of the requirements for living in Alaska is that you have to enjoy talking about either the weather or politics. A brief discussion of the latest weather disaster or local political scandal usually warmed everyone up and built a rapport taken for granted in a standard classroom setting. Students

would often end up giving advice to each other and/or arrange a time when they could talk outside of class. In addition to the initial poll and discussion, to maintain students' interest, it is important to break up the lecture every ten to fifteen minutes, with questions directed at individuals. These breaks in the lecture were ideal opportunities to share class-related problems or issues discussed during the individual weekly telephone conversations. In many cases, students experienced similar problems and the sharing of these problems somewhat alleviated their feelings of isolation.

Ultimately, we found that the classic lecture format had to be abandoned, and came to realize that peer tutoring could be a significant factor in students' successfully completing our class. We encouraged it wholeheartedly, and to aid in this process we shared e-mail IDs among class members, some of whom contacted each other. It was convenient and effective for both students and instructors to communicate by e-mail. Students were also taught to communicate with the library using the library's e-mail IDs for interlibrary loan and reference.

TEACHING USE OF TECHNOLOGY

How does one teach basic library research skills to students via the telephone? The one basic requirement for the course was some kind of access to a computer with a modem. Since much of the class was set up around dialing in to Rasmuson Library's databases, developing students' computer skills was essential to their completion of the course. Once again, their skills varied a great deal. We had students who were already experts with e-mail and other computing functions who zipped right through dial-in, sign-on, and database searching functions. For others, however, dialing in was a major hurdle that created a great deal of frustration and took many telephone calls between instructor and student. This was only the first step to get into the system, with much more ahead of them. In hindsight, more time needed to be designated for this part of the class.

Access to computing equipment proved to be a problem for more than one student. Students would be promised use of a computer at the local site, but when it was needed, access was denied and other arrangements had to be worked out. Access problems also arose from situations where the computer was located at the local public school, library, or other public facility with limited hours and competitive use.

On the up side of access issues, many students had their own PCs or had access to PCs at their workplaces. Students and instructors alike enthusiastically supported sharing e-mail IDs among class members, which fit in well with the idea of a peer tutoring network. E-mail and fax seemed to be the ideal combination, but it was not always possible or available.

TEACHING LIBRARY RESEARCH CONCEPTS

Just as the textbook for LS 100 was developed around real-life examples illustrating basic concepts important for understanding and doing beginning library research, we introduced those same alien concepts to students in a context that was familiar.

For example, the similarities between a library catalog and a catalog from L.L. Bean were used to show the elements necessary to use a catalog. Each provides information to locate one item among many. Every Alaskan has at one time or another ordered something from a catalog. This particular example worked so well that we now use the same analogy when we teach the on-campus class.

Another real-life example used to teach the concept of controlled vocabulary was the yellow pages from the local phone book. Everyone understands how to use the yellow pages and more than likely has firsthand experience doing so. If a student can understand how the telephone book uses subject headings and SEE references, he or she can understand controlled vocabularies, such as the *Library of Congress Subject Headings*.

These examples worked very well and were used as a teaching technique in addition to being integrated into specific class assignments. In conjunction with real-life examples, instructors of audioconferenced classes should be flexible, extremely patient, and open to creative solutions for problems.

CONCLUSION

Based upon objective evaluations and oral feedback, student satisfaction with the course was uniformly high. Students believed that they learned the skills necessary for accessing the library's resources electroni-

cally and, further, understood how to access any modern library electronically.

The instructors found that students needed a great deal of personal reassurance and support as they learned how electronic dial-in worked. Extensive time was spent on the telephone walking students through the initial sign-on process. It is sometimes difficult for those of us who feel competent in the "information age" to remember how much anxiety and stress can be experienced the first time we assembled a PC or dialed into our first e-mail system. During the duration of the semester, students used e-mail or remote database searching at least once a week. Frequent use of new computer skills is critical for retention.

The textbook tested out positively, especially for a first field experience. The organization and concepts worked well in sequence and built upon students' previous experiences and knowledge. Any revisions to the textbook will be based upon new technologies being introduced in the library.

NOTES

1.   Carnegie Commission on Higher Education, *Less Time, More Options: Education Beyond the High School* (New York: McGraw-Hill, 1975).

2.   Arthur Podolsky, *Public Libraries in 50 States and the District of Columbia: 1989* (Washington, DC: United States Department of Education, Office of Educational Research and Improvement, 1991), 9.

3.   University of Alaska, Fairbanks, *Core Curriculum Proposal* (Fairbanks, AK: University of Alaska, Fairbanks, 1990), 12.

4.   Sharon M. West, *Library and Information Strategies* (Fairbanks, AK: Elmer E. Rasmuson Library, University of Alaska, Fairbanks, 1991).

5.   Elizabeth Brandt, "Native American Attitudes toward Literacy and Recording in the Southwest," *Journal of the Linguistic Association of the Southwest* 4 (1981): 185-195.

GRAPHIC DESIGN FOR LIBRARY PUBLICATIONS

Mary Jane Walsh

INTRODUCTION

This is Graphic Design for Library Publications and I'm Mary Jane Walsh from Colgate University. Diane Nahl's talk yesterday about the content of print guides was a nice lead-in to this instructive session. To borrow terminology from the field of architecture, she talked about function, and I'm going to talk about form; specifically about how form affects function.

When I came to Colgate in 1984, technology consisted of telephones, microform reader printers, OCLC terminals, and two "dumb" terminals used for searching Dialog. There wasn't a microcomputer in the entire building.

In contrast, today we have an Innovative Interfaces integrated system, 12 CD-ROMs with nine different search protocols (five of them are networked), we have a PC in every librarian's office, we brought up First-Search about a month ago, and we got our Internet access during the fall semester ('92). Most of this change has occurred in the last three to five years.

We started to feel the effects of all that new technology almost immediately at the reference desk. Now, when you have five people waiting at the reference desk for help (we've all been there, right?), you have to make a decision—how long do you spend with each student? The technology—all that new technology—started to pose a problem. How long do

you spend teaching someone the commands to search a new electronic tool that they've never seen before?

We also started seeing the effects in our library instruction classes. In 50-minute sessions (we keep adding more and more things to teach our students), how long do you spend teaching the mechanics of command structure and letting that take away from the concepts?

So, a couple of years ago, as one part of the solution, we took a look at the print guides that we've been using. Now, they're a very low tech answer to a very high tech problem, but paper does have some advantages. For one thing, it supports multiple simultaneous users without a license fee. It's portable. Our campus network is almost complete (the fine arts building and the campus dorms are scheduled to be networked this summer). We anticipate even more users connecting to our systems from remote sites, so we want something portable. Updating is fairly easy on paper—if you are networked.

There are drawbacks (to paper). Primarily, the publications go out of date as fast as you can produce them. Our guide to searching ERIC went out of date while still at the print shop!

What we discovered when we looked at our print guides was that we had a real hodge-podge: we had different sizes; we had different colors; we had different typefaces. Some had been created years ago on typewriters; some had been photocopied to death; some were barely legible.

So it fell to the head of library instruction to plan and implement a program of coordinated library publications. Now, you have to understand that my

Walsh was head of library instruction and is now head of U.S. documents, maps, and microforms at Colgate University, Hamilton, New York.

previous design experience consisted of having had a roommate for one year who was an advertising layout artist for the *Buffalo Evening News*. What I want to share with you today is what I have learned while progressing from a rank beginner to a novice (i.e. the very, very basics).

PLANNING

Being a librarian, the first thing I did was a literature search. On the last page of your handout (see p. 148) is a brief list of some of the materials that I found particularly useful—it's not a comprehensive list. The first two items describe the publications program at Carnegie Mellon, and they deal with administration and planning. The third and fourth items describe the publications program at The University of California, Irvine, which won a John Cotton Dana award several years ago. They also deal with administration and planning. The last two have some very useful design guidelines. The Crawford book also discusses hardware and software, from sophisticated word processing to sophisticated desktop publishing. I will not be covering hardware or software today.

Being a beginner, the next thing I did was what most beginners do (they want a live body to talk to): I went looking for an expert. Although we are a small campus, there is a graphic designer on staff in the communications department, which is responsible for publishing the college catalog, the alumni newspaper, and the like. He was willing to sit down and talk with me, and he gave me some very handy hints that I will pass on to you later. Although he wasn't able to design our publications for us, he did look over our designs and make suggestions.

Which brought me to the next step, which was to look at what other libraries were doing. LOEX was a great source of examples. Any time my colleagues went anywhere they brought me back handouts. I talked to other librarians to see how they were using automation to help them, and I went down to Cornell University's undergraduate library to see how they were using WordPerfect to produce bibliographies from a database of citations.

Goals

We set three goals for the publication program. The first was that we wanted the publications to scream "library." Without looking for the fine print, they had to be instantaneously and clearly identifiable as coming from us. That has advantages and disadvantages: if your reading public happens to feel warm and cuddly about the library or at least has professional respect for you,

they are likely to read the publications that you send to them in the mail. If they don't think much of the library, the publications go immediately into the recycling bin.

Second, we wanted the publications to be coordinated, but not uniform in style. Uniform is boring, but in order to be identifiable as coming from the library they had to have some sort of coordinated look.

Last, but not least, we wanted to be able to produce the publications in house. That was very important. At the time, we were using a Zenith 286 computer, WordPerfect 5.0, and an HP LaserJet II printer. We also wanted to be able to photocopy the publications in our print shop.

Inventory and Classify

After setting our goals, we inventoried and then classified the publications that we currently had. We borrowed the classification scheme from Carnegie Mellon: policies and services, subject guides, problem solvers, resource guides, forms, class bibliographies, special publications. We decided to work with the first four types of publications.

Beyond following some basic design guidelines, we decided to leave the last three classes of publications alone. Forms have a long history and tradition of size and color that we didn't want to change. I wasn't going to dictate to my colleagues how the bibliographies for their classes must look, and special publications defy all attempts to coordinate (their design).

DESIGN BALANCE

Throughout the design process we were doing a balancing act. We were balancing three different things:

Good Design and Budget

First of all, we had to balance good design rules and a very natural tendency to try and cram as much information as possible on the page. We've all done that at some time. We want to cut down on printing costs, we want to be nice to the environment and use less paper, and we don't want the students using our publications as scrap paper, so we try to get as much information as possible on every page. It's like having one 50-minute session to teach "everything" about the library to a class of freshmen—you want to cram "everything" in, but then what do the students learn? Perhaps nothing. We came to the realization that a longer publication that is used for its intended purpose is much more cost effective than a short publication that isn't used at all. In order to be used, the publication must be visually attractive to the public, and, even more important, it must be easy to read. Good design helps.

Simplicity and Embellishment

Second, we had to balance the ideas of simplicity and embellishment. On the advice of our graphics designer at Colgate, the first thing we did was eliminate all the clip art in our publications. He suggested that we take it easy the first couple of years; deal with text, deal with white space, deal with simple graphical elements (we decided to use lines as our graphical elements). Then when we were comfortable with what we were doing, we could reintroduce pictorial elements like clip art.

Variety and Unity

Last, we had to balance unity (because we wanted these to be identifiable as library publications) and variety. For variety, we decided to create a unique design for each of the four major kinds of publications that we were going to create. We would have unity within each kind of publication.

For economical reasons as well as for unity, we decided that all our publications would be based on an 8.5" by 11" inch sheet of paper. That size is actually pretty flexible as we discovered. You can create three different sizes of publications simply by folding the paper different ways.

What we did with paper to help balance unity and variety was to choose one type of paper (the name is Ticonderoga) for all our publications. Then we assigned one color to each type of publication: our Problem Solvers are maize, our Resource Guides are peach, Policies and Services are seafoam green, and Subject Guides are blue. We also had the print shop reserve a library color. Every publication that is sent through campus mail to faculty, administrators, or students, regardless of what kind of publication it is, goes out on Ticonderoga Light Blue. So as soon as people see that light blue sheet of paper in their mailboxes, they know that it's from the library. No one else on campus can use that paper.

I will be talking about the terminology of typography a little later on, so just bear with me when I tell you that, for unity, we chose just two typefaces: Dutch Roman and Swiss Roman. For variety, we use different fonts, which means that we use different styles and different sizes of those two typefaces. What we were trying to avoid by limiting our typeface selection is something like this (see appendix 1). This is what Walt Crawford calls "ransom notes."[1] This is the second page of one of our publications, and it's actually a

fairly well-designed page. The problem with this publication is not the layout or the spacing; it's the fonts. Almost every paragraph is in a different font. It's very distracting.

Another unifying factor was the decision to use one citation format.

GENERAL CONSIDERATIONS IN DOCUMENT DESIGN

There are some general ideas you should keep in mind when designing a document. The first is that document design should reflect and enhance the content of the publication. If the design fights the content, it's no good.

The second idea is that documents have distinct, identifiable elements, and that these elements should form the basis of your design. They should enhance the organization of the text. It is a good idea to identify those elements before you start creating the publication. Once you think you've got the perfect document put together, it's hard to go back and shoehorn in an element that you forgot to leave space for. If you look at figure 1, you will see the elements that we identified in our various publications. Not all of our publications have all of these elements. [Examples of publications illustrating figure 1 were shown.]

PAGE DESIGN

Size

One of the first decisions you have to make about a publication is its size. As I mentioned earlier, our publications are all based on 8.5" by 11"; so that's one size. Fold that in half and you get a 5.5" by 8.5" publication. That's a good size for publications that have a single column of text. You can also fold 8.5" by 11" in thirds, a trifold, and you get publications with 3.5" by 8.5" columns [example of each shown].

Orientation

When deciding the size of a publication, also consider the orientation. This is portrait orientation [example]; it is taller than it is wide. Landscape orientation is wider than it is tall. We don't have any landscape publications, but this one, a 5.5" by 8.5", is created by printing an 11" by 8.5" landscape file. Then we fold it in half and get a portrait publication out of our landscape file.

Elements of Documents at Colgate

Banners
- Same for each publication in a series. Can be used to identify the series.
- Together with the title, the most prominent item on the first page.
- Became a unique design element for each type of publication at Colgate.

Titles
- Different for each publication.
- Together with the banner, the most prominent item on the first page.

Headings and sub-headings
- Provide organization and natural places to pause in reading.
- Use only as many as needed to organize text - no more than 5 levels.
- Be consistent in how you graphically distinguish levels. Use the following singly or in combination:
  - Size - each level 2 points lower than the preceding
  - Placement - center, flush left, indented
  - Font Styles - bold, italic

Text
- Use a serif font; size between 9 points and 12 points.

Date
- Helps to keep track of different versions

Author
- Credit where credit is due

Running footers and/or headers
- Useful for page numbers; chapter titles in longer publications.

Table of contents and/or index
- If a publication is too long to read in one sitting it should have a table of contents. Include a table of contents if more than 15 pages long. Shorter publications may need one also.
- Use common sense about inclusion of an index.
- Use dot leaders or double space to make connection between item and page number easy.

Figure 1: Elements Identified in Publications

White Space

If you take nothing else home from this talk, *please* remember the concept that white space is in-credibly important. Print only works in contrast to white space. Without white space, it's just a solid, gray, amorphous mass. No one will read it. Even if someone wanted to read it, they would have great difficulty. White space is especially important when designing 8.5" by 11" guides with only one column of text. I'll talk more about that later.

Vertical, or internal, white space enhances the organization of your publication with spacing between paragraphs, sections, and chapters. External white space frames the text and makes it more inviting. External white space also keeps your lines short enough so that they are easy to read. The eye doesn't get tired or confused and jump between lines as it tracks across the page.

There is a rule of thumb (see appendix 2) that says that no more than 50-55 percent of a page should be text block. That doesn't include banner, title, headings; just the actual text. On appendix 2, you can see what that comes out to in square inches. Now, the numbers look pretty small, but look at an actual example (see appendix 3). This publication has 42.5 square inches of text block; well within the 51 square inch maximum for an 8.5" by 11" page.

Visual Importance

When you have finished designing a publication, prop it up against a wall and step back. Can you see a hierarchy on the page; is it visible from a distance? Can you see the change from one section to the next? Tell the major changes from the minor changes? If you can't, then the page is badly organized, and you need to start again. If you can (and, in a way, this is even worse), but when you walk up and look at the text, the hierarchy of the text doesn't match the hierarchy you could see from a distance, then there's a problem with the headings and subheadings and the vertical white space. Get other people to step back and look at publications for you, especially if you have different versions that you can't decide among. Prop up the different versions, ask people which they like better, but don't tell them what the differences are. Sometimes they defy the rules. And that's okay. I always go with what people are going to read.

First Page

The first page is the most important page of the publication, because it is what you use to attract the reader's attention in the first place. The first page should identify very clearly what the publication is. That's why our titles are the biggest words on our publications. The first page also should, with longer publications, help organize what follows. For example, a newsletter may benefit from a table of contents in a box on the first page.

Line Width

One very important thing that you can do to make your publications readable is to make sure that your lines are not too wide. In appendix 2 are some guidelines for line width. There are several rules of thumb, so it's a pick your own poison sort of thing. You can count the words, you can measure the line. The thing to keep in mind is that as the font size changes, the line width changes. Line width isn't constant based on the size of the paper, but rather on the size of the type.

Appendix 4 is an example of a publication that we actually distributed to faculty members. Dutch Roman 10 point upright is used for the body text. By any one of the guidelines in appendix 2, the line's too wide. If this had less vertical white space, it would be illegible; people would say "forget it." The excuse I used was that this had to be a one-page handout, front and back, and all that information was *absolutely* necessary. I didn't see any other way of doing it until I went back to my own guidelines (see appendix 5). This is the same publication, 37 square inches of textblock, done in two columns and much, much, easier to read because the lines are much shorter.

The 8.5" by 11" page can be a real problem to design. There are two ways to solve it. One is to use columns. What we have here (in appendix 5) is an example of newspaper columns; they are equal in width, start at the top, go down to the bottom of the first column, then back up to the top of the second column, and so on. The space between the columns is known as the gutter, and it is typically one-half to one-third of the width of the left and right margins. You can also use side-by-side columns (see appendix 2). The columns are unequal in width, and they work best when you have headings that you can pull out and put in the left hand column.

The other way to address the line width problem on an 8.5" by 11", if you *really* want to use one column of text, is to use very large fonts with very large margins; or, put your banner down the side, which takes up some of the space. This publication (see appendix 6) combines all three. The text is Dutch Roman 14 point upright, which is somewhat larger than normal for text (the usual range is 9 to 12 points). There is a full one-inch margin on the right, and we ran the banner down the left. Now running a banner or title vertically flies in the face of conventional graphic design wisdom. We are comfortable breaking this rule, perhaps because we're used to seeing titles on book spines running vertically. [Question about why we face the letters in the direction that we do. Answer:

so that the eye can run from top to bottom when reading the banner, rather than from bottom to top.]

Typography

I finally will define all the terms that I've been using. Most of us use the word "font" indiscriminately to describe everything from a font to a type family. From general to specific:

A "type family" is basically an alphabet that has been designed as a unit and has one name. Dutch Roman is a type family. It includes all different sizes and styles of the same family.

A "type face" is a type family in a specific style. Dutch Roman upright is a type face and Dutch Roman italic is a different type face; Dutch Roman bold is another type face. A type face can come in a variety of sizes.

A "font," technically, is one type face in one size. 9 point Dutch Roman upright is one font; 9 point Dutch Roman italic is another font; 10 point Dutch Roman bold is a third font. Rules of thumb: With apologies to Sesame Street, typography rules of thumb are brought to you by the letter P (see figure 2). This is an example of a "serif" and a "sans serif" font. Serifs are these little lines and curves on the edges of the letter. They help to make letters more legible, which is why a serif font is recommended for the body of your text. A sans serif font lacks those little lines and curves. Use sans serif fonts for short lines like headings. We also use sans serif for search examples in our handouts for online catalogs, CD-ROMs, and the like.

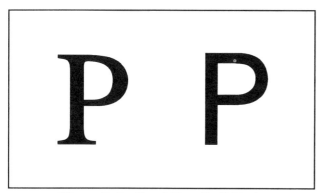

Figure 2: Serif and Sans Serif Fonts

Other typography rules of thumb:

1. If at all possible, don't underline. Underlining frequently touches the bottom of the letters, making them less legible. Italics (for titles) are easy enough to create on most word processors.

2. Words done in all upper case are more difficult to read than a combination of upper and lower

case, so limit use of upper case to one or two words, like titles. Consider making the first letter in an all upper case word one or two point sizes larger than the rest of the letters in the word.

3. Be consistent in how you use the different fonts. For example, if you use italics for titles in citations and bold for headings and subheadings, then for emphasis consider using bold and italic combined.

Leading

To adjust the "leading" of a text is to adjust the spacing between the lines of the text. The word comes from the strips of lead used to space lines of type in the bad old days when typesetting was done by hand. The appropriate amount of leading varies with the font size, and shorter lines need less leading than longer lines.

You can get by just fine without adjusting the leading in most of your print guides. The only time we use it in our publications is when we have titles or headings that run more than one line. This publication (see appendix 9) has the leading adjusted in the left column (line spacing changed from 1 to 0.8), but not in the right column.

Kerning

"Kerning" is the process of adjusting spaces between pairs of characters (i.e., letters). Some letters, like the uppercase W or A, leave more space on either side than is truly necessary. To the "educated eye," that extra space just doesn't look right.

On the top of appendix 8 are the last two lines of the kerning test for WordPerfect 5.1 done in Dutch Roman 12 point upright. You can see that there is some difference, but in fonts normally used for text (9 to 12 points), I doubt that most people would notice whether or not you have kerned the text. Text done in large fonts, however, often looks better when kerned.

You need, at the very least, a sophisticated word processor to kern. On WordPerfect, you can adjust the amount of kerning, but I find that it's simpler to either turn the kerning feature on and then forget about it, or leave it turned off. I trust their judgment as to the amount of kerning needed for each font.

If you find that you don't like the look of your text when it is kerned (and there will be times when you don't) there is still one instance when it may be useful. I confess that I turn on the kerning when I need to squeeze one more word on a line. Sometimes it even works!

Justification

I wouldn't worry too much about either leading or kerning in your publications, especially when you first get started. You may, however, wish to experiment with "justification."

There are four types of justification: center, left, right, and full. You may want to use center justification for signs or headings in columns, and right justification for special effects. Mostly, however, you will be concerned with left and full justification.

Left justified text (see bottom of appendix 8) is also known as ragged-right text. The text lines up neatly at the left margin; it doesn't at the right margin. The is an equal amount of space between all the words in left justified text.

In fully justified text (see appendix 9), spaces between words (or sometimes between letters) are adjusted so that the text on each line fills up the entire line. Both the left and right margins line up neatly. Full justification is used only with proportional fonts, never with monospaced fonts. In monospaced fonts (like the right hand column of appendix 9), the same amount of space was allocated for each letter, regardless of the width of the letter. In proportional fonts (like the left hand column of appendix 9), the space allocated for each letter is determine by its width.

Theory says that left justified text is easier to read than fully justified text because of the equal spacing between the words, and because there is less hyphenation at the end of the line. However, tests have shown that readers prefer to read fully justified text, especially for longer documents (have you read a book recently that wasn't fully justified?). So much for theory.

In some circumstances, you should still use left justification, regardless of what readers prefer. Look at this overhead again (see appendix 9). Notice the "rivers of white"[2] running through the text? It's much more obvious in the monospaced font than in the proportional font (which is why you don't fully justify monospaced fonts). It's easy to get that unwanted white space in documents with narrow columns and fully justified text.

So what's a poor publications coordinator to do? Compromise. We use full justification in publications with only one column, and left justification in publications with more than one column. It seems to work.

A final word about justification. If you use hyphenation in fully justified text to eliminate those rivers of white, or in left justified text because you just can't stand that big space at the end of a line, don't hyphenate more than two lines in a row.

OUTCOMES AND CONCLUSIONS

There are three outcomes of our library publications program:

1. We've produced a Library Publications Handbook that contains some general design guidelines and excruciatingly detailed directions for producing Policy and Services Guides, Subject Guides, Problem Solvers, and Resource Guides. The handbook is available from LOEX.

2. We have the good beginnings of a database of citations commonly used in publications, which greatly reduces the time to produce the bibliographic portions of some publications.

3. I've just about finished creating templates for our four types of publications. When done, they will make creating a publication much easier. All the initial margins and font settings, the banners, and titles will be in files, ready to retrieve.

Use

Evidence regarding the amount of use our publications get is mostly anecdotal, but use appears to vary with the kind of publication. The Policy and Services Guides are really a form of PR. We distribute them to new students and new faculty at their respective orientations, but they don't get much use from the display racks.

We don't have a good handle on how much use the Subject Guides get because we haven't produced many of them—they are the most time consuming to write and to format.

The Resource Guides and Problem Solvers get heavy, heavy use. In BI classes, we can concentrate on teaching the concepts involved in computerized searching, like keyword or Boolean or truncation; demonstrate a particular computer resource (we don't have a set-up for hands-on participation); and give the students the Resource Guide for that particular tool. We emphasize that they should bring the guide with them when they come to the library to use that resource. Then, and this is important, we validate the usefulness of that guide by referring to it when we work with students at the reference desk.

We also use the Resource Guides and Problem Solvers at the reference desk during those crunch periods when it feels more like triage than research assistance. We can hand students a publication about finding book reviews, very quickly point out a couple of sources to start with, and point them in the right direction. They seem to find what they need.

We also see a lot of use of Resource Guides at our network terminals (Internet and networked CD-ROMs). It seems that I'm constantly putting back into the display case the guides for searching the Hamilton College, Cornell, and Syracuse University catalogs. And we refill some of those resource guides on a regular basis.

Conclusion

I hope that this talk has convinced you that this low tech approach to a high tech problem is not so much "low tech" as "appropriate tech." Administrators like it: it's fairly inexpensive and it doesn't require powerful equipment. Directors like it: it's good PR. Reference librarians like it: we don't have to have perfect memories. The BI librarian likes it: I can teach concepts, not mechanics, and it reaches students who have different learning styles. Users like it, or seem to, anyway. Either they are desperate for scrap paper, need a little more roughage in their diet, or we're providing them with something that they need and use.

NOTES

1. Walt Crawford, *Desktop Publishing for Librarians* (Boston: G.K. Hall, 1990), 152.

2. Crawford, 142.

SUGGESTED READINGS

Bube, Judith Lynn. "A Coordinated Library Publications Program." *Library Journal* 111:17 (1986): 46-50.

Burbank, Lucille, and Dennis Pett. "Designing Printed Instructional Materials." *Performance and Instruction Journal* 25:8 (1986): 5-9.

Crawford, Walt. *Desktop Publishing for Librarians*. Boston: G.K. Hall, 1990.

Eldredge, Jon. "Managing a Library Publications Program." *College & Research Library News* 46:11 (1985): 620-624.

Library Publications Guidelines. Pittsburgh: Carnegie Mellon University Libraries, 1988.

Naismith, Rachael. "Establishing a Library Publications Program." *College & Research Library News* 46:2 (1985): 59-63.

Search Hints

Keyword Searching

Some catalogs, like Mondo, offer keyword searching as a separate option. In some catalogs, all searches are keyword searches. A keyword search may search every word in every record, or it may search one or more fields. On Mondo, for example, a Subject Keywords search searches the title, subject, and notes fields.

In keyword searching:
1. you enter a word or words.
2. the computer retrieves records which contain your keywords, without regard to the order in which you entered them or the order in which they appear in the records.

The computer:
1. looks for *exact* matches; it will not find COLOUR or COLORS if told to look for COLOR.
2. will not retrieve records that do not contain your keyword(s), even if the record is about your topic.
3. may retrieve irrelevant records if your keyword(s) have more than one possible meaning or if they form part of a larger subject heading. For the example, the keyword CONDUCTOR may retrieve records about music and/or railroads and/or electricity.

You should:
1. use different spellings or forms of words (e.g. color, colour, colors) or truncate.
2. use synonyms (e.g. teenager, adolescent, youth).

You may tell the computer to look for more than one word at a time (see Boolean Operators, Nesting, and Proximity Operators).

Truncation

Truncation symbols are used to retrieve, in one step, different spellings and forms of words (e.g. symphony, symphonies or symphonic). Truncation symbols vary from system to system. Some systems may use two symbols; one for single character truncation, and one for multiple character truncation. Commonly used symbols include * # : $?

Boolean Operators

Boolean operators (AND, OR, NOT) are used to search more than one keyword at the same time. Using them may increase or decrease the number of records retrieved.

OR Use to broaden a search; use between synonymous words or concepts. At least one of the words combined with an OR will appear in all records retrieved.

AND
Use to narrow a search; use between different concepts. All words combined with an AND will appear in all the records retrieved. Some catalogs treat a space as an AND.

NOT
Use to narrow a search; use to eliminate unwanted concepts. Records with the word following the NOT will not be retrieved.

The order in which AND, OR, and NOT are processed varies from system to system.

Nesting

Some systems allow you to group together words using parentheses. E.g. (PAINTING OR WATERCOLORS) AND (BRITAIN OR BRITISH OR ENGLISH OR ENGLAND). Operations within parentheses are processed before all other boolean operations.

Proximity Operators

Some systems allow you to tell the computer how close together your keywords must be in a record. This is a specialized form of boolean AND; all words entered must be present in each record. Proximity operators vary from system to system. There are, for example, three different proximity operators commonly used to indicate adjacency: ADJ, a blank space, and a hyphen (NEW ADJ YORK, NEW YORK, NEW-YORK).

Limits

Some systems allow you to limit your keyword searches. You may be able to limit where the computer searches for your keywords (e.g. limit to the subject headings) or you may be able to limit by language, date of publication, or type or material.

Rules of Thumb

White Space

Primary text block (minus banner, title, headings, footers) should be no more than 55% of page.

Page size	Text size (square inches)
8½ x 11	51
5½ x 8½	26
3½ x 8½	17½

Line Width

1. Maximum 10 - 12 words, 60 - 70 characters
   Ideal 7 - 10 words, 55 - 60 characters

2. 1½ times the length of the lowercase alphabet (about 50 characters). Range: 25% narrower to 50% wider.

Font	Width	Range
9 pt Dutch Roman	2.25"	1.69" - 3.38"
10 pt Dutch Roman	2.55"	1.91" - 3.83"
12 pt Dutch Roman	3.06"	2.30" - 4.59"

3. Two times the point size, measured in picas.

Font	Width picas	Width inches	Range inches
9 pt Dutch Roman	18	3.00	2.25 - 4.5
10 pt Dutch Roman	20	3.33	2.50 - 5.0
12 pt Dutch Roman	24	4.00	3.00 - 6.0

4. Two columns: 18 - 22 picas = 3 - 3.67 inches

5. Three columns: 12 - 14 picas = 2 - 2.34 inches

Justification

Use full-justification with proportional fonts only.

Don't hyphenate more than 2 lines in a row.

Use left-justification in multi-column publications.

Typefaces

Select one serif typeface for text. Use a size between 9 points and 12 points.

Don't use more than two different typefaces in a single publication. Headings and sub-headings should all be in the same typeface as the text, a single contrasting typeface, or some combination of the two.

If you choose different typefaces for text and headings, choose distinctly different ones.

You may not need a different typeface for headings.

Finding
BOOK REVIEWS

**Problem
Solver 2**

INTRODUCTION

Book reviews are published in periodicals, usually shortly after the book being reviewed has been published. Reviews generally provide enough information about a book to enable a reader to decide whether or not to read it. Reviews may be descriptive or critical. They may include a summary of the book, discuss its style, compare it with other books on the same subject, or provide background information about the author. Reviews show the reactions to a book at the time it was published, and can be an important source of evaluation, allowing you to compare your opinion with those of various critics.

Remember that a book review records one individual's impression of a particular book, and that impression may be biased in some way. Consequently, one should:

1. Consult several reviews (if available) of the same book in order to obtain a more balanced assessment of the book.
2. Note the author of the review and, if desired, look for information about the reviewer.
3. Look to see if the periodical in which the review appears might have a built-in bias. What are the titles of the articles? Who publishes the periodical?

PRELIMINARY STEPS

In order to locate a book review you should know the:
1. author's name
2. title of the book
3. year in which the book was *first* published.

If you lack any of this information, consult Mondo, the title page and verso of the book, or ask a Reference Librarian for assistance.

IDENTIFYING REVIEWS

Book review indexes can be used to identify which periodicals published reviews of a particular book. These indexes are shelved with the other periodical indexes and abstracting services in Case Library. Book review indexes typically are arranged alphabetically by author's name, and some also have a title index. Most are published monthly and cumulate annually. That is why year of publication is so important. Begin your search in the volume for the first date of publication, and check the following year or two. There often are delays in reviews appearing in the index.

Other periodical indexes may cover book reviews, either in a special section or as part of the regular arrangement. They are particularly useful for finding reviews in scholarly journals. Reviews in scholarly journals may appear as many as 5 years after the publication of the book.

BOOK REVIEW INDEXES

Book Review Index. Detroit: Gale Research, 1965-- .
       LIB HAS 1965--
       LOCATION Case Indexes
                Online (make appointment at Reference Desk)
  CALL NUMBER Z1035 .A1 B6

Indexes reviewing journals, general interest magazines, and scholarly journals. Arranged alphabetically by author of book being reviewed. Title index refers you to author. Published bi-monthly; cumulated annually.

Book Review Digest. New York: H.W. Wilson, 1905-- .
       LIB HAS vol. 1 (1905)--
       LOCATION Case Indexes
  CALL NUMBER Z1219 .C96

Indexes and excerpts reviews of books written in English and published in the U.S. and Canada. Arranged alphabetically by author; subject and title indexes. Published bi-monthly; cumulated annually.

Index to Book Reviews in the Humanities. Williamston, MI: Phillip Thomson, 1960-- .
       LIB HAS vol. 1 (1960)--
       LOCATION Case Indexes
  CALL NUMBER AI3 .I45

Indexes reviews of books about language and literature, history, philosophy, the arts, classics, travel, folklore, sports and recreation. Arranged alphabetically by author. Published annually.

OTHER INDEXES WITH BOOK REVIEWS

Readers' Guide to Periodical Literature. New York: H.W. Wilson, 1905-
       LIB HAS 1890/99--
       LOCATION Case Indexes
                Network terminals (Firstsearch, 1983--)
  CALL NUMBER AI3 .R48

Separate book review section begins in volume 36, 1976/77.

Newspaper Abstracts. Ann Arbor, MI: University Microfilms International, 1985-- .
       LIB HAS 1985--
       LOCATION Case Catalog Area (CD-ROM)
                Online (make appointment at Reference Desk)

Search last name of author or title of book. Combine with ty(review).

New York Times Index. New York: New York Times, 1851-- .
       LIB HAS 1851--
       LOCATION Case Indexes
  CALL NUMBER AI21 .N44

Use subject heading **Book Reviews.**

THE COLGATE UNIVERSITY LIBRARIES   EVERETT NEEDHAM CASE LIBRARY   GEORGE R. COOLEY LIBRARY

Internet
Guide
Number 2

Search
Basics

The ability to access the Internet opens up an almost overwhelming number of information resources to members of the Colgate community. Campus wide information systems, Electronic bulletin boards, bibliographic, numeric and full text databases, and library catalogs are just some of the possibilities. This series of library publications will concentrate on library catalogs and full text and bibliographic databases.

This handout is designed to cover some of the things you should know before you start searching an unfamiliar database, whether it be a library catalog or other bibliographic database.

How to Select a Catalog or Database
While there are many guides to the Internet available, we recommend beginning with HYTELNET, a program mounted on our VAX. See *Searching HYTELNET* (Internet Guide 1) for a description of and help with this program.

Connecting and Exiting
Use HYTELNET to connect to a catalog or database or, if you know the domain name or the IP address of the institution you wish to contact, you can connect directly by typing TELNET followed by the name or address.

Many catalogs will ask what kind of terminal you are using. Unless you know that you are using a different terminal, answer VT100.

If the directions tell you to exit a catalog by using the Telnet escape key, or if your computer locks-up, try one of the following:
    <Ctrl>-<Shift> 6, q
    <Ctrl>-], q
If none of the above works, you can always turn off your computer and try again.

Scope of the Catalog/Database
Many libraries do not have their entire holdings on their online catalogs. Older materials, special collections, and certain kinds of materials may not be cataloged and are not accessible over the Internet. For libraries with large collections, you will find that online catalogs frequently include materials *cataloged* from the mid 1970's to the present.

Some libraries make available over the Internet more than their library catalog. On the first screen may be listed various databases that you may connect to, including in some instances, popular bibliographic databases like *Art Index* or *General Science Index*. The search commands for these additional databases may be the same as for the library catalog, or they may be different for each database.

THE COLGATE UNIVERSITY LIBRARIES   EVERETT NEEDHAM CASE LIBRARY

Internet
Guide
Number 2

Search
Basics

Introduction
The ability to access the Internet opens up an almost overwhelming number of information resources to members of the Colgate community. Campus wide information systems; electronic bulletin boards; bibliographic, numeric, and full text databases; and library catalogs are just some of the possibilities.

This handout is designed to cover some of the things you should know before you start searching an unfamiliar database, whether it is a library catalog or other bibliographic database.

How to Select a Catalog or Database
HYTELNET, a program mounted on our VAX, lists a variety of information sites, including library catalogs and databases. HYTELNET gives directions for logging into those sites, and makes the initial connection to the computer at the site. See *Searching HYTELNET* (Internet Guide 1) for help with this program.

If you need advice on choosing a library catalog, inquire at the Reference Desks. We have sources that list which libraries have good collections in which subject ares.

Connecting and Exiting
Use HYTELNET to connect to a catalog or database or, if you know the domain name or the IP address of the institution you wish to contact, you can connect directly by typing TELNET followed by the name or address.

Many catalogs will ask what kind of terminal you are using. Unless you know that you are using a different terminal, answer VT100.

It is important to exit and disconnect from the database you are searching. Disconnecting improperly can cause problems for the host institution. If the directions tell you to exit a catalog by using the Telnet escape key, hold down, all at once, the <Ctrl> <Shift> and 6 keys, release, type q.

Scope of the Catalog/Database
Many libraries do not have their entire holdings in their online catalogs. Older materials, and certain kinds of materials such as archives, journals, or sound recordings may not be in the online catalog. For libraries with large collections, you will find that online catalogs frequently include materials **cataloged** from the mid 1970's to the present.

Some libraries make available over the Internet more than their library catalog. On the first screen may be listed various databases that you may connect to, including in some instances, popular bibliographic databases like *Art Index* or *General Science Index*. The search commands for these additional databases may be the same as for the library catalog, or they may be different for each database. Many libraries limit use of some databases to their own users.

Help
Most systems offer online help. The two most common ways to get help online are to type HELP <Enter> or EXPLAIN <Enter>. Librarians can help you with the commands for different catalogs or databases, and there are help sheets in the libraries and the Computer Center.

Correcting Typing Errors
Different systems allow you to correct errors in different ways. If the <Backspace> key doesn't work, position the cursor with the arrow keys and type over the error, using the space bar for blanks.

Printing
The print function of the host database will not work. Your communications software may have the ability to capture your entire search. If not, use the <Print Screen> key on your keyboard to print each screen, one at a time.
The database may allow you to download your results to disk, which you can then print using your word processor or statistical package.

THE COLGATE UNIVERSITY LIBRARIES   EVERETT NEEDHAM CASE LIBRARY

THE COLGATE UNIVERSITY LIBRARIES
SERVICES & POLICIES 7

EVERETT NEEDHAM CASE LIBRARY

GEORGE R. COOLEY LIBRARY

Library Users' Bill of Rights

As users of Case and Cooley Libraries, you are entitled to certain expectations about the use of your libraries:

1. Library users have the right to an environment that is quiet enough for reading and study; one that is free of boisterous or disruptive activity.

2. Library users have the right to have access to all library materials and to have them recalled as regulations allow.

3. Library users have the right to surroundings free of food, beverages, and their resulting problems.

Know your rights. Questions? Ask a librarian.

Asking for HELP

Problem Solver 3

The reference librarians at Case and Cooley Libraries are available to help you find the information you need. You will help us to help you if you keep the following in mind:

What do you want first: the good news, or the bad news?

The good news is that reference librarians can help you to do better work. The bad news is that research is work, and quality research is time consuming work. Start your research early. We can not make any of the work disappear.

The Library helps those who help themselves.

One of your jobs as a student is to become as self sufficient a learner as you are able. When you know how to do something yourself, go ahead and do it. For example, if you are looking for a specific title in the libraries' collections, try Mondo before asking a reference librarian if we own it. We don't have the collection completely memorized--yet!

There are no stupid questions.

The mission of the University and the libraries is to help students learn what they don't know. If you need to know something related to the library or about finding information, ask a reference librarian. Don't be embarrassed to ask "simple" questions. Simple questions are not always as simple as they seem.

Ask for what you need, not where you think you'll find what you need.

"I need articles about restoration and preservation of stained glass, and my professor says to use scholarly journals" is better than "Where's the *Readers' Guide*?" Don't limit yourself to just the sources that you already know. We may be able to show you new sources that will help you do better work, often in less time.

If you plan to be here a while, learn the language.

Libraries have a language all their own. There's a difference between a book and a periodical article, and between a biography and a bibliography. Knowing the differences can affect your success as a student. If you don't know what a term means, ask. Remember, there are no stupid questions. Try to explain fully and clearly what information you need.

The best answer to a question is often another question.

When you ask a question, we will often ask you a question right back. We're not being nosy. We're trying to get a better idea of what you need, so that we can help you.

If you don't know how you got here, you're lost.

Keep a record of where you have searched and what subject headings, keywords, authors, and titles you've used. If you do, we can suggest changes in your search strategy or different sources that you might use.

What's personal is personal, even when you need to share it.

Librarians have a code of ethics that guarantees your right to confidentiality and your right to seek information without being subjected to judgment. Don't worry about asking potentially embarrassing questions, or questions you think might expose you to the judgment of others. If you feel that you need to speak with a reference librarian in a more private forum than at the reference desk, make an appointment to see one of us.

Your needs are fully--and only--as important as everyone else's.

When a reference librarian is working with you, others should be expected not to interrupt. When a reference librarian is working with another patron, please don't interrupt (unless there's fire or blood involved). You affirm your own rights and those of others by waiting until the librarian is available to help you.

There's a time and a place for everything.

While a restaurant may be open into the wee hours, the dinner menu may be unavailable hours before the doors close. A similar principle applies to many of the library services you may need, including reference help. Reference librarians are available many hours a week, but not every hour that the libraries are open. Hours are posted at the reference desk and at the front door. The place to ask for reference help is at the reference desk. If there's no one at the desk when scheduled, the librarian on duty is helping someone. Patience! The librarian will return to the desk. Please don't ask for reference help from circulation staff or a passing librarian.

THE COLGATE UNIVERSITY LIBRARIES   EVERETT NEEDHAM CASE LIBRARY   GEORGE R. COOLEY LIBRARY

— MARY JANE WALSH —

Word Perfect Kerning Test

Unkerned:
WordPerfect AVAILABLE Available Kerning available wonderful you Wonderful You

Kerned:
WordPerfect AVAILABLE Available Kerning available wonderful you Wonderful You

Left-Justified

Theory says that left-justified text (i.e. ragged-right text) is easier to read than fully-justified text. The reason why? In left-justified text there is an equal amount of space between all words in the text. In fully-justified text, the amount of space between each letter or between individual words is adjusted to make each line of text completely fill the line of the page. This can create unintentional "rivers" of white space that snake through the text, which is very distracting. Hyphenation can be used to close-up some of that excess white space, but it must be used very carefully. The general rule of thumb is that no more than two lines in a row should be hyphenated.

Readers, however, defy the theories. Studies of reader preferences have shown that they would rather read fully-justified text than left-justified text. Do we all long for the orderly look of an even right-hand margin?

Fully-Justified

Proportional font

Theory says that left-justified text (i.e. ragged-right text) is easier to read than fully-justified text. The reason why? In left-justified text there is an equal amount of space between all words in the text. In fully-justified text, the amount of space between each letter or between individual words is adjusted to make each line of text completely fill the line of the page. This can create unintentional "rivers" of white space that snake through the text, which is very distracting. Hyphenation can be used to close-up some of that excess white space, but it must be used very carefully. The general rule of thumb is that no more than two lines in a row should be hyphenated.

Readers, however, defy the theories. Studies of reader preferences have shown that they would rather read fully-justified text than left-justified text. Do we all long for the orderly look of an even right-hand margin?

Monospaced font

Theory says that left-justified text (i.e. ragged-right text) is easier to read than fully-justified text. The reason why? In left-justified text there is an equal amount of space between all words in the text. In fully-justified text, the amount of space between each letter or between individual words is adjusted to make each line of text completely fill the line of the page. This can create unintentional "rivers" of white space that snake through the text, which is very distracting. Hyphenation can be used to close-up some of that excess white space, but it must be used very carefully. The general rule of thumb is that no more than two lines in a row should be hyphenated.

Readers, however, defy the theories. Studies of reader preferences have shown that they would rather read fully-justified text than left-justified text. Do we all long for the orderly look of an even right-hand margin?

REMOTE ACCESS OPAC SEARCHING

Cheryl Blackwell

Albion College is a small liberal arts college with about 1,600 students. The Albion College library installed an integrated Innovative Interfaces OPAC in August 1989. Innovative is a powerful yet very user-friendly system. We are also fortunate to have an extremely capable technical services staff. Our database is second to none. We own approximately 275,000 volumes. These facts—excellent system, clean database, and a relatively small number of holdings—help make our OPAC easy to use. Because our OPAC is so easy to use, I have often wondered how effectively our students search other OPACs. Can they transfer what they know about our system to another?

I have taught a 1/2-credit library research methods course at Albion College for the past five years. The last five weeks of this 15-week course are devoted to the electronic library (i.e., online catalogs, CD-ROM, Boolean searching, databases). In November 1992, the Albion College library gained limited dial-up access to Internet—limited in that access is available only through the head of public services' PC and our access to Internet does not include e-mail or FTP. I felt it was essential to provide my students with some hands-on Internet experience. Due to the limited options, I decided to have them search the OPACs of several colleges and universities via Internet.

Shortly after we gained access to Internet, two things happened. First, the Fall 1992 issue of *LOEX News* arrived (with a call for conference abstracts). Second, the college began working on an Internet grant proposal. Since I had to design a lecture and assignment

on remote OPAC searching for my class, I decided to submit an abstract proposal based on that assignment to LOEX. I also recognized that I could begin preparing some Internet training for when we have campuswide access to Internet. Thus, the assignment I am going to discuss with you today served many purposes.

My students' assignment consisted of three components. First, each student had to schedule a 90-minute block of time so that they could perform a half dozen or so carefully selected searches apiece on four different OPAC systems. They were instructed to take notes so that they could recall searches that gave them trouble, features they liked or disliked, and so on.

The second component of the assignment required each student to present a 5-minute instruction session based on some aspect of his or her OPAC search. The presentation was touted as an opportunity to "teach the stuff you think should be taught, the way you think it should be taught." Handouts earned extra points.

The last component was a brief (1- to 2-page) summary/review of the assignment. This served as an opportunity for them to reflect upon what they learned. The summary was to include the objectives of their presentations (in case I was not certain what they were talking about) and any difficulties they encountered while working on their presentations. Finally, I asked them to list and comment on the difficulties they had during their OPAC search sessions.

The way I saw it in January, when I submitted my abstract to LOEX, the assignment offered many benefits:

1. My students were introduced to Internet.

Blackwell is B.I./reference librarian at Stockwell-Mudd Libraries, Albion College Library, Albion, Michigan.

2. My students played an active role in educating each other. They were responsible for schoolin' their classmates.

3. I got to evaluate my OPAC instruction. Was my instruction transferable? Were my students able to use other systems effectively?

4. I gained insight into how my students *really* searched OPACs. What aspect of remote OPAC searching was most difficult for them? Why was it difficult?

5. With a bit of luck, I could use some of their ideas, handouts, and experiences for future OPAC searching instruction.

6. My students got to experience how difficult my job is!

7. I gained some valuable experience as a presenter at a LOEX conference.

Selecting which OPACs to use was time consuming. I spent more time than I care to remember searching various systems at numerous colleges and universities. I finally settled on four installations. The NOTIS OPAC was located at a large state university, GEAC was located at a small liberal arts college, Dynix was located at a mid-sized university, and an Innovative Interfaces installation was located at a large state institution. Even though we already have an Innovative OPAC, I wanted to know if my students would have difficulties searching an installation with a larger database and multiple branch libraries.

Since I wanted to challenge my students but not overwhelm them, devising "good" searches was even more labor intensive than selecting OPACs had been. I settled on five questions for each system. I have included a copy of the questions for each OPAC at the end of this article (see student work sheets, p.163-164). Rather than devise different questions for each system, I used the same questions or the same types of questions for each system. I felt this would make it easier for students to make comparisons between the systems. I did not include long involved searches that would involve multiple Boolean, truncation, or limiting.

Eight students completed the assignment. The class was a mixture of males and females representative of upper- and lower-class divisions. Since the students were searching Internet through a dial-up connection on a PC, I was present for each student's search session. We used a gopher at the University of Michigan to get to a classified menu listing of library OPACs. To save time, I logged the students on and off the OPACs.

The average student search session was 90 minutes. They all searched the OPACs in the same order: Innovative, NOTIS, Dynix, GEAC. The systems, in my opinion, went from the easiest to the hardest. Since the questions for each system were so similar, I will only discuss the questions and the systems that gave my students the most trouble.

Most students felt comfortable with the Innovative OPAC and started keying away. The OPAC's author and authority control made questions 1-3 very easy to search. Just about every student faltered on question 4: "Find the May 7th 1992 issue of *Nature*." With the exception of one student, they all wanted to look in *Expanded Academic Index*. *Expanded Academic Index* is loaded on our OPAC as a file and is available as a main menu option. Even after I explained that they were looking for the location of the journal *Nature* and that *Expanded Academic Index* was *not* available on this particular OPAC, some of them were still confused.

On the NOTIS OPAC, things started heating up right away. The system's authority control for the first question about Tom Peters presented them with two authors. Next, their search under the author Samuel Clemens did not turn up the title *A Connecticut Yankee in King Arthur's Court*. NOTIS installations please note that *all* of the students missed the entry at the top of the Samuel Clemens listing that instructed them to also look under Mark Twain. But, no sweat, since most of them just did a title search. Every student received the message that no titles matched his or her request. After reading the help screen that offered suggestions on why their searches had failed, they discovered why they came up empty-handed—no initial articles can be used in NOTIS title searches. Our Innovative system is forgiving and skips over initial articles.

Also, the multiple holdings on the journal *Nature* caused some concern but turned out to be nothing they couldn't handle. In regard to question 5, after their title search for the play *Funeral Games* failed, they were a bit slow, but eventually performed a keyword search.

The students' biggest search headaches were with the Dynix and GEAC systems. Neither of these systems had author or, more importantly, subject authority control. For the most part, they were able to circumvent this shortcoming by performing term word searches in Dynix and Boolean searches in GEAC. From their keyword searches they were able to search relevant records and ascertain which LCSH to use. They adapted quite well to this kind of keyword searching. Dynix's plethora of options was confusing to most of the students. They also disliked having to scroll through two or three screens in some instances of information to get call numbers.

I saved the worst for last. As I mentioned earlier, the GEAC installation did not have authority control. It also did not list a keyword menu option. Instead, the GEAC Boolean menu option does both Boolean and keyword searches in the author, title, and subject fields—effective, but not very straightforward. The lack of authority control was trouble. The subject search for Samuel Clemens yielded 12 entries. It even listed a source of criticism on *The Adventures of Huckleberry Finn*. Unfortunately, it did not include a "see also" reference to Mark Twain. The students were annoyed when I performed a subject search under "Mark Twain" that yielded over 100 titles, four of which specifically discussed *The Adventures of Huckleberry Finn*. "Why didn't the system tell me to look there?!" they exclaimed.

Question 6 in GEAC imparted two pieces of knowledge. First, some libraries have *not* listed out the titles of plays, short stories, and so on in anthologies. This can limit the usefulness of keyword searching. For example, a keyword search for the short story "Bernice Bobs Her Hair" yielded no hits. However, from their searches in other OPACs my students knew that "Bernice Bobs Her Hair" was located in the book *Flappers and Philosophers*. A title search showed that the GEAC library did indeed own a copy of *Flappers and Philosophers*, but that the short stories had *not* been listed in the bibliographic record. This question provided a wonderful example of how remote OPACs can help one find information in one's own OPAC.

STUDENT PRESENTATIONS AND REVIEWS

As I expected, some presentations were better than others. I was disappointed that only two students opted to use handouts. One set of handouts addressed Boolean searching and was not very good while the other set of handouts was fun, but not particularly useful. The students took two approaches to their presentations. The majority of the class briefly discussed the strengths and weaknesses of each system. The second group took a broader approach and addressed OPAC searching in general. If I had to list the theme that was addressed most frequently in these presentations it would be the similarities of the systems. Several presentations specifically stated that the similarities in the systems far outweighed the differences:

> In my presentation I just want to high-
> light some helpful hints, or difficulties I
> came across in my searching. Also, I wanted

to list some things that are universal to all systems.

> ...mostly, the idea is if you can under-
> stand one system you can understand others.

In many instances, they felt it was just a matter of deciphering the language, the menus. As one student phrased it: "The most difficult aspect of searching was understanding the particular lingo for each system. Sometimes the same search is called something different on another system. For example, how do I get more bibliographic information— FUL, MORE, COMPLETE etc.?"

Most students also took the stance that it all makes sense. There is nothing magical or evil about OPACs or OPAC searching. As a matter of fact, the underlying theme of two presentations was common sense. One student's summary/review stated:

> My experience with searching remote
> library catalogs was definitely a learning one.
> If I had to sum up what I learned in one
> sentence it would be something like this: I
> learned to be patient; not all catalogs are
> created equal and some take longer to figure
> out. You have to experiment to figure things
> out, think logically, and read the screens
> carefully. Well, I guess that would be more
> than one sentence, but the important concepts
> are contained.

Many of the students' comments and suggestions were predictable. They liked systems that offered help screens (i.e., authority control) and had clearly marked and defined menu options. Some statements, however, caught me completely off guard, such as:

> One must look at the rewards of doing
> a good search (i.e., a good paper, etc.).

> I really preferred systems that gave lots
> of bibliographic information.

Was the assignment successful? Like many library assignments, some aspects were more successful and worthwhile than others. Since I was present during their searches, I noted many of the students' comments and frustrations. It seems that the most straightforward way to present my observations is to list point-by-point what I had hoped to accomplish and then briefly discuss what actually occurred.

BENEFITS

1. My students are introduced to the world of Internet—While hardly an ideal Internet experience, considering the limitations, we did all right.

2. My students play an active role in educating each other. They become responsible for schooling their classmates—Although the students' presentations were not bad, I had hoped they would be more concerned with the task of educating their classmates. Most of the presentations were grade-driven. I don't think anyone felt compelled to provide a meaningful and thoughtful learning experience for the class. On the bright side, several did mention that they had discussed the online search component and their presentations with classmates.

3. I get to evaluate my OPAC instruction. Was it transferable? Were my students able to use other OPACs effectively—I think my class OPAC instruction was adequate, but by no means perfect. For the most part the students were able to use other OPACs effectively. But, of course, they had a reference librarian leaning over their shoulders to answer their questions. As I mentioned earlier, the students were confused by questions that asked them to locate specific issues of journals. Everyone wanted to look in *Expanded Academic Index* (which is loaded as a file on our OPAC). I don't have a clue what they planned to do once they found a citation from the 7 May 1992 issue of *Nature*.

Considering that we spent a fair amount of time in class discussing keyword searching, initially they were slow to use keyword searching to find records and get subject headings. However, they were very good at using subject headings (tracings) to expand and focus searches. They were also willing to try Boolean searches and usually in appropriate types of searches!

4. I gained insight into how my students *really* searched OPACs. What aspect of remote access searching was most difficult for them? Why was it difficult?—I was surprised at how many of the students expressed extreme irritation at rather minor inconveniences. I tend to focus on broader conceptual aspects when I teach, but my class was very concerned with the mechanics of searching. They were especially critical of systems that required a lot of commands and key strokes to get at the information they needed. They were not impressed with systems that forced them to do "extra work." For example, all eight students complained about having to press **RETURN** after most commands in every system except Innovative.

I felt the biggest disadvantage to NOTIS was the need to press the RETURN button every time.

...the system [Innovative's subject authority controls] gives you options to choose from so you don't have to retype what you want.

Their complaint regarding the inability on most systems to backspace and correct typos was, given their poor typing skills, well deserved. However, even after I explained that they would be able to backspace if they were searching the OPAC at the installation's library, they were not moved. They were concerned with the here-and-now, and presently there was no backspacing!

Several other observations are worth mentioning. Disbelief and shock were voiced regarding the default bibliographic display in several OPACs. "Subject headings aren't displayed for heaven's sake!!!" The majority felt it was inconvenient to have to request important bibliographic information through yet another command. The system that requested a **SEND** to execute a search threw every student for a loop! Several students actually typed the word s-e-n-d. Systems that didn't specifically list and define keyword searching in the menu also caused a bit of panic. Students were very literal. It was as though all our discussions on synonyms could not apply to other aspects of the OPAC.

Most of my students were willing and able to learn from their mistakes—perhaps too willing. If something "worked," they were eager to try it again. But in several instances, I don't think they could explain why it worked. There was a lot of reaction and not much thinking. The students were not afraid of the computer. They were willing to experiment.

Knowing the capabilities of the system was very important. To find out the capabilities you need to experiment and get a feel for the system.

5. With luck, I will be able to use some of their ideas, handouts, and so on for future OPAC searching instruction—Unfortunately, I will not be able to use any of the presentations as complete segments in an introductory Internet remote OPAC searching lecture. Most of the presentations assumed that the audience was very familiar with OPAC searching. However, many of the narrative passages and quotes that I've used throughout my LOEX presentation, relate important ideas and observations from my students. Many of these student observations are ideal BI commentary. In past instruction sessions I have noticed that students'

interest is peaked by comments, questions, observations, and so on derived from other students.

6. My students get to experience how difficult my job is—My students were not interested in discovering how trying teaching can be. In a classic example of not being able to see the forest for the trees, one benefit that I did not list in my LOEX abstract was that the OPAC searching allowed the students to apply what they had been learning in class in a new hands-on environment. Nearly every student commented that this aspect of the assignment was particularly helpful. The assignment was also good at showing them why libraries do things the way they do. They were able to see why authority control, additional subject headings, and so on are useful. They were amazed to learn that a lot of "that stuff" actually makes sense!

In regards to my time and energy, the assignment was extremely demanding. Since we should have campus access to Internet in Spring 1994, I plan on using the search component of the assignment as an in-class exercise. That way, the students will be able to help each other and I won't burn. I also believe that, with some modifications, I should be able to use the search component of the assignment in generic Internet training sessions.

STUDENT WORK SHEETS
QUESTIONS USED FOR EACH
ONLINE CATALOG SYSTEM

INNOVATIVE

1. What is the call number of the book written by Tom Peters in 1984 or 1985? It has something to with business.

2. How many books ABOUT Samuel Clemens does the library own? Find a title of literary criticism that discusses *The Adventures of Huckleberry Finn*.

3. Find some books on the subject "Latinos." What are some other subjects that might list material on this topic?

4. Find the May 7th 1992 issue of *Nature*.

5. There is a new(er) book that discusses the cultural influences of Elvis Presley. Does the library own this book?

NOTIS

1. What is the call number of the book written by Tom Peters in 1984 or 1985? It has something to with business.

2. How many books BY Samuel Clemens does the library own? How many copies of his novel *A Connecticut Yankee in King Arthur's Court* does the library own?

3. How many titles on the subject "movies" does the library own? What other subjects might also have information on this topic?

4. Locate the November 1992 issue of *Nature*.

5. Find a copy of the play *Funeral Games*. It was written in the 1970s by a famous British homosexual playwright. Where is it located?

DYNIX

1. What is the call number of the book written by Tom Peters in 1984 or 1985? It has something to with business.

2. How many books ABOUT Samuel Clemens does the library own? Find a title of literary criticism that discusses *The Adventures of Huckleberry Finn*.

3. The topic of your history paper is the Chicano movement. What is the easiest way to find information on this subject?

4. Does the library carry the title *Science News*? Where is it located?

5. Find a copy of the short story "Bernice Bobs Her Hair."

GEAC

1. What is the call number of the book written by Tom Peters in 1984 or 1985? It has something to with business.

2. How many books ABOUT Samuel Clemens does the library own? Find a title of literary criticism that discusses *The Adventures of Huckleberry Finn*.

3. Find some books on the subject "Latinos." What are some other subjects that might list material on this topic?

4. Find the December 1992 issue of *Nature*.

5. Find a copy of the short story "Bernice Bobs Her Hair."

LIBRARY INSTRUCTION IN THE CARTHAGE COLLEGE HERITAGE STUDIES PROGRAM

Eugene A. Engeldinger, Brent McClintock, and Dennis L. Unterholzner

COURSE-INTEGRATED LIBRARY INSTRUCTION AT CARTHAGE COLLEGE

Eugene A. Engeldinger

The Heritage Program and Course-Integrated Instruction at Carthage College: An Introduction

I would like to discuss two aspects of BI at Carthage in order to set the stage for my two colleagues, Dennis and Brent, who will address the details of our instructional program. They will describe what occurs in the classroom and what effect it has on the quality of student assignments.

In order for you to have a better sense of what the Carthage library instruction program entails, first let me say a few words about two basic elements, the Heritage program itself and a definition of "course-integrated instruction" as we see it.

WHAT IS HERITAGE?

The Heritage program is a four-course sequence required of all Carthage students and taken during the freshman and sophomore years. Four credits are earned

Engeldinger is vice president for academic information services, *McClintock* is assistant professor of economics, and *Unterholzner* is head of public services, Ruthrauff Library, Carthage College, Kenosha, Wisconsin.

each term. The program is interdisciplinary, with a concern for learning content and process, an appreciation for cultural differences and the improvement of communication skills. There is an emphasis on our American heritage, which includes contributions not only from Europe and the West but also from Asia, Africa, the Americas, and the rest of the world. All have helped make America what it is today.

What are students expected to learn? Besides insights into the various readings, they should improve their oral and written communication skills, critical thinking skills, and their information finding or research skills.

What are the readings like? Heritage I and II "The Western Experience" extends throughout both terms of the freshman year and includes work with Shakespeare's *Tempest*, Shelley's *Frankenstein*, Beethoven's *Ninth Symphony*, selections from the Bible, Locke, Mill, Conrad's *Heart of Darkness*, Chinua Achebe's *Things Fall Apart*, Marx, Freud, and many, many other creative and thoughtful works.

Heritage III is devoted to intercultural studies with Japan as the subject. Four books are used to investigate various aspects of Japanese life, culture, history, and society with the unavoidable comparisons and contrasts with American life and customs.

Heritage IV is devoted to American cultures, using four books to show different aspects of the "American experience." These readings act as springboards to reflection, discussion, research, and writing about what it is to be an American. During the current year they are:

- Richard Rodriguez, *Hunger of Memory*;

- Zora Hurston, *Their Eyes Were Watching God*;

- Timothy O'Brien, *The Things They Carried*; and

- Louise Erdrich, *Love Medicine*.

In order to show better what this has to do with the library, I will read what the program description says about library research. The booklet is addressed to the Heritage students and says in part:

LIBRARY LITERACY: From the first unit of Heritage I, all students will begin learning and demonstrating their ability to find and incorporate basic information into their writing and speaking. By the time students reach Heritage IV, they will be expected to have learned and demonstrated repeatedly in various contexts all the skills necessary to generate a well-researched paper.

In order to deepen your cultural literacies and stimulate your curiosity about basic culture, you will be expected to learn and practice some strategies for gathering and evaluating information. Some of your writing and speaking assignments will require you to locate, examine, and incorporate information from both print and nonprint sources beyond course texts. You will be (re-) introduced to the sources (sic) of Ruthrauff Library and will be expected to learn how to use them appropriately.

In different ways, most of your courses at Carthage might be expected to cultivate your competence, confidence, and comfort with libraries.[1]

From this it is clear that the Heritage program has as one of its stated purposes the fostering of library research skills.

WHAT IS COURSE-INTEGRATED INSTRUCTION?

The second idea I should discuss is the term "course-integrated" instruction. Just what does this mean? We all know and use the term, but do we all define it the same way?

When defining the term "course-integrated" instruction, it is easier sometimes to begin with the notion of course-related instruction. With course-related instruction, the classroom instructor and the BI librarian are interested in introducing students to library research in a particular discipline. The library instruction may or may not be tied to a particular assignment; and even

if it is, the instruction may or may not occur at a time in the term when students need it most. Typical of this type of instruction might be that for the history professor who wants the class introduced to the most important history sources because the students will be doing a project such as a speech, term paper, panel discussion, or other report later in the term. In this scenario the sources included in the instruction will be history-related but not necessarily related to the specific topics.

On the other hand, course-integrated instruction implies that the professor has specifically and intentionally incorporated the library activity as a significant feature in the course—and usually has planned it in conjunction with the librarian, who assists students in completing the library research assignment.

In course-integrated instruction the library element is an integral part of the assignment but is secondary to the course assignment. The library assignment may have value in its own right but it is not necessarily presented in that way. It is presented as a means to an end (i.e., a course project) that would be less satisfactory without the integrated instruction. Implicit also is the notion that the information-searching strategies can be used in other similar situations, that the strategies are not of value only in completing the assignment at hand.

How does this work in actual practice? That is the truly interesting part and I will leave it to Dennis and Brent to discuss their experiences with library instruction at Carthage and to provide you with their insights.

NOTE

1. *Heritage Studies Program for 1992-1993* (Kenosha, WI: Carthage College, 1992), 8.

COURSE-INTEGRATED BIBLIOGRAPHIC
INSTRUCTION IN ECONOMIC AND HERITAGE
STUDIES: A TEACHING PROFESSOR'S
PERSPECTIVE

Brent McClintock

INTRODUCTION

The relationship between librarians and teaching faculty on many university campuses can be an uneasy one. On the one hand, many professors, perhaps reflecting some of their own inexperience with libraries in their student days, tend to point their students in the general direction of the college library and say, "Go to it." On the other hand, some librarians may act as if the library is some inner sanctum to which only those suitably initiated in the library sciences may be admitted. As a consequence of such attitudes, librarians may face periodic onslaughts of student researchers who have only dim ideas of their assignments and who are ill-equipped to undertake library searches for relevant information. Quite naturally, this set of circumstances may lead to little progress in the overall learning process, create tension between library and teaching faculty, and leave students unconvinced that library research is an effective way to improve their knowledge.

The library and research experience need not produce these outcomes. One way to improve the experience is to engage in course-integrated bibliographic instruction (BI), a method that has been applied across the curriculum at Carthage College. The process of BI at Carthage may be illustrated by using case studies from the Heritage Studies program and economic courses. Particular attention in the following discussion is placed on the objectives, procedures, results, and evaluation of course-integrated BI *from the perspective of a teaching professor*.

INTEGRATING BI WITH THE CLASSROOM EXPERIENCE

There are two types of objectives that teaching faculty might wish to achieve when introducing BI into the learning experience. First, students should develop transferrable skills in searching for information that they may use elsewhere in their studies and in later lives. Examples of these skills might include learning how to use a catalog, where to look for certain types of information, how to define subject headings, and how to conduct an efficient computer search using key terms.

The second category of goals are specific to the course or discipline. For example, how can improved knowledge of an issue be attained by an efficient information search and how does an economist, historian, or biologist use research to practice his or her craft or discipline? Thus, specific objectives should not only allow the student to complete class assignments but also provide a sense of the process by which economists, for instance, work through and solve economic problems.

THE PROCESS OF COURSE INTEGRATION

The first step in integrating BI into a class occurs *before* the term begins with a meeting between library and teaching faculty to discuss the need for instruction in a particular course. Issues to be discussed may include how BI will help achieve course objectives, the class assignments to be set, and library exercises that would help complete these assignments.

The professor in introducing the course to students aims to clearly set out the role of research in the learning process and its importance to overall success in the course. Prior to visiting the library, the class may carry out preparatory work, which could include selection of a topic, writing an abstract of a paper proposal, or reading a book for which reviews are to be found.

The next step is the class visit to the library or the librarian may visit the classroom. Students may receive a short introduction to search techniques and possible forms of information. The majority of library time is best allocated to student activities focused on "learning by doing." Follow-up, where appropriate, may involve student consultation with a reference librarian as and when needed, meeting with the instructor, or a further visit to the library for the whole class.

Finally, assessment of the bibliographic experience is conducted. This evaluation by the librarian, course instructor, and students allows improvements to be made the next time a similar library exercise is scheduled or the course is offered.

CASE STUDIES IN THE HERITAGE PROGRAM AND ECONOMICS

The process of integrating BI into courses may be given concrete illustration by discussing case studies in the Heritage Program and in economics at Carthage College. Two examples of BI in the third Heritage III (Non-Western Cultures) on Japan and one in intermediate macroeconomics are discussed here.

Heritage Studies

At the beginning of the Heritage III course, students are asked to prepare a cultural background report on Japan once they have received BI. The general objective is to expose students to the idea that they can expand their own limited knowledge on *any* issue by searching out the work of others. Specific objectives are to move students beyond the myths and stereotypes of Japan to some factual accounts of Japanese culture; to encourage teamwork (a practice valued by the Japanese) to allow students to directly experience the requirements of such work; and to integrate library research with classroom work and the use of computer software (e.g. PC Globe).

CARTHAGE COLLEGE
Heritage Studies Program

Heritage III: Non Western Cultures -- Japan

CULTURAL BACKGROUND REPORT ON JAPAN

Assignment:

In cooperation with your team, prepare a 3-4 page backgrounder on your assigned
_____ topic. This involves adopting a comparison and contrast of the topic as
it exists in Japan and the U.S.

Sources:

The library, PC Globe computer software, and other sources you may think of (eg. faculty &
students with particular knowledge).

Output & Deadline:

i)   A 3-4 page report from your team on your topic to be delivered to Brent
        McClintock's office (LH 206) by 12 midday, Friday, Sept. 18.

ii)   A brief personal evaluation of the work/contribution of other members of your
        group to completion of the assignment. **YOUR REPORT WILL BE KEPT
        CONFIDENTIAL.** Hand in during class on Monday Sept. 21.

Figure 1: Cultural Background Report on Japan

The class assignment requests each small group to research a topic (e.g., family gender issues in Japan) and to prepare a three- to four-page report, including a bibliography (see figure 1). The whole class visits the library for BI by a librarian. The course instructor attends and assists in answering questions on the assignment. Once reports are completed, their quality is evaluated by the class and instructor while individual contributions to teamwork are evaluated confidentially by group members.

Lastly, all reports on the various topics are combined into one volume which students use as a background resource during the term (including a short bibliography). This volume provides a starting point for sources for oral presentations and written work later in the term. The same research procedure may be used at the beginning of other courses as a way of rapidly moving students from a position of little to greater knowledge.

A second assignment in the Heritage III course involving BI is a book review of a course text, Yukio Mishima's *The Temple of the Golden Pavilion*. The general goal of the assignment is to introduce students to search procedures for reviews of books and films. More specific goals are to expose students to differing points of view of the same text and to compare these with their own assessment of the text. The assignment asks students to find two reviews of Mishima's book, which they are to summarize, analyze, and compare to their own reaction to the book each in a one- to two-page paper. Upon completion of these papers, the class discuss their results. Additional perspectives from outside the class may also be introduced.

Intermediate Macroeconomics

While BI is incorporated into the economics major at Carthage College from the freshman through the senior levels in such courses as principles of micro-economics, international economics, and the senior seminar, discussion here will be limited to the experience in intermediate macroeconomics. This course is usually taken during the junior or senior year.

The goal of integrating BI into this course at the general level is to make the connection between academic theory and the real world (i.e., to provide students with "hands-on" experience). Specific goals are to introduce students to the ways in which macro economists practice their craft (e.g. numerical competency and the debates over economic problems and their solution).

Classroom time is assigned to preparing students for the research process *prior* to the library visit (see figure 2). On their own and in small groups, they work on topic definition, linkages to other issues, possible sources of information, and search strategies. The library visit centers around an exercise, which engages students in the collection and analysis of data that track economic performance since 1945 (see figure 3). The same materials are used for a more detailed investigation of the most recent few years of economic activity later in the term, Additionally, students use the data collected through library research to complete quantitative, computer-based analysis on the business cycle (e.g., when was the last recession, how big a recession was it, and how does it compare to previous recessions?).

Evaluation of Course-Integrated BI

From an instructor's perspective, the results are positive. After such course-integrated BI, there is a greater realization among students that the difficulty facing them in solving most problems is usually not too little information, but too much. As Kenneth Boulding once put it, they come to appreciate that "knowledge is the orderly loss of information." Armed with this insight, students are highly motivated to find more efficient search strategies. BI also tends to generate much higher quality research papers—in terms of content, data use, bibliography, and sophistication of analysis. Students make better connections between economic theory and applications. They also become more aware of the debates within economics and there is a greater willingness by students to challenge "the

economics experts" *and the instructor*! Students are likely to be better prepared for the workplace and graduate school through a greater appreciation of the importance of teamwork, report writing skills, and exercising one's judgment. Perhaps most importantly, students display a greater *passion* for what they are doing.

Of course, the process may always be improved. For example, a second library visit during the term to reinforce the impact of the first may be desirable. Library and classroom work might be more closely integrated. Finally, the process reveals the need to update and add library resources related to classroom work.

Student assessment of BI tends to be mixed. Course evaluations over a two-year period specifically targeted at assessing BI reveal a 50-50 split over whether BI is useful or not. These evaluations tend to be closely dependent on particular assignments and the related BI. One word of caution is in order: I have found students tend to underreport the benefits they appear to gain from BI. For many students, it is somehow risking being called a nerd to admit that they actually gained something out of using the library or other information sources. As an evaluator of their written work and quality of class discussion, I see a significant improvement in the quality of the learning experience.

Some comments of students in intermediate macroeconomics are indicative of the process that many students undergo:

> Well, my first response is "library from hell!" It was a lot of research and hard work, but I feel a little more excited and interested in my topic and economics as a whole. I was actually typing with enjoyment and excitement. I never thought economics could be interesting and fun. I feel that I own the library, I know it so well.

> This paper took up a lot of time. There was a lot of research needed and I found there was too much information for some parts of my paper. Although it was a lot of work, I was pleased with my work and sense of accomplishment. I learned to enjoy reading the *Wall Street Journal*, along with other economic sources. The reason for this is once you understand how to read economic articles, they can be interesting.

> ... I feel I can intelligently discuss the recent, present, and future economy. The main problem that I had with this paper was the tremen-

CARTHAGE COLLEGE
Department of Economics

ECON 252: INTERMEDIATE MACROECONOMICS

ASSIGNMENT #1

TOPIC IDENTIFICATION AND PRELIMINARY RESEARCH

Instructions: Spend some time thinking through the issues raised in this assignment related to your topic (along with jotting down some thoughts) in order to prepare yourself for a productive in-class discussion with your group. Take notes on your group discussion. After class, write up the results of both your group and your own thinking on the topic. Hand-in a 1-2 page note so that I am able to gauge your current understanding and plans. Later, add this note to your economic journal.

1.   Define your topic, eg what is meant by the topic, _____

2.   What reasons led YOU to select this topic as opposed to other topics?

3.   Why is _____ a topic or issue that involves economic problems? How does _____ affect economic activity and the everyday lives of citizens?

4.   What do you know or speculate are some of the "cause and effect" relationships associated with the _____ topic?
      In other words, what factors are likely to cause your topic, _____ _____, to occur or are linked to it. What are some of the effects or outcomes in terms of the health of the economy?

5.   Based on your answers to questions 1-4 and other thoughts you may have, what kinds of information do you think it may be important to gather in your economic journal and for writing your paper? What types of data might you look for? How will you start looking for this information and where will you look for it?

Figure 2: ECON 252: Intermediate Macroeconomics

dous amount of information. It was difficult to organize it and tie it all together....It was a good, practical, and "learning experience" paper. After it was finally completed, I achieved a great feeling of accomplishment and relief. I smoked a big cigar to celebrate!

REFLECTIONS OF A PROFESSOR ON THE COURSE-INTEGRATED APPROACH TO BI

The following observations are offered as suggestions to librarians, from a teaching professor's perspective, as to how teaching faculty might be encouraged to introduce or expand BI in their classes:

Fall 1992
B. McClintock

CARTHAGE COLLEGE
Department of Economics

ECON 252: INTERMEDIATE MACROECONOMICS

ASSIGNMENT #1

TOPIC IDENTIFICATION AND PRELIMINARY RESEARCH

Instructions: Spend some time thinking through the issues raised in this assignment related to your topic (along with jotting down some thoughts) in order to prepare yourself for a productive in-class discussion with your group. Take notes on your group discussion. After class, write up the results of both your group and your own thinking on the topic. Hand-in a 1-2 page note so that I am able to gauge your current understanding and plans. Later, add this note to your economic journal.

1. Define your topic, eg what is meant by the topic, _____

2. What reasons led YOU to select this topic as opposed to other topics?

3. Why is _____ a topic or issue that involves economic problems? How does _____ affect economic activity and the everyday lives of citizens?

4. What do you know or speculate are some of the "cause and effect" relationships associated with the _____ topic?
In other words, what factors are likely to cause your topic, _____
_____, to occur or are linked to it. What are some of the effects or outcomes in terms of the health of the economy?

5. Based on your answers to questions 1-4 and other thoughts you may have, what kinds of information do you think it may be important to gather in your economic journal and for writing your paper? What types of data might you look for? How will you start looking for this information and where will you look for it?

Figure 2: ECON 252: Intermediate Macroeconomics

dous amount of information. It was difficult to organize it and tie it all together....It was a good, practical, and "learning experience" paper. After it was finally completed, I achieved a great feeling of accomplishment and relief. I smoked a big cigar to celebrate!

REFLECTIONS OF A PROFESSOR ON THE COURSE-INTEGRATED APPROACH TO BI

The following observations are offered as suggestions to librarians, from a teaching professor's perspective, as to how teaching faculty might be encouraged to introduce or expand BI in their classes:

— EUGENE A. ENGELDINGER AND OTHERS —

LIB 199—THE ELECTRONIC LIBRARY—SPRING, 1993
(March 30 - May 18, 11:00-12:20 UH;
Classes in the IMC-Studio B
Internet Classes in the Computing Center)

Instructors: Sara Brownmiller, 282 Knight, 6-2368
Bob Felsing, Level 5 (Coll. Dev.), 6-1857
Paul Frantz, 282 Knight, 6-1880
Joanne Halgren, Level 3 (ILL), 6-1876
Isabel Stirling, Science Library, 6-3076

Text: Library course packet, Campus Copy Center, EMU

SCHEDULE

Mar 30 - Introduction; overview of the UO Library system

Apr 1 - No class; attend exhibits at OLA conference

Apr 6 - Principles of database searching

Apr 8 - Janus/Expanded Academic Index

Apr 13 - Technical services: MARC record; authority control
(Guest: John Helmer, Systems Librarian)

Apr 15 - Accessing other library catalogs; bibliographic format

Apr 20 - FirstSearch/ILL/ARIEL

Apr 22 - Periodical databases: print, electronic access

Apr 27 - Internet I: Introduction to the Internet

Apr 29 - CD-ROMs; downloading

May 4 - Internet II: Gopher library catalogs

May 6 - NEXIS/LEXIS

May 11 - Internet III: Introduction to Gopher Resources

May 13 - Government documents databases
(Guest: Documents librarian)

May 18 - Reports on annotated bibliographies; course wrap-up

Poster session 2 (Frantz): Part 2 - Syllabus

READINGS:

Periodically, the instructors in this course may ask you to read an article on some facet of the electronic library or to read a user's guide in preparation for working with a particular electronic resource. The indicated materials will be placed on reserve in the Knight Library.

ASSIGNMENTS:

You can expect assignments on the Janus online catalog, on databases providing access to periodical articles, and on Internet searching. (Other brief assignments or quizzes may be added.) These assignments will give you practice in using the above resources.

Assignments will account for 50% of the final grade.

FINAL PROJECT:

Your final project will be to compile a 30-item annotated bibliography on a nicely focused topic. Ideally, your topic should be related to whatever course work or research you are engaged in or to an area of personal interest. Whatever the topic, you must have your topic approved by one of the instructors by April 15.

We will discuss the requirements of this annotated bibliography at greater length as we get into the course. Two things to remember at this point: first, the project is due on the last class day, May 18, for which you will report on your bibliography project; and second, the final project is worth 50% of the final grade.

Poster session 2 (Frantz): Part 2 - Syllabus (continued)

204   LOEX-93   — PAUL FRANTZ —

SOME GUIDELINES FOR YOUR ANNOTATED BIBLIOGRAPHY

A bibliography is a list of sources of information on a given subject. To annotate such a bibliography is to provide a summary of each of the sources, with an evaluative note added.

1. Your annotated bibliography should be at least 30 items. It should be handed in at or before the last class period (May 18).

2. Arrange the sources in alphabetical order by the last name of the author. If a source has no clear author, then place in alphabetical order by the title of the work.

3. You may use any of the more common style manuals as your guide in citing your sources (APA, Chicago, MLA, Turabian), but employ only one style throughout your bibliography.

4. Your annotations should be approximately 75-100 words long, should summarize the content of the source, and should include some "evaluative" opinion as to the usefulness or worth of the source. (As a guide to writing annotations, consult James L. Harner's On compiling an annotated bibliography, pp. 21-26 "Writing the entries"—on reserve in the Knight Library under LIB 199.) Note: you do not need, nor do you have time, to read through each of your 30 items in order to write an annotation.

5. For the purposes of the course, please try to find a mix of formats in your bibliography. That is, ideally your 30 items should comprise books, periodical articles, perhaps government documents, and "other materials" (pamphlets, media, newspaper articles, institutional sources, etc.).

6. For the final class period, please prepare a 5"x7" card on which you summarize your project, commenting on which electronic technologies were most helpful, difficulties (and triumphs) of your research, and any interesting experiences in your research you wish to share with the class. You will be asked to hand in the card, with your bibliography. You will also be asked (time permitting) on the last class day to give an oral report of no more than four minutes on your bibliography experience.

7. Qualities we will look for in grading the project:

*   a mix of sources, if possible;
*   well-constructed annotations;
*   a bibliography free of grammatical or spelling errors;
*   a well-presented oral report.

Poster session 2 (Frantz): Part 3 - Assignment

LIBRARY COURSE EVALUATION

Instructor_____

Course Number_____

Term_____

Please mark this evaluation sheet according to the instructions below. Record your reactions honestly.

YOU NEED NOT PUT YOUR NAME ON THIS PAPER

Circle the number in each line that most closely reflects your attitude between the two extremes given. Circling a #3, for instance, would indicate no particularly positive or negative attitude on that question. If a question is not relevant to your course, circle N/A.

THE COURSE

Organization of the course	HAPHAZARD	1 2 3 4 5	WELL ORGANIZED	N/A
Class meetings	USELESS	1 2 3 4 5	PROFITABLE	N/A
Assignments	BUSY WORK	1 2 3 4 5	SUPPORTS INSTRUCTION	N/A
Tests	IRRELEVANT TO COURSE CONTENT	1 2 3 4 5	VERY RELEVANT TO COURSE CONTENT	N/A
Grades	UNFAIR	1 2 3 4 5	VALID	N/A
Materials distributed in class	WASTE OF PAPER	1 2 3 4 5	VERY HELPFUL	N/A
Audio/visual materials (transparencies, etc.)	INEFFECTIVE	1 2 3 4 5	EFFECTIVELY SUPPORTS INSTRUCTION	N/A
Time spent on class preparation in relation to other courses with the same credit hours	BELOW AVERAGE	1 2 3 4 5	ABOVE AVERAGE	N/A
Did you use the textbook/packet (e.g. Kinko's)?	NO	1 2 3 4 5	FREQUENTLY	N/A
Value of the textbook/packet in helping to understand course material	NONE	1 2 3 4 5	GREAT	N/A
Did you use materials placed on reserve?	NO	1 2 3 4 5	FREQUENTLY	N/A
Probable long-range value of course	NONE	1 2 3 4 5	VERY VALUABLE	N/A
Would you recommend this course to others?	NO!	1 2 3 4 5	ENTHUSIASTICALLY!	N/A

THE ROOM

Was the environment (acoustics, temperature, etc.) a good one for learning?	NO!	1 2 3 4 5	VERY GOOD ENVIRONMENT	N/A

--CONTINUES ON REVERSE SIDE--

Poster session 2 (Frantz): Part 4 - Evaluation Form

— PAUL FRANTZ —

THE INSTRUCTOR	Negative Extreme		Positive Extreme
General attitude of the instructor	COLD AND DISTANT	1 2 3 4 5	CONCERNED AND HELPFUL
Clarifies course objectives	POORLY	1 2 3 4 5	VERY WELL
Knows the subject	POORLY	1 2 3 4 5	VERY WELL
Shows own enthusiasm for the subject	SHOWS NO ENTHUSIASM	1 2 3 4 5	SHOWS GREAT ENTHUSIASM
Is prepared for class	SEEMS HAZY AND HURRIED	1 2 3 4 5	ALWAYS WELL PREPARED
Makes class sessions profitable	SELDOM	1 2 3 4 5	ALWAYS
Answers class questions	WITH RELUCTANCE	1 2 3 4 5	CLEARLY AND ENTHUSIASTICALLY
Is available for extra help when needed	HARDLY EVER	1 2 3 4 5	ALMOST ALWAYS
Respects the student	NOT AT ALL	1 2 3 4 5	EXCELLENT

THE STUDENT

In general, what is your attitude toward your University work so far?	DISAPPOINTED	1 2 3 4 5	VERY POSITIVE
Class standing	Grad Senior Junior Sophomore Freshman Special		

Below is space for written comments. These may commend the instructor, suggest improvements, or indicate changes in content and emphasis that you think the course needs.

Your instructor values your opinions and will have a chance to read these comments, AFTER FINAL GRADES HAVE BEEN TURNED IN. SIGNED COMMENTS WILL ALSO BE PLACED IN THE INSTRUCTOR'S PERSONNEL FILE.

Poster session 2 (Frantz): Part 4 - Evaluation Form (continued)

DOES PSYCHOLOGICAL TYPE AND TEACHING METHOD AFFECT STUDENT LEARNING OF BASIC LIBRARY SKILLS?

by
Diane Prorak, Tania Gottschalk,
and Mike Pollastro

University of Idaho Library
Reference Department
Moscow, ID 83843

ABSTRACT

Will students learn more if librarians teach using a small group, active-learning method rather than a lecture method? Will students with a particular psychological type (and thus a preferred learning style) learn more with one teaching method than another? To investigate these questions, we designed a study involving students enrolled in twelve sections of the University of Idaho (UI) freshman composition course in the spring of 1992 (n=246). Six of the sections were taught basic library skills using a lecture/demonstration method. The other six were taught using a small group, active-learning method. Pre- and post-tests of knowledge and confidence in using the library were administered to students in the 12 sections. As well, the Keirsey Temperament Sorter, a 70-item test identifying four pairs of Jungian psychological indicators, was administered to predict students' learning styles.

T-tests on the difference between pre- and post-test scores and confidence levels indicated a significant difference at the .001 level. Linear analysis indicated that test scores and confidence levels were not dependent on teaching method or Keirsey type. However, linear analysis revealed a relationship between test scores and librarian providing the instruction. Qualitative analysis revealed a mixed reception to both small group and lecture methods. The most consistent comment was "more hands on." Students indicated sessions would be improved if taught in a computer lab setting.

These results suggest that 1) students may not necessarily learn more if a small group, active-learning method is used rather than a lecture method and 2) students with a particular psychological type may not necessarily learn more with one teaching method than another. More research needs to be done on a) the most effective small group teaching methods for bibliographic instruction; b) factors that make one instructor more effective than another; and c) student preferences for and success in one teaching method over another.

Poster session 3 (Prorak): Part 1 - Research Study: Psychological Type and Teaching Methods

① PROBLEM

■ Will students learn more if librarians teach using a small group, active-learning method rather than a lecture method?

■ Will students with a particular psychological type (and thus a preferred learning style) learn more with one teaching method than another?

---

② METHOD

■ Twelve sections of University of Idaho (UI) freshmen composition courses in the Spring of 1992 (n=246) were selected for the study.

■ Three librarians each taught:

Two sections using a lecture/demonstration method (six sections total)

Two sections using a group, active-learning method (six sections total)

■ All students were administered the Keirsey Temperament Sorter (n=246).

■ All students were administered pre- and post-tests of knowledge and confidence in using the library (n=246).

Poster session 3 (Prorak): Part 1 - Research Study: Psychological Type and Teaching Methods (continued)

③ LECTURE METHOD

FORMAT
- Librarian lectures for about 35 minutes in each of two class sessions.
- Lecture includes demonstration of computer using a projection panel.
- Librarian solicits student input by asking questions throughout lecture.
- Books and periodicals are shown as "props" in lecture.
- Students use rest of class session to individually complete worksheets in library and return them to the librarian for grading.

CONTENT
- First session's lecture covers how to use the library's catalog (LaserCat) to find books.
- Second session covers how to find articles using paper indexes and, using LaserCat, how to find out if the UI Library owns the periodicals.
- Both sessions use whole class input and overhead projector in creating a list of information that a cataloger or indexer would put into a record for a particular book or article.

---

④ GROUP METHOD

FORMAT
- Librarian gives a brief introductory lecture (5 minutes).
- Students work in small group of 4-6 members.
- Groups are given books and indexes to use.
- Groups report to whole class. Some demonstrate computer use with a projection panel.
- Librarian summarizes.
- After class, students individually complete worksheets in library and return them to the librarian for grading.

CONTENT
- In the first session, student groups create a record for a book and then determine how they would use the computer to search for their book.
- In the second session, groups create a record for an article, use an index to compare their record to one in a standard index and then determine how to find out if the UI Library owns the magazine.

Poster session 3 (Prorak): Part 1 - Research Study: Psychological Type and Teaching Methods (continued)

⑤ PSYCHOLOGICAL TYPE AND LEARNING STYLE

KEIRSEY TEMPERAMENT SORTER
■ A 70-item test identifying four pairs of Jungian psychological indicators
■ Results provide students with 4 letters indicating their preferences in each pair and a combination psychological type:
  ■ **E**xtraverted vs. **I**ntroverted
  ■ I**N**tuiting vs. **S**ensing
  ■ **T**hinking vs. **F**eeling
  ■ **J**udging vs. **P**erceiving
  ■ **X** = no clear preference

PSYCHOLOGICAL TYPES IN OUR SAMPLE (N=246)

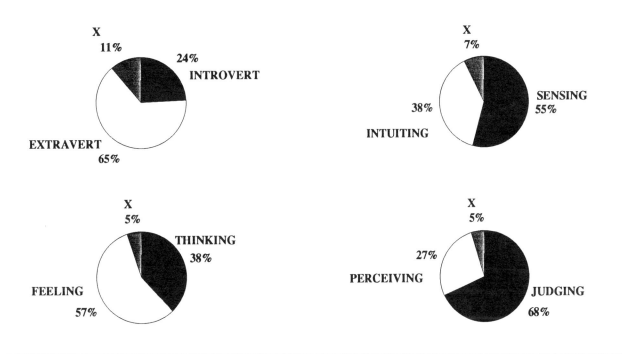

LEARNING STYLE
■ Based on previous research, individual or combinations of Keirsey type letters can be used to predict student learning preferences
■ For example, "**E**" or "**NF**" students would be predicted to like, and thus, learn more effectively in a small group setting (See *Please Understand Me* by D. Keirsey and M. Bates, 1984)

Poster session 3 (Prorak): Part 1 - Research Study: Psychological Type and Teaching Methods (continued)

⑥ QUANTITATIVE RESULTS

Table 1: T-Test of Difference Between Pre- and Post-Test Scores

N	Mean	Std Dev	Std Error	T	Prob > |T|
246	0.87	2.06	0.13	6.67	0.0001

Table 2: T-Test of Difference Between Pre- and Post-Confidence

N	Mean	Std Dev	Std Error	T	Prob > |T|
244	2.03	2.25	0.14	14.10	0.0001

Table 3: Linear Analysis of: Difference Between Pre- and Post-Test Scores (Dependent Variable)

Independent Variable	DF	Type III SS	F Value	Pr > F
1. Instruction Method Used	1	3.41	0.81	0.37
2. *Librarian Providing Instruction*	*2*	*38.65*	*4.57*	*0.01*
3. Gender of Student	1	0.01	0.00	0.96
4. Students' Preferred Instruction Method	2	4.45	0.53	0.59
5. Attendance of Instruction Sessions	3	14.28	1.13	0.34
6. Pre-Confidence in Using Library	4	24.54	1.45	0.22
7. Introverted/ Extraverted	2	4.45	0.53	0.59
8. Intuiting/ Sensing	2	0.87	0.10	0.90
9. Feeling/ Thinking	2	1.24	0.15	0.86
10. Judging/ Perceiving	2	0.20	0.02	0.98

Poster session 3 (Prorak): Part 1 - Research Study: Psychological Type and Teaching Methods (continued)

⑦ QUALITATIVE RESULTS

Representative student comments about the teaching methods:

■LECTURE METHOD

☺ " [The most valuable part was] when she actually showed the LaserCat on the overhead to show how it worked."

☺ "It went pretty much step-by-step."

☹ "It was effective to a certain point, but there is always that point in the lecture when students get bored with the subject."

☹ "The instructor did a great job, but I had trouble staying awake."

☹ "More class involvement [is needed] in the session."

■GROUP METHOD

☺ "Better than a lecture."

☺ "It was a good method because it made the students get involved."

☺ "It was good to have us work in groups to be able to cooperate everyone's knowledge."

☹ "I learn better through the lecture method."

☹ "The groups were not helpful because only one or two people did all the work."

☹ "I felt more work needed to be done individually."

☹ "Going and reviewing what every group had done was very boring."

■BOTH METHODS

The most consistent comment was "more hands on". Students indicated sessions would be improved if taught in a computer lab setting.

Poster session 3 (Prorak): Part 1 - Research Study: Psychological Type and Teaching Methods (continued)

⑧ SUMMARY

■ Test scores showed a significant difference in student knowledge and confidence after instructional sessions.

■ No significant relationship was found between student scores and teaching method or Keirsey Type.

■ A significant relationship was found between student knowledge scores (but not confidence scores) and librarian providing instruction.

■ Students in both lecture and group sessions indicated that they thought sessions would be improved if taught in a hands-on, computer lab setting.

---

⑨ CONCLUSIONS

■ Students may not necessarily learn more if a small group, active-learning method is used rather than a lecture method.

■ Students with a particular psychological type may not necessarily learn more with one teaching method than another.

■ More research needs to be done on:

    a) the most effective small group teaching methods for bibliographic instruction

    b) factors that make one instructor more effective than another

    c) student preferences for and success in one teaching method over another

"Using an Online Search Assignment
to Teach Students Critical Thinking Skills"

Jan Davis Tudor
Willamette University

A professor of political science and I developed an assignment for use in an undergraduate senior seminar that involved teaching students how to search the DIALOG information retrieval system using planned search strategies. Our goal was to explore whether an assignment that requires students to formulate and execute an online search and evaluate the search results is an effective method of teaching critical thinking skills. The emphasis of the assignment was not to teach students the detailed techniques of online database searching, but rather to teach them how to ask questions while doing research. We examined two methods of administering the assignment. The first semester I taught the students how to search DIALOG using command language, and the second semester I taught DIALOG's Menus system. At the end of the second semester, I was able to compare the two methods and determine which type of DIALOG search is best suited for this undergraduate assignment.

I taught students enrolled in two political science courses the basis of searching DIALOG using DIALOG's Classroom Instruction Program. After their topics were approved by the professor, students were taught how to select appropriate databases, how to formulate and conduct a search, and how to evaluate the search results. I prepared a handout and guide on source analysis. Prior to executing the searches, students were required to turn in a completed list of questions from the handout regarding choice of databases and search strategies. Students were asked to select the five "best" articles from their retrieved list of citations, and were required to write a bibliographic essay based on the selected citations and the evaluation criteria they used.

This assignment was successful because students enjoyed and appreciated learning how to find library materials using a new technology while making informed, analytical decisions during the entire search process. Because of cost and staff time considerations I will not use DIALOG next year, but the assignment can and will be applied to CD-ROMs and the online catalog.

Poster session 4 (Tudor): Part 1 - Introduction

SEARCH STRATEGY FORM
(This form must be completed and
given to a reference librarian
before searching DIALOG)

1. What is your search statement?

2. What database(s) will you search?

2a. Why did you select the database(s)? What is the scope of the database?

3. What are your search terms? (Complete the DIALOG search worksheet)

4. If you retrieve too many records, how will you modify your search?

5. If you retrieve too few records, how will you modify your search?

Poster session 4 (Tudor): Part 2 - Search Strategy Form

THE CLASS:

Fall semester: Asia and the International System (16 students, juniors and seniors). Students and professor met with librarian for 1-1/2 hours. Librarian lectured on basics of database structure and searching and source analysis. Students spent approximately 45 minutes doing hands-on exercises using command language.

Spring semester: Senior Seminar in International Relations (11 students, all seniors). Students and professor met with librarian in library for a one-hour lecture on source analysis and DIA-LOG searching with Menus. Because of time limitation, no hands-on work was incorporated.

COMPARISON OF METHODS:

Without a doubt teaching students how to search Menus was much more effective than teaching command language for this assignment. Although the majority of students understood command language and could do the class exercises without much problem, most had forgotten how to search by the time they came to the library to do their searching. Of the students who were in both classes, only one preferred command language.

ADVANTAGES OF THE ASSIGNMENT:

• Students had to make several decisions about their topics/research before "turning on the computer."
• Students were exposed to a different method of finding information (the "world of online databases").
• Students were exposed to different types of information (e.g., military intelligence reports).
• The assignment fostered faculty/librarian cooperation.
• The assignment can be applied to CD-ROMs and online catalogs.

DISADVANTAGES OF THE ASSIGNMENT:

• It impacted on getting the librarian's time. The librarian met with each student individually.
• DIALOG Menus is not exceptionally user-friendly. Librarian involvement with students' searches is necessary.
• Many students firmly believed that DIALOG was going to provide them with everything they needed.
• The cost was about $15 a student.

WHAT WOULD I DO DIFFERENTLY NEXT TIME?

• I would meet with students as a group twice so I could spend more time explaining how to formulate a search and the use of Boolean logic.
• I would incorporate more active learning techniques in my source analysis lecture.

Poster session 4 (Tudor): Part 2 - Search Strategy Form (continued)

Adapting to Technological Change:

Coping with Multiple Forms of a Data Source

Katherine M. Weir

Background

Illinois State University (ISU) is a comprehensive public university with an enrollment of over 21,000 and an emphasis on undergraduate education. The university library is arranged by subject areas: the arts and humanities, social sciences and business, science and technology, and education, psychology, and philosophy are on separate floors, with subject librarians to provide specialized reference service. A general reference area on the main floor serves as the initial reference contact for students. At the online catalog terminals, students have access to a statewide online catalog (IO) that can be scoped for local, remote, or statewide searching. In addition, these terminals provide access to two periodical index utilities, CARL and IBIS. Multiple CD-ROM products by various vendors are installed at workstations scattered throughout the building. The general reference librarians conduct basic library instruction for incoming students, and the subject librarians provide library instruction related to their disciplines. Each year, over 8,000 students receive some form of formal library instruction.

The university has a commitment to prepare students for lifelong learning. The goal in library instruction is to enable students to function in a complex information environment and to satisfy their information needs as both the needs and the technologies change throughout their lives. With the multiplicity of resources and technologies in use and yet to come, source-based library instruction cannot suffice. Increasingly, students need to learn research strategies that enable them to approach new sources, evaluate them, and use them effectively.

Presenting Multiple Forms of a Database

Formerly, we could teach students how to use the major resources in their discipline while introducing them to the scope and content of these publications. However, with the multiplication of access vehicles, we must also teach students that the same data may be available to them in various packages. For example, users at ISU have several H.W. Wilson indexes available in three forms: traditional paper index, Wilson CD-ROM product, and access through the online Illinois Bibliographic Information Service (IBIS). As each form has a different appearance, requires a different search protocol, and permits searching on different keys, they appear to be three different sources of information rather than three ways of accessing the same information.

To cope with the multiple packages available, several teaching strategies can be used in combination. The instructor can introduce students to sources appropriate for their subjects, discuss source identification, selection, and evaluation techniques, and teach search strategies and concepts. By examining the headers on computer screens, reading the introductory screens, and learning to access the help utilities, a student can identify the databases being searched, determine its scope, and formulate search statements properly. Sample computer screens used to demonstrate these points are included as Appendix C. Through demonstration, discussion, and hands-on exploration, students learn to use Boolean operators in constructing a search, to observe the differences between keyword and controlled vocabulary indexing, and to employ truncation. A brief outline for a 75-minute class session follows:

5 min.	Introduction to subject librarian and outline of material to be covered
5 min.	Overview of appropriate print and electronic sources; distribute handouts
10 min.	Evaluation and selection of databases: Scope, access, and special features
5 min.	Search strategy
10 min.	Overview and demonstration of electronic databases
20 min.	Group exercise
15 min.	Discussion of exercise results
5 min.	Closure and review of material covered

During the demonstration, the mechanical aspects of database searching are covered as well as the conceptual aspects, such as formulating complex search statements. The topics for sample searches have been selected to illustrate broadening a search or substituting terms to obtain better results and narrowing topics when too much information is retrieved. With eight terminals and one projection unit available in the classroom, students can be assigned to search the same topic or different topics on several different databases simultaneously, yielding a rich variety of results for discussion. Detailed outlines for typical 75-minute and 50-minute class sessions, two sample

---

Poster session 5 (Weir): Part 1 - Summary: Technological Change and Multiple Database Forms

demonstration search scripts, a class exercise form, and sample class handouts will be found in the appendix.

Other Forms of Instruction

In addition to formal instruction in database searching during bibliographic instruction sessions, the library provides informal and individualized forms of instruction. Traditional guides and bibliographies are available on each subject floor and are distributed to classes starting library assignments. Detailed handouts are available at most computer workstations for point-of-use self-instruction on the mechanical operation of the workstation and the manipulation of the database(s) accessible through that terminal. The handouts illustrate how to activate the system, give commands, print, download, and quit. Sample point-of-use instruction sheets are included in Appendixes F and G. Each semester the systems librarian also offers walk-in workshops for various databases or access vehicles. In the workshops students practice all types of searches available on the databases, see the results of common errors, and learn to access the help utilities for each database.

Conclusion

The introduction of multiple access vehicles for the same data sets has prompted a switch from traditional source-based bibliographic instruction to a more rewarding type of instruction. Classroom discussion and demonstration center on the types of sources useful for the completion of students' assignments and the concepts used in conducting their bibliographic research. Active learning predominates, as students explore the resources and are drawn into discussion of their strategies, search statements, and the results they obtain. In conducting such classes, there is little time for the discussion of particular sources. Instead, handouts and annotated bibliographies are used to introduce the basic sources for the discipline.

APPENDIX

Weir is business librarian at Milner Library, Illinois State University, Normal, Illinois.

Poster session 5 (Weir): Part 1 - Summary: Technological Change and Multiple Database Forms (continued)

Outline for 75-Minute Class Session

5 min.   Introduction to subject librarian and outline of material to be covered
5 min.   Overview of appropriate print and electronic sources [distribute handouts]
10 min. Evaluation and selection of databases [provide basis, define concepts, demonstrate]
       Scope
          Subjects/disciplines covered
          Number and types of publications indexed
       Access
          Keyword or controlled vocabulary
          Boolean logic
          Nesting
       Special features (Commands, truncation, etc.)
5 min.   Search strategy
       Problem formulation
       Resource identification and selection
       Search statement formulation and search execution
       Evaluation of search results
       Search revision
10 min. Overview and demonstration of electronic databases
       Librarian executes search on projection unit
       Students follow along on own active terminals
20 min. Group exercise
       Librarian assigns topic and database to groups at each terminal
       Students formulate search statements, execute search, and evaluate results
15 min. Discussion of exercise results
       Comparison of results among databases
       Comparison of results using differing terminology
5 min.   Closure and review of material covered

Outline for 50-Minute Class Session

5 min.   Introduction and overview of print and electronic sources [distribute handouts]
10 min. Evaluation and selection of databases [provide basis, define concepts, demonstrate]
       Scope
       Access
       Special features
5 min.   Search strategy
15 min. Group exercise
10 min. Discussion of exercise results
5 min.   Closure and review of material covered

Poster session 5 (Weir): Part 2 - Appendix A - Outline of Classes

Sample Demonstration Search #1

Topic: *Drug Testing in the Workplace*
Purpose: To demonstrate the substitution of terms to locate articles on a given topic
Use the Wilson CD-ROM version for this demonstration

Select BROWSE mode to demonstrate the subject heading approach
Type in: **DRUG TESTING**
>	No subject headings match this entry.

Scan to find the heading which most closely matches: **Drugs / Testing**.
Display the first few articles for this heading
>	Note that articles under this heading are about the testing of new drugs for approval, NOT testing for drug use by employees

Switch to WILSEARCH mode
Type in: **DRUG TESTING**
>	Yields 558 articles, including a mix of articles about testing new drugs for approval and testing for drug abuse, primarily among employees

Look at subject headings of one or two useful articles: **Drug abuse / Testing**
Switch back to BROWSE mode
Type in: **DRUG ABUSE / TESTING**
>	Yields 323 articles about testing for drug abuse, primarily among employees

Press < ESC > to return to the subject heading list in BROWSE
Highlight the heading **DRUG ABUSE / TESTING**
Press the **F8** key for the *see also* list of related subject headings
>	Note the heading: **Employee drug problem**, which lists 370 articles that may also prove useful

Poster session 5 (Weir): Part 3 - Appendix B - Sample Demonstration Searches

SAMPLE DEMONSTRATION SEARCH #2

Topic: *Mergers*
Purpose: To demonstrate narrowing a topic by adding terms
Use the Wilson CD-ROM version first for this demonstration, then repeat on IBIS

Select WILSEARCH mode
Type in: **MERGERS**
     Yields 16,744 articles. Searches yielding so many items indicate a need to narrow the topic
Switch to BROWSE mode
Type in: **MERGERS**
     No subject headings match this entry
Scan to **Mergers and acquisitions**, the heading which most closely matches
Note the asterisk (*) to the left of this heading
     Explain that this is not a subject heading, but that other terms are used for this topic. To see a list
     of subject headings that can be used to search the topic, you must press the **F8** key.
Press the **F8** key for the *see* list of related subject headings
Note the heading: **Corporate acquisitions and mergers**
     This is a valid subject heading for the topic, but 595 articles are listed. This may still be
     too many articles to deal with. The sub-headings of this subject heading may provide suggestions
     for narrowing the topic further.
Return to BROWSE mode
Type in: **CORPORATE ACQUISITIONS AND MERGERS**
Scan the sub-headings listed below the main subject heading
Note the sub-headings: / **EMPLOYEE BENEFIT PROBLEMS** (27 articles) and
     / **PUBLIC RELATIONS** (12 articles), which may be suitable topics.
Switch to IBIS
Select *Business Periodicals Index*
Type in: **MERGERS**
     Yields 17,110 documents.
Press **F1** for Help
     Use the Help utility to try to narrow the topic. Note the explanation at *"subject searching"* to use
     .de. to limit the search to terms used as subject headings.
Return to IBIS and type in: **MERGERS.DE.**
     Yields 16,336 documents. Ask for suggestions for ways to limit the search further. Try adding the
     subject heading *"acquisitions."*
Type in: **ACQUISITIONS.DE.**
     Yields 16,465 documents
Type in: **2 and 3** to combine the terms in one search
     Yields 16,336 documents. No documents have been eliminated.
Display the first few articles
     Gives little help in narrowing the topic. Ask students for additional words to add to limit the topic.
     If none are offered, suggest consulting the paper index or BROWSE mode on the compact disc to
     get suggestions for narrower aspects of this topic. Also encourage experimenting with the use of hyphens
     between terms and the logical and proximity operators: AND, OR, SAME, WITH, ADJ.

Poster session 5 (Weir): Part 2 - Appendix B - Sample Demonstration Searches (continued)

Current Database: Business Periodicals Index

DISC SEARCH MENU

Search Compact Disc

1. BROWSE ....Subject Search
2. WILSEARCH ....Multi-term Search
3. QUIT

Press ENTER on HIGHLIGHTED selection or press the number of desired choice

F1 - HELP   F3 - Change Database / Disc   ESC - To Quit

Examine Labels and Headers to Identify the Database

IBIS: ILLINOIS BIBLIOGRAPHIC INFORMATION SERVICE
Wilson Databases

1. Business Periodicals Index   (WBPI)
2. General Science Index   (WGSI)
3. Humanities Index   (WHUM)
4. Reader's Guide Abstracts   (WRGA)
5. Social Sciences Index   (WSSI)
6. All available Wilson databases   (WLSN)

To choose a Wilson database file, type the number that appears to
the left of its name. (For help and database descriptions, type H.)

Make your selection, then press ENTER:

Type   B to backtrack   H for help   Q to quit   X to exit IBIS

Poster session 5 (Weir): Part 3 - Appendix C - Sample Computer Screens

```
MODE: (Browse)        BROWSE Mode - Searching for Citations        PANEL: BPAN002


    You have accessed the BROWSE Mode search entry screen.

    The database which you are searching and the date range of that database are
    listed at the top of the screen.

    Enter your subject in the window provided at the bottom of the screen.

    If you are searching for a name, i.e., for a person as a subject, type in the last
    name first, followed by a comma, a space and the first name, for example,
    Reno, Janet.  When you have typed in the subject, press ENTER to begin the
    search.

    To return to the BROWSE screen in order to enter your subject, press the ESC key.



        END of this HELP Path
  Press ESC to EXIT Help
```

Use Help and Introductory Screens to Determine the Scope

```
            IBIS:  ILLINOIS BIBLIOGRAPHIC INFORMATION SERVICE
                   Searching:  Business Periodicals Index


(c) H. W. Wilson Co.
   Dates covered:  1982-present.  Contains citations to articles in over 300 English
language journals.  Subjects covered:  accounting, advertising, banking, chemical
industry, communications, computer science, construction industry, drug and cosmetics
industries, economics, electronics, finance and investments, personnel administration,
marketing, occupational health and safety, paper and pulp industry, petroleum and gas
industries, printing and publishing, public relations, public utilities, real estate, regulation
of industry, and transportation. Producer:  H. W. Wilson.






Make your selection, then press ENTER:
Type    B to backtrack      H for help        Q to quit         X to exit IBIS
```

Poster session 5 (Weir): Part 3 - Appendix C - Sample Computer Screens (continued)

start with what you typed. For example if you enter:

Subject words   / employee training

WILSEARCH ends it with a colon, searches it as employee training:, and would find references under such headings as Employee Training, Employee Training as a profession, and Employee Training Departments. The three primary ways of entering subject words may be combined in a single search. For example:

Subject words   any computer# microcomputer#
2nd subject   training evaluat:
3rd subject   / college students

could find information on the training of college students to evaluate microcomputers or computers.

Press ESC to EXIT Help

Press <PgDn / PageDown> KEY for NEXT Screen
Press <PgUp / PageUp> KEY for PREVIOUS Screen

Use Help Utilities to Learn How to Formulate Search Statements

IBIS: ILLINOIS BIBLIOGRAPHIC INFORMATION SERVICE
Help Searching H. W. Wilson Databases (WBPI)

author searching
: To search for articles by author, type the last name, a hyphen, first initial, and dollar sign truncation symbol.
Example: gunderson-j$

title searching
: To search for keywords within the title of an article, use proximity operators ADJ or WITH.
Example: desert adj shield or cool with style

journal searching
: To search for journal titles, enter the title with hyphens between each word. If the title contains only one word, add the source field qualifier .so.
Example: readers-digest or nation.so.

subject searching
: To search for articles in a particular subject, enter the subject followed by the descriptor field qualifier .de. Enter multi-word subjects with hyphens. Combine subjects with Boolean operators AND or OR, or proximity operator SAME.
Example: taxation.de. same pension-plans

Make your selection, then press ENTER:
Type   B to backtrack   H for help   Q to quit   X to exit IBIS

Poster session 5 (Weir): Part 3 - Appendix C - Sample Computer Screens (continued)

LIBRARY RESEARCH IN MARKETING

DATABASE SEARCHING EXERCISE

Database searched: _____

Search statement: _____

Type of search: _____

        (Subject, title, keyword, Browse, etc.)

Results:

    How many items retrieved? _____

    Too much, too little, just right? _____

    Good fit, poor fit, just right? _____

    Example of good or poor item _____

_____

Did you revise your search statement or type of search?

    To what: _____

Results of revised search:

    How many items retrieved? _____

    Too much, too little, just right? _____

    Good fit, poor fit, just right? _____

    Example of good or poor item _____

_____

Comments:

Poster session 5 (Weir): Part 5 - Appendix D - Class Group Exercise

LIBRARY RESEARCH IN MARKETING

Evaluating Databases

Scope
Disciplines/subjects covered
Number and types of publications indexed
Dates covered

Access
Keyword, controlled vocabulary, multiple approaches
Single term or multiple term or concept searching
Boolean logic and operators (AND and OR searching)
Nesting

Database idiosyncrasies
Special commands, including truncation and truncation symbols
Format of input or search results

Search Strategies
Devising and following a strategy for your library research can ensure that you consult all likely sources of information using terminology and searching methods suited to each source. While no one search strategy is suited to all topics and circumstances, the following strategy should help you perform a more efficient and effective search for information.

1. Formulate a clear statement of the topic or problem.
2. Identify likely sources of information: books, articles, survey data, etc.
3. Identify resources to lead you to the data: catalogs, indexes, reference books, etc.
4. Select a resource. Taking into account the nature and scope of the resource, formulate a search statement. Generally, the search statement will NOT be the same as your topic or problem statement. It will be more precise, or address only a part of the topic or problem.
5. Perform the search and evaluate the results: good or poor fit; too much or too little retrieved.
6. Adjust the search strategy to obtain better results:
   Too much data / too many items retrieved: Narrow the search by adding a search term or selecting more restrictive terms. Items already identified may suggest terms to use.
   Too little data / too few items retrieved: Broaden search by omitting a search term or substituting broader, or inclusive terms. Select another resource.
   Nothing / poor fit retrieved: substitute synonyms for original search terms, rephrase the search statement. Select another resource.
7. Repeat search steps 4, 5, and 6 for each likely resource.

Poster session 5 (Weir): Part 6 - Appendix E - Sample Class Handouts

LIBRARY RESEARCH IN MARKETING

ELECTRONIC SOURCES TO ACCESS INFORMATION

IO - the on-line catalog
Use to identify books, reports, and journal titles
Timeliness: current within a few days of cataloging
Access points: author, title, keywords in title, subject headings, series titles
Strategies: user friendly interface guides the search; may sort or limit
Scoping: default is ISU library; can broaden or select the libraries searched

Business Periodicals Index on CD-ROM - journal index
Use to identify articles in business journals
Timeliness: updated monthly, but indexing lags by weeks (i.e., index current to the end of December
    may only cover journal issues through October)
Access points:
    BROWSE - subject heading search only; use for single subject searches
    WILSEARCH - title, keyword in title and subject, personal name, journal title, organization;
        default is AND search, use ANY or OR for OR searching; for nesting use all three subject
        lines
Truncation: use the number sign (#) for a single letter; the colon (:) for multiple letters

IBIS - collection of journal indexes available on-line
Currently contains ERIC, an education database, and five indexes published by H.W. Wilson
Use to identify journal articles in any one of six indexes
Timeliness: updated monthly; indexing may lag by weeks
Access points: keyword and descriptor searching of subject headings, titles, and the contents of abstracts
    (ERIC and Readers Guide Abstracts only)

CARL/Uncover - on-line journal index
Use for current indexing of articles in any discipline
Timeliness: updated daily during the check-in of journals at libraries in the CARL system
    Covers October 1988 to the present
Access points:
    NAME for authors
    WORD for keywords in article and journal titles - NO SUBJECT SEARCHING
    BROWSE for journal titles (not articles)
Strategies: user friendly or commands (//N, //W, //T); combination searches using AND only

InfoTrac - journal index on CD-ROM
Use for current indexing or articles in any discipline; includes the National Newspaper Index
Timeliness: covers from 1989 to approximately four weeks prior to current date
Access points:
    SUBJECT GUIDE search - use for broad subjects; single subject only
    KEYWORD search - use for searching subjects that contain two or more concepts

Poster session 5 (Weir): Part 6 - Appendix E - Sample Class Handouts (continued)

IBIS
AT
MILNER LIBRARY

An Introduction for Library Users

IBIS
"IBIS" stands for "Illinois Bibliographic Information Service." IBIS is a collection of subject-based, online indexes available through the ILLINET Online network. Use IBIS to obtain references to articles in journals and magazines in many subject areas. For example, ERIC indexes articles and research reports in education and related fields. IBIS should not be used to find books - use ILLINET Online to locate books located in this library and other libraries throughout Illinois.

IBIS Is a New System
The IBIS interface is still in its development and early testing phase. Some screens will direct you to optional services that are not yet in place.
Even at this stage of development, it is hoped that you will find IBIS helpful in conducting your research. To further improve the system, your suggestions and reports of problem are very important.

Using IBIS
IBIS is available during the following times:

Monday Friday	7:00a.m. - Midnight
Saturday	8:00a.m. - Midnight
Sunday	Noon - Midnight

You may use IBIS on public terminals throughout the library.

Selecting a Database

After connecting with IBIS, type "c" to choose a database. ERIC and five "Wilson" databases are currently available. The Wilson databases are *Business Periodicals Index, General Science Index, Humanities Index, Readers' Guide Abstracts, and Social Sciences Index*. There is also an option which will allow searching of all five Wilson databases at one time. If you are uncertain about which database to select from the menu, type "h" for database descriptions and help in choosing a database.

To begin your search, type the corresponding database number from the menu or use the four character label for your database. At any time while you are searching, you may change databases by typing "c/" followed by the four character label for the new database; for example, type "c/eric" to change to the ERIC database.

Poster session 5 (Weir): Part 6 - Appendix F - Sample Class Handouts

Searching IBIS

Basic Information
1. You do not need to use capital letters.
2. Use the back arrow key and retype if you make a typing error.
3. Each time the "enter" key is pressed, IBIS creates a numbered search statement. To see the search statements you have used, type "r" for a review.
4. IBIS automatically searches for both singular and plural forms of words (e.g. "dog" also finds "dogs").
5. You may truncate words by using the symbol "$".

Searching for SUBJECTS:

IBIS searching makes use of Boolean operators (AND, OR, NOT) and proximity operators (ADJ, WITH, SAME) to combine terms. For an explanation of these concepts see the IBIS help screens. To search for references on a single subject, choose words that you think will appear in the titles of articles or that will be keywords or index terms. Use the Boolean operator OR to combine any synonyms for your topic.

> EXAMPLE: to search for articles on smoking,
> Type: **smoking or tobacco or cigarettes** < enter >

Combining Search Terms

To search for articles that include more than one topic or concept, combine terms using the Boolean operator AND.

> EXAMPLE: To search for articles on smoking and cancer in women:
> Type: **smoking and cancer and women** < enter >

Use the proximity operator "ADJ" (adjacent) to specify that two words occur next to each other, in the order typed. Use a space or the proximity operator "WITH" to specify that two words appear in the same sentence in the record. Use the proximity operator "SAME" to specify that two words occur in the same field of a record.

> EXAMPLE: To search for articles on "the greenhouse effect" or "global warming":
> Type: **(greenhouse adj effect) or (global with warm$)** < enter >

PRINTING YOUR RESULTS

The **Print** command shown on the screen is not yet operational. Printing is currently possible only if you are at a terminal which is attached to a printer. To print your results, press the "Shift" and "Prt Scr" keys simultaneously. You can print only one screen at a time with this method.

Poster session 5 (Weir): Part 6 - Appendix F - Sample Class Handouts (continued)

BUSINESS PERIODICALS INDEX ON CD-ROM

You can search *Business Periodicals Index* in Milner Library by two modes of access: **BROWSE** and **WILSEARCH. BROWSE** searches by subject, company name, or personal name. **WILSEARCH** combines subjects/topics, authors, titles, journals, and organizations. Consult the paper copies of the *Business Periodicals Index* (Index Table 8) for subject headings if you need help determining what terms to use.

BROWSE

1. Press <Enter> to see the search menu.

2. Select **BROWSE SEARCH** from the Search Menu. Use the arrow keys to highlight your choice, or press the number for your choice. If Wilsearch searching is on the screen, press the Escape key <ESC> until the Main Menu appears. Select **BROWSE** and press <Enter>.

3. Type in the subject term or phrase, company name, or personal name and press <Enter>.

4. An alphabetic list of subjects will appear, with the term closest to the words you typed highlighted. The number to the left indicates the number of articles cited.

5. Press <Enter> to view the article citations. WAIT - the machine takes 10-15 seconds to search the disc.

6. If your subject appears with an asterisk (*) there are no citations listed under this subject heading, but another subject heading is used for articles on the topic. Press the <F8> key to see the terms related to your subject choice.

7. If the new terms have citations listed, use the arrow keys to highlight a term. Press <Enter> to see the articles.

TO PRINT

Press the <F4> key on the left side of the keyboard to print one article citation.
Press the <F6> key to print all citations up to ten at one time. Press any key to interrupt the printer. To continue printing, press "Y" for yes; to stop printing type "N" for no.

TO END SEARCH

Press <ESC> (Escape) repeatedly until you return to the Main Menu.

- OVER FOR WILSEARCH -

Poster session 5 (Weir): Part 6 - Appendix G - Sample Class Handouts

BUSINESS PERIODICALS INDEX ON CD-ROM

You can search *Business Periodicals Index* in Milner Library by two modes of access: **BROWSE** and **WILSEARCH**. **BROWSE** searches by subject, company name, or personal name. **WILSEARCH** combines subjects/topics, authors, titles, journals, and organizations. Consult the paper copies of the *Business Periodicals Index* (Index Table 8) for subject headings if you need help determining what terms to use.

WILSEARCH

1. Select WILSEARCH from the Search Menu. Use the arrow keys to highlight your choice, or press the number for your choice. If Browse searching is on the screen, press the Escape key <ESC> until the Main Menu appears. Select **WILSEARCH** and press <Enter>.

2. When the search screen appears, enter terms on as many of the lines as you need. You do not need to fill out the entire screen.
   Use one or more of the three **Subject words** lines for subject searches. Several terms may share a line, or one term may he typed on each line.
   Use the **Title words** line to search for the title of a specific article. You do not need to enter the entire title; a few key words will do.
   Use the **Personal name** line to search for articles BY or ABOUT a person.
   Use the **Journal name** line to search for journal titles. You must type the full, exact title; if you type keywords from the title, the search will fall.

3. Press <End> and then <Enter> to perform the search. WAIT - the machine takes 15-30 seconds to search the disc.

4. Press <Enter> to see the articles.

TO PRINT

Press the <F4> key on the left side of the keyboard to print one article citation.
Press the <F6> key to print all citations up to ten at one time. Press any key to interrupt the printer. To continue printing, press "Y" for yes; to stop printing type "N" for no.

TO END SEARCH

Press <ESC> (Escape) repeatedly until you return to the Main Menu.

- OVER FOR BROWSE -

Poster session 5 (Weir): Part 6 - Appendix G - Sample Class Handouts (continued)

Creating "MILT": A Multimedia Interactive Library Tour

Orange County Community College, Middletown, New York

Sarah Vasse

THE COLLEGE

Founded in 1950 as the first county-sponsored community college in the State University of New York system (SUNY), Orange County Community College (OCCC) offers 62 academic programs designed for transfer and career preparation for over 6,000 full-time and part-time students on the main campus in Middletown and at the Extension Center in the city of Newburgh, 27 miles east. The Learning Resource Center (LRC) at the Middletown Campus contains 93,000 books, subscribes to 500 periodicals, and holds back issues on 30,000 microforms. Videotape, audiotape, compact disc, and computer software collections and equipment are also available, as well as CD-ROM indexes, interlibrary loan and online database search service. While a small reference library of basic resources is being developed at the Newburgh Extension Center, students are invited to use the resources of main campus library.

Orange County Community College may be typical in finding itself facing an increasingly daunting combination of factors that have a direct impact on library services and the need for effective library instruction:

- Dramatic increases in enrollment, with students at two campuses;

- Diversity of age and cultural background among students;

- The time constraints of commuting students who also have jobs and family responsibilities;

- Open admissions, resulting in a student body with an extremely wide range of academic preparation, from the semi-literate, to the ESL student, to the traditionally "college-prepared" student who continues on to complete a baccalaureate degree;

- Service to the area's high school students and other citizens, for whom the OCCC Learning Resource Center is the only public college library; and

- A small staff of librarians (4.5) to serve this large and diverse population of students, faculty, staff, and community patrons.

In attempting to meet some of these challenges, we recognized that we now live in a "visual age" in which television is the most pervasive and effective educational medium for a population increasingly reluctant to read. The photo-CD tour grew out of a slide program originally designed when the Newburgh Extension opened in 1990. At that time, we attempted to instruct students in library skills without the use of a library on site, by showing slides of the facilities, resources, and people at the Middletown Campus Library. As one of the instruction librarians, I took the photographs for this slide program.

THE DEVELOPMENT OF MILT

The development of "MILT", the Multimedia Interactive Library Tour, began when a colleague in graphic design, Joe Litow, was looking for material to use in the development of a multimedia PC-based prototype for an interactive instruction program. The slide-tour of the Library/LRC answered that need, and the "MILT" idea served the Library/LRC's need for new instruction methods for both campuses.

In 1992 the Kodak Photo-CD became available as a new technology that makes it possible to provide a photographic tour, customized to meet a variety of different group- and course-related interests. The photos on a CD can be rearranged in selected patterns to meet particular needs. This serves as a general introduction to a library, as a course-related visual tour of library resources, and as a means for an individual patron or instructor to select parts of the program for focus on a particular area. As an enthusiastic but amateur photographer, I again did the photography for this part of the project with my 35mm camera. A "script book" with prints of each picture provides a basis for narration of the program and its variations. This was developed in consultation with my fellow librarians at OCCC.

Poster session 6 (Vasse): Part 1 - Introduction

A photo-CD can also be set to change at pre-set intervals to provide an automatic photo-tour, making it continuously available, if desired. In early 1994, according to Kodak, it will be possible to add sound, text, graphics, and interactive branching to the photographs on a photo-CD, with minor additions to existing equipment. It will then be possible to provide *images and sound for a narrated photo-tour*, set to run automatically and viewed by a group or by an individual.

COSTS:

Kodak Photo CD Player (PCD 850)	$479.95
Developing of 3 rolls of film into a photo CD (Kodak print film, total of 109 images)	$217.13 (Cost of *2 CDs, for use in PC program development and in Kodak Photo CD-version for immediate use).
Developing of 2nd photo-CD, for additional pictures and replacement of "bad shots"	FREE (Kodak bonus for purchase Photo CD Player)
Developing of 3rd photo-CD to combine best of photos on CDs 1 and 2, plus addition of selected photos from original slide program.	$153.04 (Photo CD developing always provides prints of each image for use in "script book.")

TOTAL COST: **$850.12**

The Kodak Photo-CD is an excellent new tool for library instruction. It has the advantage of being visual, flexible, expandable, and interactive. The instructor can stop it at any time for discussion, further explanation, or use of handouts and other devices for more detailed instruction. New sections can be added to a photo CD, as long as the total number of images does not exceed one hundred. There is great potential in this new format. The biggest challenge is in getting ourselves to change to new ideas and methods for instruction.

Suggested resource for further information: Larish, John *Photo CD: Quality Photos at Your Fingertips* (Torrence, CA: Micro Publishing Press, 1993).

Poster session 6 (Vasse): Part 1 - Introduction (continued)

THE FUTURE DEVELOPMENT OF "MILT"

The technology has now become available to display pictures from a photo-CD with an IBM-compatible PC projecting through an LCD panel; and to combine this with *graphics, narration*, and background *music*.

This turns the photo-CD tour into an *interactive presentation*

- with *animated words* moving to sections on a *map of the library*,

- with *pictures* to explain procedures and identify resources, and

- with *people seen in active roles* to make the process of library use familiar and easily understood with the ability to *focus on selected parts* of the total program, for concentration on specific sections.

It will soon be possible to add *moving images* in a "video overlay" and 3-D animation. The ultimate goal is to try to get this to be a user product in a kiosk, with a "mouse" for individual operation, and with the whole system resident in the computer.

The computer hardware necessary for the interactive PC version of the tour includes the following:

- IBM-compatible PC / DX2/66,

- 8 MB RAM with a 200 MB hard disk,

- SuperVGA display card, capable of displaying 16 million colors,

- Color LCD panel or projection panel,

- NEC intersect CD-ROM with an XA-format,

- SOFTWARE: Windows 3.1, Assymetrix Toolbook, Corel Draw, and Micrografix Picture Publisher, and

- Kodak Photo CD access software.

Cost is approximately $3,000 for computer and CD hardware, software, and peripherals; and $5,000 for LCD projection panel, if not already available.

Multimedia Developer is Joe Litow, Department of Music, Art, Speech, and Theatre.

Instruction Librarian/Photographer is Sarah J. Vasse Learning Resource Center, Orange County Community College, 115 South Street, Middletown, NY 10940.

Vasse is librarian, writer, and photographer, Orange County Community Collge, Middleton, New York.

Poster session 6 (Vasse): Part 2 - Future Development

BIBLIOGRAPHY

LIBRARY ORIENTATION AND INSTRUCTION—1992

Hannelore B. Rader

The following is an annotated list of materials dealing with information literacy including instruction in the use of information resources, research, and computer skills related to retrieving, using, and evaluating information. This review, the nineteenth to be published in *Reference Services Review*, includes items in English published in 1992. A few are not annotated because the compiler could not obtain copies of them for this review.

The list includes publications on user instruction in all types of libraries and for all levels of users, from small children to senior citizens and from beginning levels to the most advanced. The items are arranged by type of library and are in alphabetical order by author (or by title if there is no author) within those categories.

Overall, as shown in the example below, the number of publications related to user education and information literacy has increased by 11 percent from 1991 to 1992. This is also the second largest bibliography since this particular literature review began in 1973. The largest list so far appeared in 1984.

These figures are approximate and are based on the published information that was available to the reviewer; however, since the availability of this information does not vary greatly from year to year, these figures should be reliable.

Publications dealing with user instruction in academic libraries continue to be the largest number, with a nineteen percent increase. The number of publications about user instruction in public libraries decreased, while those about schools or libraries increased by 70 percent: Special library publications decreased as did items for all levels.

User education publications in libraries continue to deal with teaching users how to access and organize information, including online searching, online system use, and bibliographic computer applications. An increasing percentage deal with evaluative research of user education. It is noteworthy that in 1992 articles dealing with instruction in the use of CD-ROMs and online catalogs increased substantially, as did articles dealing with information literacy, resource-based and active learning, and integrating information literacy into the curriculum. Likewise, several articles began to address training for the Internet.

ACADEMIC LIBRARIES

Adams, Mignon. "The Role of Academic Libraries in Teaching and Learning." *College and Research Libraries* 53 (July-August 1992): 442-445.

Describes an interview with the Middle State Association of Colleges and Schools Executive Director of the Commission on Higher Education, Howard Simmons. Advocates the library's important role in the teaching/learning process and the empowerment of librarians.

Rader is director, University Library, Cleveland State University, Cleveland.

Type of Library	# of 1991 Publications	# of 1992 Publications	% Change
Academic	118	140	+ 19%
Public	05	04	- 80%
School	33	56	+ 70%
Special	16	11	- 31%
All Types	23	06	- 74%
TOTAL	195	217	+ 11%

Adler, A. Emmeli. "Advanced Library Instruction for Undergraduate Students." *PNLA Quarterly* 56 (Winter 1992): 22-23.

Describes a library instruction program for education students at St. Martin's College.

Affleck, Mary Ann. "Bibliographic Instruction in Community Colleges: Current Practice and the New Standards." *Research Strategies* 10 (Winter 1992): 24-33.

Reports the results of a survey of 120 library directors of two-year U.S. colleges. Compares those findings with the ACRL's "Standards for Community, Junior and Technical College Learning Resources Programs." Findings indicate that directors are committed to user instruction but should examine further how to meet more closely the standards, especially in the area of critical thinking.

Arp, Lori, and G. Schafer. "Connecting Bibliographic Instruction and Collection Development: A Management Plan." *RQ* 31 (Spring 1992): 398-406.

Summarizes a systematic data collection and analysis between bibliographic instruction and collection development departments at the Auraria Library in Colorado and how this affects instructional program design, collection evaluation, and planning.

Barclay, Donald A. "Understanding the Freshman Writer: The Pedagogy of Composition and Its Relevance to Bibliographic Instruction." In *Academic Libraries: Achieving Excellence in Higher Education.* Ed. by Thomas Kirk, 133-135. Chicago: Association of College and Research Libraries, 1992.

Advocates that instruction librarians become concerned about the pedagogy of freshman writing in order to improve user instruction and help students become more knowledgeable about library research.

Becker, Karen A., and S.T. Huang. "Implications of CD-ROM Usage for Bibliographic Instruction." In *Academic Libraries: Achieving Excellence in Higher Education.* Ed. by Thomas Kirk, 136-144. Chicago: Association of College and Research Libraries, 1992.

Based on user survey at Northern Illinois University. Librarians determined that users needed formal instruction for searching the more sophisticated and advanced CD-ROM databases.

Bergman, Emily, and L. Maman. "Aims of User Education: Special Library Results." *Special Libraries* 83 (Summer 1992): 156-160.

Summarizes a survey of special libraries regarding the provision of library instruction. The survey conducted by ALA's Library Instruction Round Table Journal determined that such instruction is done to encourage more effective use of the library and to articulate information needs.

Beth, Amy, and E.I. Farber. "Lessons from Dialogue. Technology Impacts Teaching/Learning." *Library Journal* 117 (15 September 1992): 26-30.

Discusses how technology changes teaching and affects faculty and user instruction. Based on a study at Earlham College; findings are provided regarding technology's impact on teaching and learning in the undergraduate environment.

Bodi, Sonia. "Collaborating with Faculty in Teaching Critical Thinking: The Role of Librarians." *Research Strategies* 10 (Spring 1992): 69-76.

Describes an enhanced role for librarians in course-integrated library instruction that promotes critical thinking as an important component of research. Cites North Park College in Illinois as an example.

Bodi, Sonia. "Learning Style Theory and Bibliographic Instruction: The Quest for Effective Bibliographic Instruction." In *Academic Libraries: Achieving Excellence in Higher Education.* Ed. by Thomas Kirk, 145-148. Chicago: Association of College and Research Libraries, 1992.

Examines David A. Kolb's theory of experiential learning and applies it to bibliographic instruction programs at North Park College in Illinois in order to address the diverse learning styles of students.

Borah, Eloisa G. "Beyond Navigation: Librarians as Architects of Information Tools." *Research Strategies* 10 (Summer 1992): 138-142.

The author challenges librarians to forge tools for future information users. Describes three computer-based projects that serve as examples of how librarians can increase their involvement in the development of reference tools.

Breivik, Patricia S. "Education for the Information Age." *New Directions for Higher Education* 20 (Summer 1992): 5-13.

Individuals need information literacy to be effective in the current changing information environment. Undergraduate education should focus on resource-based learning to prepare people for problem solving.

Buchanan, Nancy L., et al. "The Effectiveness of the Projected Computerized Presentation in Teaching Online Library Catalog Searching." *College and Research Libraries* 53 (July 1992): 307-318.

Describes a computerized presentation teaching NOTIS commands and search strategies to freshman composition students. Presents a comparison of teaching students with and without the computerized presentation and finds that students who received the computerized presentation learned search strategies more effectively.

Burnheim, Robert. "Information Literacy—a Core Competency." *AARL* (December 1992): 188-196.

Redefines the collection, analysis, and organization of ideas and information as a broader concept of information literacy to train young people for competency in the workplace. Provides and describes competencies for information literacy as part of the curriculum development process.

Burnheim, Robert. *Information Literacy: The Keystone of the Bridge*. ERIC Reproduction Service, 1992. ED 356 775.

Discusses information literacy skills and procedures to analyze information resources. Describes a research project supporting the delivery of competency-based training curricula. Describes how librarians and teachers should cooperate in developing information skills.

Burns, Charles A., et al. *Colleague: An Annual Collection of Articles on Academic and Administrative Issues Facing Community Colleges of the State University of New York*. ERIC Reproduction Service, 1992. ED 342 454.

Butterworth, Margaret. "Making a Video about On Line Searching." *Audio-Visual Librarian* 18 (February 1992): 29-31.

Describes the production of a video to teach online searching to students at Edith Cowan University in Australia involved in distance education.

Carpmael, Steve M., and J. Nichols. "Library Orientation: A Workable Alternative?" *Library Review* 41 (1992): 16-30.

Describes a library orientation program at the University of the West of England. Gives objectives, a workbook description, methodology, practical considerations, and practical application findings.

Chambers, Joan. "Access vs. Ownership: How Far Can We Shift?" *Colorado Libraries* 18 (June 1992): 18-20.

At present many libraries are having problems offering adequate support for instruction, research, and scholarship.

Clay, Rudolph J., and C.P. McLeod. "Using a For-Credit Course to Increase Access to a Diverse Collection." In *Academic Libraries: Achieving Excellence in Higher Education*. Ed. by Thomas Kirk, 149-153. Chicago: Association of College and Research Libraries, 1992.

Describes a three-credit course to prepare students for effective library use, developed at Washington University. One goal of the course is to increase utilization of diversified collections.

Cox, Jennifer, and R. Johnson. "Transfer Students in the Library: The Forgotten Population." *Research Strategies* 10 (Spring 1992): 88-91.

Discusses how many colleges and universities do not offer library orientation for transfer students and provides information on the University of Arizona's program for such a population.

Crawford, Gregory A. "The Effects of Instruction in the Use of PsychLit on Interlibrary Loan." *RQ* 31 (Spring 1992): 370-376.

Examines the impact of user instruction on interlibrary loan. Findings indicate that requests for journal articles indexed in Psychological Abstracts actually decreased after the installation of PsychLit. Emphasis was placed on having users rely on journals owned by the Rutgers State University libraries. Describes a three-credit course to prepare students for effective library use, developed at Washington University. One goal of the course is to increase utilization of diversified collections.

Crea, Kathleen, et al. "The Impact of In-House and End-User Databases on Mediated Searching." *Online* 16 (July 1992): 49-53.

Culbertson, Michael. "Analysis of Searches by End-Users of Science and Engineering CD-ROM Databases in an Academic Library." *CD-ROM Professional* 5 (March 1992): 76-79.

Reports on a study that analyzed CD-ROM searches in five science and engineering databases. It was found that instruction in CD-ROM database searching was needed.

Downard, Karen. "User Education in Academic Libraries." *Library Management* 13 (1992): 29-38.

Reviews user education in academic libraries and provides arguments, pro and con. Provides guidance on how to set up a user education program from planning to evaluation.

Drueke, Jeanetta. "Active Learning in the University Library Instruction Classroom." *Research Strategies* 10 (Spring 1992): 77-83.

Describes a successful conversion of a research methods lecture to an active learning session at the University of Nebraska. Provides useful hints on how to do this.

Dupree, Sandra. "Videotaping Bibliographic Instruction." *Arkansas Libraries* 49 (October 1992): 8-11.

Describes rationale and details of videotaping bibliographic instruction at the University of Arkansas at Monticello. Uses a combination of in-house produced and commercial products.

Eadie, Tom. "Beyond Immodesty: Questioning the Benefits of BI." *Research Strategies* 10 (Summer 1992): 105-110.

Questions the real value of traditional approaches to bibliographic instruction. Feels that users can get whatever assistance they need at the reference desk. Discusses various parts of user instruction in terms of ineffectiveness in its outcome.

Egan, Philip J. "Bridging the Gap Between the Student and the Library." *College Teaching* 41 (Spring 1992): 67-70.

Discusses the reluctance of college students to use libraries and promotes the idea that teachers should require library research and library conferences for students to help them overcome psychological barriers.

Engeldinger, Eugene. "Frustrating Management in a Course-Integrated Bibliographic Instruction Program." *RQ* 31 (Fall 1992): 20-24.

Stresses the importance of developing a philosophical basis for user instruction programs, marketing it on campus, and integrating it into the curriculum. Links needs assessment with quality management focused on users.

Ensor, Pat. "Knowledge Level of Users and Nonusers of Keyword/Boolean Searching on an Online Public Access Catalog." *RQ* 31 (Fall 1992): 60-74.

Summarizes a study at Indiana State University to assess characteristics of users and nonusers of keyword searching on the online catalog. Some results indicate that users become better as they gain more experience; however, there is also a need to develop more online instruction and simplify both terminology and online systems.

Ensor, Pat. "User Characteristics of Keyword Searching in an OPAC." *College and Research Libraries* 53 (January 1992): 72-80.

Elaborates on a user study at Indiana State University to determine their use of keyword and Boolean search modes. (see also above)

Farmer, D.W. "Information Literacy: Overcoming Barriers to Implementation." *New Directions for Higher Education* 20 (Summer 1992): 103-112.

In order to implement effective information literacy programs fundamental changes in attitude and behavior must take place in the higher education environment.

Feinberg, Richard, and Charles King. "Performance Evaluation in Bibliographic Instruction Workshop Courses: Assessing What Students Do as a Measure of What They Know." *Reference Services Review* 20, no. 2 (Summer 1992): 75-80.

Reviews bibliographic instruction program at SUNY Stony Brook where students read workbooks and review questions before they attend workshops held by librarians. Provides an individualized learning situation.

Fister, Barbara. "Common Ground: The Composition/Bibliographic Instruction Connection." In *Academic Libraries: Achieving Excellence in Higher Education*. Ed. by Thomas Kirk, 154-158. Chicago: Association of College and Research Libraries, 1992.

Describes three major trends in the teaching of writing and shows how they relate to user instruction issues. Collaboration between these two areas is outlined.

Fister, Barbara. "The Research Processes of Undergraduate Students." *Journal of Academic Librarianship* 18 (July 1992): 163-169.

Presents findings from 14 undergraduates comparing their research processes with search strategies taught in B.I. Describes differences between student approaches and what is taught in library instruction, and explores implications for the future.

Frick, Elizabeth. "The Think Tank Papers: Are We in the Ball Park?" In *The Evolving Educational Mission of the Library*. Ed. by Betsy Baker, et al., 9-19. Chicago: Association of College and Research Libraries, 1992.

Places the first think tank in 1981 into perspective to the second, held in 1989. Discusses bibliographic instruction in terms of the evolving concept of information literacy.

Gaunt, Marianne I., and S. Nash. "Expository Writing and Information Literacy: A Pilot Project." *New Directions for Higher Education* 20 (Summer 1992): 83-90.

Describes a program at Rutgers University to integrate information literacy into freshman composition courses. Evaluation of the program showed successful techniques and areas for improvement.

George, Mary W. "First Things First: Thoughts on Teaching the Concept of Source." In *Academic Libraries: Achieving Excellence in Higher Education*. Ed. by Thomas Kirk, 159-162A. Chicago: Association of College and Research Libraries, 1992.

Suggests methodology to teach the concept of source regarding primary versus secondary sources. Demonstrates how undergraduates can look at sources critically using nine different perspectives.

Giguere, Marlene. "An Introduction to Services Accessibility on the Internet." *Education Libraries* 16 (Summer 1992): 5-9.

Gorman, Michael. "Practical Problems, Practical Solutions." *Research Strategies* 10 (Summer 1992): 117-119.

Discusses the necessity of library instruction especially in the setting of an academic library, where first-generation college students need library skills to succeed academically and where practical and successful instruction programs are a necessity in tight budget times.

Hale, Martha. "Education for the Second Generation of Bibliographic Instruction Librarians." In *The Evolving Educational Mission of the Library*. Ed. by

Betsy Wilson, et al., 128-139. Chicago: Association of College and Research Libraries, 1992.

Explores library education in relationship to current changes and proposes several changes in the library/information science education curriculum.

Hansen, Kathleen A. "Information for Mass Communication." *Research Strategies* 10 (Spring 1992): 92-96.

Describes a journalism and mass communications program at the University of Minnesota in which a required four-credit course on information gathering and evaluation has to be taken prior to any other course work.

Hardesty, Larry, et al. "Earlham's BI Enhances Teaching and Learning." *College and Research Libraries News* 53 (June 1992): 402-403.

Describes the fifth Earlham College-Eckerd College Bibliographic Instruction Conference held 5-7 February 1992. Sixty-five librarians, faculty, and administrators from 40 institutions discussed integrating library instruction into the curriculum using Earlham College's model.

Helsel, Sandra K. "Virtual Reality as a Learning Medium." *Instruction Delivery Systems* 6 (July/August 1992): 4-5.

Henning, Joanne. "A Light Hearted Look at CD-ROM Service—What We Taught Them and What They Learned." *PNLA Quarterly* 56 (Winter 1992): 15-16.

Describes end-user instruction in CD-ROMs for students at the University of Calgary Library.

Henri, James, and K. Dillon. "Learning to Learn. Reflections upon Enquiry, Information Literacy and Critical Thinking." *Australian Library Journal* (May 1992): 103-117.

The authors argue that educators need to restructure the instructional programs from teaching a fixed body of knowledge to resource-based learning and involving students in the teaching/learning process. Information literacy should also become part of this.

Hubbard, Willis M. "Shifting Paradigms for Librarians. A Report from EDUCOM '92." *College and Research Libraries News* 53 (December 1992): 707-708.

Discusses how the term "bibliographic instruction" should be changed because it is very narrow in concept.

Huber, Kris, and B. Sherman. "Scholarly Networking in Action." *Research Strategies* 10 (Winter 1992): 40-43.

Shows how to teach students to trace the flow of ideas through informal connections such as electronic networking. Gives specific examples within psychology.

"Information Retrieval and Evaluation Skills for Education Students." *College and Research Libraries News* 53 (October 1992): 583-598.

This statement represents a complete revision of the ACRL Education and Behavioral Sciences Section 1981 Bibliographic Competencies for Education Students, and gives a new conceptual foundation for instructional objectives to facilitate the teaching of information retrieval and evaluation skills in an electronic information environment. The statement includes broad goals and terminal objectives as well as two sample applications.

Irving, Ann. "Quality in Academic Libraries: How Shall We Know It?" *Aslib Information* 20 (June 1992): 244-246.

Looks at user problems from three perspectives: the student, the faculty, and the librarian. Reveals that much of the students' time is spent trying to find information rather than critically evaluating information. Advocates monitoring users' experiences to improve quality of information services.

Jackson-Brown, Grace. "Comparisons of Graduate and Undergraduate End-Users of ERIC and PsychLit on CD-ROM." In *Academic Libraries: Achieving Excellence in Higher Education*. Ed. by Thomas Kirk, 160-167. Chicago: Association of College and Research Libraries, 1992.

Summarizes a survey examining user satisfaction with searching PsychLit and ERIC CD-ROMs at Indiana University-Bloomington. The results are compared in two different library settings, an education library and a university reference department.

Jacobson, Frances F., and M.J. Jacobson. "Bibliographic Instruction in the Electronic Environment: Incorporating Recent Cognitive Theories of Learning." In *Academic Libraries: Achieving Excellence in Higher Education*. Ed. by Thomas Kirk, 168-174. Chicago: Association of College and Research Libraries, 1992.

Examines recent cognitive theories of learning in terms of applying them to bibliographic instruction in the electronic environment. Provides ideas to apply new views of learning, to teach conceptual knowledge, and to improve students' learning in an environment that is variable and unpredictable.

Jacobson, Trudi E. "All I Need Is in the Computer: Reference and Bibliographic Instruction in the Age of CD-ROMs." In *Assessment and Accountability in Refer-*

ence Work. Ed. by Susan G. Blandy, et al. Binghamton, NY: Haworth Press, 1992.

Discusses the need for education students in the use of CD-ROMs. Explains the need to teach students critical thinking skills so they are able to evaluate information.

Jacobson, Trudi E. "Good Acting Secret of Successful B.I." *College and Research Libraries News* 53 (July/August 1992): 441.

Discusses techniques for successful user instruction.

Jacobson, Trudi E., and J.R. Vallely. "A Half-Built Bridge: The Unfinished Work of Bibliographic Instruction." *Journal of Academic Librarianship* 17 (January 1992): 359-363.

Describes a study of the bibliographic instruction literature in nonlibrary journals where it was found that of 74 articles in a ten-year period, 18 were written by faculty and only three were positive.

Jones, Linda B. "Linking Undergraduate Education and Libraries: Minnesota's Approach." *New Directions for Higher Education* 20 (Summer 1992): 27-35.

In an effort to improve undergraduate education, resource-based learning and information literacy skills play important roles in the Minnesota State University system.

Jurgens, Jane C., and D.J. Villa. *Academic Libraries as Dynamic Classrooms*. ERIC Reproduction Service, 1992. ED 349 014.

Discusses problems encountered by nontraditional university students regarding library research skills and how librarians can assist them. Describes two approaches to teach such students at Northeastern Illinois University.

Kalin, Sally W. "Support Services for Remote Users of Online Public Access Catalogs." *RQ* 31 (Winter 1992): 197-213.

Kaufman, Paula T. "Information Incompetence." *Library Journal* 117 (15 November 1992): 37-39.

Discusses how existing library instruction programs have not provided citizens with adequate information skills. Information skills education must be part of the core curriculum in schools, colleges, and universities to provide citizens with information competency.

Kenney, Donald. "Bridging the Gap Between the Think Tanks." In *The Evolving Educational Mission of the Library*. Ed. by Betsy Baker, et al., 1-8. Chicago:Association of College and Research Libraries, 1992.

Summarizes ACRL's Bibliographic Section think tanks on the future of bibliographic instruction and provides some comparisons.

Kenney, Richard F., and E. Schroeder. "An Evaluation of a Training and Assistance Program for the CD-ROM Databases: Reflections on the Process." *Reference Services Review* 20, no. 2 (1992): 41-50.

Experience gained at SUNY-Cortland is shared regarding designing an instructional program for end-users. Provides insights into evaluating such search processes.

Kilman, Leigh A. "Public Justice Information Sources: A Teaching Partnership." *Research Strategies* 10 (Summer 1992): 129-133.

Provides details about a Public Justice Information Sources undergraduate course at St. Mary's University for public justice students. Includes the course syllabus.

King, Richard L. "Bibliography and the Decades: Freshmen Experience the Library." *Research Strategies* 10 (Fall 1992): 178-181.

Describes a motivating library assignment for students to help them create bibliographies focusing on the events of a particular decade.

Knapp, Amy F., and M Whitmore. *Bridging the Cultural Gaps: A Workshop for International Students*. Washington, DC: Document Reproduction Service, 1992. ED 345 738.

Kurman, Tina. "Coping with Change and Computer Lists." *Illinois Libraries* 74 (December 1992): 506-608.

LaBaugh, Ross T. "BI Is a Proper Noun." *Research Strategies* 10 (Winter 1992): 34-39.

Explores the parallels between composition theory and emerging theory of B.I. and urges instruction librarians to focus on the rhetorical needs of students. Students should be taught the importance of journal information to their research and a critical approach to computers.

LaGuardia, Cheryl. "Renegade Library Instruction." *Library Journal* (October 1992): 51-53.

Advocates teaching students what they need to know rather than what librarians want to teach them. Questions many of the fundamentals of B.I. Discusses need for very basic library instruction.

Laney, Gretchen. "Two Models of Bibliographic Instruction at Belhaven Library." *Mississippi Libraries* 56 (Spring 1992): 8-10.

Describes library instruction in the context of a freshman orientation course at Belhaven College, allowing librarians four contact hours with students to instruct them in information skills.

Lenox, Mary, and M.L. Walker. "Information Literacy: Challenge for the Future." *International Journal of Information and Library Research* 4 (1992): 1-18.

Discusses the necessity to teach information literacy on all educational levels. Identifies five challenges as follows: shifting from acquisition of information products to access; realization that information is a commodity and must be treated like a business; recognition of diversity; need for information products to provide dynamic options; and need for teachers, librarians, and administrators to become facilitators of life-long learning.

Lewis, Patricia. "Using Dictionaries to Create a Product Name." *Research Strategies* 10 (Fall 1992): 174-177.

Describes how students at St. Olaf College in Minnesota are introduced to critical writing skills and how librarians are providing innovative assignments using dictionaries to help in this endeavor.

Liestman, Daniel. "Implementing Library Instruction for International Students." *PNLA Quarterly* 56 (Winter 1992): 11-14.

Describes a user education program for international students.

Mackey, Neosha, et al. "Teaching with HyperCard in Place of a Textbook." *Computers in Libraries* 12 (October 1992): 22-26.

"Making Sure We're in 'In Compliance'." Editorials. *Research Strategies* 10 (Winter 1992): 2-3.

Discusses how bibliographic instruction librarians can become leaders in removing communication barriers between libraries and handicapped students. Gives several examples of how librarians can help the handicapped achieve access to information.

Marais, J.J. "Evolution of Information Literacy as Product of Information Education." *South African Journal of Library and Information Science* 60 (June 1992): 75-79.

Marley, Judith L., and H.E. Price. "Bringing Music History Alive: Using Artifacts to Explore Historiography." *Research Strategies* 10 (Summer 1992): 134-137.

At the University of Alabama music students are required to take a graduate course in music research materials, resources, and methodologies. Musical artifacts are chosen to be examined as part of a term project.

McClure, Charles. "A User Perspective on Developing Internet Services." *Computers in Libraries* 12 (April 1992): 53-55.

Discusses development of networked information services from user perspective including user instruction.

McHenry, Kelley E., et al. "Teaching Resource-Based Learning and Diversity." *New Directions for Higher Education* 20 (Summer 1992): 55-62.

Discusses how faculty and librarians at Seattle Community College revised the general curriculum to link information literacy and resource-based learning.

McWeeney, Mark G. "Computer-Assisted Instruction to Teach DOS Commands: A Pilot Study." *Research Strategies* 10 (Winter 1992): 17-23.

Reports on a pilot study at the University of Missouri-Columbia to investigate the teaching of DOS commands through computer-assisted instruction to graduate students in library science. Includes a survey of research in CAI.

Metoyer-Duran, Cheryl. "Tribal Community College Libraries: Perceptions of the College Presidents." *Journal of Academic Librarianship* 17 (January 1992): 364-369.

Examines the perceptions of tribal community college presidents as they relate to information literacy.

Miller, William. "The Future of Bibliographic Instruction and Information Literacy for the Academic Librarian." *The Evolving Educational Mission of the Library*. Ed. by Betsy Baker, et al., 140-157. Chicago: Association of College and Research Libraries, 1992.

Discusses the role of academic librarians as teachers of information literacy as well as changing student populations. Outlines several challenges.

Nahl-Jakobovits, Diane, and L.A. Jakobovits. "A Content Analysis Method for Developing User-based Objectives." *Research Strategies* 10 (Winter 1992): 4-16.

Explains content analysis using oral and written library user commentaries to formulate user-based instructional objectives.

"Need Help with Your Information Literacy Program?" *College and Research Libraries News* 53 (December 1993): 718-719.

Provides a list of information literacy advisors to help librarians who are in need of assistance to set up, expand, or improve information literacy programs.

Nelson, Frederick E. "Bibliographic Instruction in the Undergraduate Research Methods Course." *Journal of Geography* (May-June 1991): 134-140.

Describes an undergraduate research methods course at Rutgers University for geography students. Outlines the course and assignments.

Nolan, Anne C., and M.P. Whitmore. "An Awareness Program for Tests and Measurement." *Research Strategies* 10 (Winter 1992): 44-48.

Describes how librarians at the University of Pittsburgh developed an in-class instructional component to teach students majoring in electronic resources in the area of measurement. The result of this teaching was an increase in the use of these library resources.

Norlin, Dennis A. "We're Not Stupid You Know: Library Services for Adults with Mental Retardation." *Research Strategies* 10 (Spring 1992): 56-68.

Few programs exist for adults with mental retardation to help them in using the library. Provides a description of a project that was aimed at studying the effects of group bibliographic instruction for adults with mental retardation in the Lincoln Trail Library System in Illinois.

Norton, Melanie. "Effective Bibliographic Instruction for Deaf and Hearing Impaired College Students." *Library Trends* 41 (Summer 1992): 118-150.

Describes how librarians at the Rochester Institute of Technology devised a way to instruct deaf students in library and information skills. Provides practical guides and examples.

Notess, Greg. "Gaining Access to the Internet." *Online* 16 (September 1992): 27-34.

O'Hanlon, Nancy. "Good Intentions Are Not Enough: Toward Cooperative Teaching of Basic Information-Seeking Competencies." *Ohio Media Spectrum* 44, no. 1 (1992): 14-19.

Reports on Ohio's school and academic librarians joint task force to implement information-seeking skills from high school to college. Lists and defines each recommended skill.

Olsen, Jan K. "The Electronic Library and Literacy." *New Directions for Higher Education* 20 (Summer 1992): 91-102.

The definition of literacy has been changed by technological advances and this has an impact on preparing academically literate people. At Cornell University four years of evaluation of literacy instruction programs have increased the understanding and teaching of information literacy.

Osborne, Nancy S., and M.H. Maier. "Service to International Users: The Case of a Brazilian Biologist." *Research Strategies* 10 (Spring 1992): 84-87.

Describes how one librarian's personal relationship with an international researcher helped to enhance the researcher's work.

Pastine, Maurine, and L. Wilson. "Curriculum Reform: The Role of Academic Libraries." In *The Evolving Educational Mission of the Library*. Ed. by Betsy Baker, et al., 90-108. Chicago: Association of College and Research Libraries, 1992.

Discusses how academic librarians can become involved in curriculum development on the campus, especially in an environment of curriculum reform. Suggests various new opportunities for librarians to become more actively involved in the educational process.

Payne, Rob. "Classroom BI, No Apology Needed—Just More Cooperation." *Arkansas Libraries* 49 (October 1992): 12-15.

Offers practical hints and advice to improve user instruction in the academic setting.

Pence, James L. "Transforming Campus Culture through Resource-Based Learning." *New Directions for Higher Education* 20 (Summer 1992): 113-122.

Information literacy and availability of information technology must be encouraged by the campus to bring about resource-based learning as part of college instruction.

Penchansky, Mimi B. *Merging Technologies and Instruction at CUNY: An Annotated Selective Bibliography*. ERIC Reproduction Service, 1992. ED 349 972.

This bibliography was produced for a faculty development colloquium at CUNY and includes a section on information literacy.

Poirier, Gayle. "The Cassette Tour: An Effective Efficient Orientation." *Research Strategies* 10 (Summer 1992): 143-144.

Describes an orientation tour on cassette at Louisiana State University and how it has been effective.

Polly, Jean. "Surfing the Internet." *Wilson Library Bulletin* 66 (June 1992): 38-42.

Popoola, M. Ola. "The Role of Libraries in the Promotion of Independent Study in Developing Countries." *Research Strategies* 10 (Fall 1992): 161-169.

Provides a discussion on the role of academic librarians in developing countries in creating self-directed learners and self-reliant researchers among nontraditional students.

Porter, John R. "Natural Partners: Resource-Based and Integrative Learning." *New Directions for Higher Education* 20 (Summer 1992): 45-53.

Describes resource-based learning projects at the Philadelphia College of Pharmacy and Science to help students become better informed about information resources in the sciences. Addresses faculty motivation, benefits, and disappointments.

Prorak, Diane, et al. "Faculty and Librarians: Colleagues in Education." *Idaho Librarian* 44 (July 1992): 89-90.

Discusses a workshop to encourage cooperation between faculty and librarians in the area of library instruction.

Rader, Hannelore B. "Adapting BI to Changing Information Needs." *Research Strategies* 10 (Summer 1992): 120-121.

Shows how BI can be successful if planned properly and if integrated into the curriculum. Use of student focus groups can help determine what students need and want in BI.

Rader, Hannelore B. "Library Orientation and Instruction—1991." *Reference Services Review* 20, no. 4 (1992): 69-84.

The annual review of library instruction and information literacy review for all types of libraries and all levels of users.

Rader, Hannelore B., and W. Coons. "Information Literacy: One Response to the New Decade." *The Evolving Educational Mission of the Library*. Ed. by Betsy Baker, et al., 109-127. Chicago: Association of College and Research Libraries, 1992.

Offers definition of information literacy and how it can fit into and expand current bibliographic instruction programs. Discusses impact of effective information literacy programs in the area of business, lifelong learning, and librarians.

Robertson, Joan E. "User Education for Overseas Students in Higher Education in Scotland." *Journal of Librarianship and Information Science* 24 (March 1992): 33-51.

Discusses issues surrounding international students in Scotland universities and how to prepare them to use the library. Reports on a survey of international students to assess the extent of the problem and offers suggestions to solve the problems.

Rockman, Ilene F. "Challenges in Teaching End Users Access to Internet Resources." *National Online Meeting* New York: Learned Information, 1992.

Describes a course in teaching users access to the Internet at California State Polytechnic University.

Roecker, Fred. "The Gateway: User Education in a Changing Environment." *Research Strategies* 10 (Summer 1992): 111-114.

Discusses the development of the Gateway project at Ohio State University, a front-end user education project to educate students within the electronic environment in the use of periodicals and research materials. Indicates that user education remains a valid and important academic library concern.

Rumsey, Eric. "HyperCard for Bibliographic Instruction." *Computers in Libraries* 12 (May 1992): 43-45.

Provides information on how to teach users searching on MEDLINE CD-ROM.

Rupp-Serrano, Karen, and N. Buchanan. "Using Presentation Software for Computerized Instruction." *On Line* 16 (March 1992): 60-64.

Describes the development of a computerized library instruction program using presentation software at Texas A&M University.

Russo, Michelle C. "Recovering from Bibliographic Instruction Blahs." *RQ* 32 (Winter 1992): 178-183.

Addresses the problem of instruction librarian burnout by providing solutions involving institutional support and using the principles from the "Twelve Steps" of Alcoholics Anonymous.

Ryan, Susan M. "The 1990 Decennial Census on CD-ROM: New Opportunities for Instruction." *Research Strategies* 10 (Fall 1992): 170-173.

Discusses the availability of census data in electronic format, the nature of the files and software, and what methods to employ instructing students in the use of this data.

Sapp, Gregg. "Science Literacy: A Discussion and an Information-Based Definition." *College and Research Libraries* 53 (January 1992): 21-30.

Reviews the current crisis in science literacy and defines the role of librarians in teaching effective information-seeking behavior to science students.

Saule, Mara R. "User Instruction Issues for Databases." *Library Trends* 40 (Spring 1992): 596-613.

Teaching methods must be reviewed because of special needs in the humanities. Analyzes attitudes of humanities students and scholars toward technology and discusses how these attitudes can be incorporated into effective computerized literature searching instruction.

Schuck, Brian R. "Assessing a Library Instruction Program." *Research Strategies* 10 (Fall 1992): 152-160.

Reports on a study of general library skills, online catalog skills, and attitudes about use of the library among undergraduates at Indiana University in South Bend. Provides an analysis of frequency of computer use, grade point average, library instruction, and online catalog use as related to library skills test scores.

Seaman, Scott. "On-line Catalog Failure as Reflected Through InterLibrary Loan Error Requests." *College and Research Libraries* 53 (March 1992): 113-120.

Summarizes a study at Ohio State University using data from interlibrary loan to determine why users failed to find entries in the online catalog. Gives implications for bibliographic instruction.

Shedlock, James. "The Changing User and the Future of Bibliographic Instruction: A Perspective from the Health Sciences Library." In *The Evolving Educational Mission of the Library.* Ed. by Betsy Baker, et al., 54-89. Chicago: Association of College and Research Libraries, 1992.

Presents a comprehensive profile of health sciences libraries in the last decade of the twentieth century and how they can address their user needs, especially in the area of library instruction. Provides background and suggestions to deal with technological changes and diverse user populations.

Shelly, Diana. *Looking into Resource-Based Learning.* ERIC Reproduction Service, 1992. ED 357 739.

This booklet outlines techniques and concepts for teaching resource-based learning in a setting of self-managing teams.

Sheridan, Jean. "WAC and Libraries: A Look at the Literature." *Journal of Academic Librarianship* 18 (May 1992): 90-94.

Discusses opportunities for librarians to become involved in programs that focus on writing across the curriculum.

Simmons, Howard L. "Information Literacy and Accreditation: A Middle States Association Perspective." *New Directions for Higher Education* 20 (Summer 1992): 15-25.

This accrediting agency believes that information literacy should be included in undergraduate programs with emphasis on resource-based learning strategies.

Stanford, Lois M. "An Academician's Journey into Information Literacy." *New Directions for Higher Education* 20 (Summer 1992): 37-43.

Describes how one college teacher applied information literacy principles to his teaching. Examines instructional development, classroom application, and student services as related to information literacy.

Stanley, Nancy M. "Computer-Assisted Instruction and the Library: A Case Study in Disappointment." *Computer-Assisted Instruction and the Library* 39 (1992): 35-43.

Reports on a project to provide remedial instructional support to re-entry students in the library and whether this is appropriate.

Stierman, John P. "A Hands-On Approach: The Missing Ingredient in Online Searching Instruction." *Illinois Libraries* 74 (December 1992): 513-515.

Stripling, Barbara K. "Tom, Tom, Quite Contrary: How Does Your Garden Grow?" *Research Strategies* 10 (Spring 1992): 115-117.

Discusses the importance of library skills instruction in the school setting and how its success can be measured.

Suale, Mara R. "User Instruction Issues for Databases in the Humanities." *Library Trends* 40 (Spring 1992): 596-613.

Provides an overview of problems and opportunities in the area of teaching database searching to humanities scholars, and a methodology to serve these highly specialized researchers.

Svenningsen, Karen. *Instructing and Implementing Dow Jones News/Retrieval into an Academic Setting*. ERIC Reproduction Service, 1992. ED 343 595.

Describes how the City University of New York, College of Staton Island Library incorporated the Dow Jones News/Retrieval Service into the collection and library instruction program.

Swan, John, et al. "Mediation and the Electronic World." *Reference Librarian* 17 (1992): 65-90.

Addresses computer-assisted instruction, online catalogs, computer networks, and reference service.

"Teaching Portfolios: How Are We Doing." Editorial. *Research Strategies* 10 (Summer 1992): 102-103.

Suggests ideas for setting up a teaching portfolio for instruction librarians based on a model from academic teaching faculty.

Thompson, Dot S., and J.A. Van Fleet. "Developing a Model of Library User Education for Freshman Science Students." *Research Strategies* 10 (Summer 1992): 122-128.

Describes the library instruction program for freshmen at Bucknell University in Pennsylvania, where librarians in cooperation with faculty have developed a library instruction module for a required science course.

Tierney, Judith. "Information Literacy and a College Library: A Continuing Approach." *New Directions for Higher Education* 20 (Summer 1992): 63-71.

Describes the experience of Kings College in Pennsylvania in integrating information literacy and resource-based learning into the curriculum.

Van Noate, Judith E. *Afro-American Studies: A Research Guide*. ERIC Reproduction Services, 1992. ED 343 566.

This guide, prepared at the University of North Carolina at Charlotte, helps to locate materials on topics in Afro-American studies.

Walton, Graham, and S. Nettleton. "Reflective and Critical Thinking in User Education Programmes: Two Case Studies." *British Journal of Academic Librarianship* 7 (1992): 31-43.

Describes two innovations in British higher education to teach critical thinking in the context of library use education. Findings indicate that user education programs must be part of curriculum development if students are to be educated for life-long learning. Librarians must become partners with faculty to make such endeavors successful.

Warmkessel, Marjorie M. "Assessing the Need for Bibliographic Instruction in Honors Sections of Freshman Composition." In *Academic Libraries: Achieving Excellence in Higher Education*. Ed. by Thomas Kirk,

175-178. Chicago: Association of College and Research Libraries, 1992.

Evaluates a cooperative user-instruction program in an honors section of freshman composition in terms of students' attitudes toward the university library. Indicates that students were less apprehensive and more willing to ask for help after the instruction.

Weaver-Meyers, Pat, and J.C. Smith. "The Academic Library Training and Instructional Design: Opinions and Practice." In *Academic Libraries: Achieving Excellence in Higher Education*. Ed. by Thomas Kirk, 179-194. Chicago: Association of College and Research Libraries, 1992.

Describes a study of librarians regarding instructional design. Indicates that lack of time and resources were the cause for lack of knowledge regarding instructional design. It is suggested that more commitment from administrators is needed to ensure adequate instructional training for librarians so they may become more effective teachers in user instruction.

Welsh, Erwin. "Hypertext, Hypermedia and the Humanities." *Library Trends* (Spring 1992): 614-646.

Provides historical background. Focuses on the use of hypertext in the humanities, shows libraries' role in this area, and presents opportunities for librarians in implementing such systems.

West, Sharon M. "Teaching Library Skills from a Long, Long Distance." *PNLA Quarterly* 56 (Winter 1992): 21-22.

Describes a library skills program offered by the Rasmuson Library in Alaska as part of distance education.

White, Herbert. "Bibliographic Instruction, Information Literacy and Information Empowerment." *Library Journal* 117 (January 1992): 76-78.

Criticizes bibliographic instruction and information literacy goals because they do not advocate abdication of librarians' role as information intermediaries. Promotes information empowerment specialists to teach understanding of information.

Whitlock, Jo Bell. "Getting Close to the Customer." *Journal of Library Administration* 18 (November 1992): 281-282.

Williams, Karen, and J. Cox. "Active Learning in Action." *RQ* 31 (Spring 1992): 326-331.

Describes a successful transition from a lecture format to one based on active learning at the University of Arizona for a freshman population of more than 5,000 students. Involves a careful planning process with faculty and setting affective goals.

Wilson, Lizabeth A. "Changing Users: Bibliographic Instruction for Whom?" In *The Evolving Educational Mission of the Library*. Ed. by Betsy Baker, et al., 20-53. Chicago: Association of College and Research Libraries, 1992.

Discusses the changing user population in academic institutions and libraries. Places demographics and technology into an ever-changing environment and offers perspectives on how these changes will affect instruction librarians.

Wiggins, Marvin E. "Information Literacy at Universities: Challenges and Solutions." *New Directions for Higher Education* 20 (Summer 1992): 73-81.

Discusses why it is more challenging to introduce information literacy within a university environment compared to a small college environment. Describes the Brigham Young University program where information literacy is integrated into the curriculum.

PUBLIC LIBRARIES

Adatto, Shelley. "Helping Users Help Themselves." *PNLA Quarterly* 56 (Winter 1992): 9-10.

Details information on user workshops for patrons at the Seattle Public Library to support school assignments.

Bell, Anita C. "A Term Paper Resource Center." *School Library Journal* 38 (January 1992): 34-36.

Describes how to create a self-help center in the public library.

de Beer, Johanna, and C.H. Fransman. "Library Orientation." *Cape Librarian* 36 (February 1992): 24-25.

Describes library orientation sessions at Lotus River Public Library in South Africa. Offers guidance and how to set up programs for children and other patrons.

Paramore, Pamela J. "Developing a Model Public Library Orientation Program for Senior High School Students." Ph.D diss. Denton, TX: Texas Woman's University, 1992.

SCHOOL LIBRARIES

Ayres, Ann, et al. "Teaching Library Skills Using Non-Print Media." *Arkansas Libraries* 49 (October 1992): 18-19.

Provides practical hints on teaching elementary school students information skills to prepare them for the year 2000. Explains how to make lessons interesting, creative, accountable, and worthwhile.

Bankhead, Elizabeth. "Multi-Media Snapshots." *Colorado Libraries* 18 (March 1992): 14-18.

Provides examples of school library projects using multiple technologies.

Barnett, Judith M. "Information Power: Using the Library Media Center in the Curriculum." *Colorado Libraries* 18 (March 1992): 22-23.

Describes a credit class for Colorado Springs High School teachers designed by media specialists.

Barron, Daniel, and T.J. Bergen, Jr. "Information Power: The Restructured School Library for the Nineties." *Phi Delta Kappan* (March 1992): 521-525.

Advocates more effective use of school library media programs to improve the educational process.

"Basic Information Seeking Competencies: High School to College." *Ohio Libraries* 5 (January/February 1992): 16-17.

Describes basic information literacy competencies as compiled jointly by various Ohio library associations.

Bell, Michael, and H.L. Totten. "Cooperation in Instruction between Classroom Teachers and School Library Media Specialists." *School Library Media Quarterly* 20 (Winter 1992): 79-85.

Describes a study of the characteristics of Texas elementary school teachers as compared to school library media specialists.

Buttlar, Lois, and M. Tipton. "Library Use and Staff Training in Curriculum Material Centers." *Journal of Academic Librarianship* 17 (January 1992): 370-374.

Examines the rationale for educating prospective teachers in library skills. Reports a study of the extent of user instruction in Curriculum Material Centers.

Chemotti, Janet T. "From Nuclear Arms to Hershey's Kisses; Strategies for Motivating Students." *School Library Media Activities Monthly* 8 (June 1992): 34-36.

Describes the attention-relevance-confidence-satisfaction model to motivate students toward library skills instruction.

Cleaver, Betty P., and M.E. Shorey. "Teaching Media Skills to Visually Impaired Students." *Ohio Media Spectrum* 44 (1992): 22-27.

Describes experiences in preparing teachers to instruct visually impaired elementary students in media skills. Provides special techniques, materials, and implications for teachers.

Curtis, Ruth V. "Taking AIM: Approaches to Instructional Motivation." *School Library Media Activities Monthly* 8 (April 1992): 32-34.

Provides an introduction to the ARCS model of motivational design to increase the appeal of instructional presentations.

Daly, Jean M. "Public and Private Lives: Connecting Classroom and Library." *School Library Journal* 38 (September 1992): 146-148.

Discusses the integration of library skills into the curriculum for fifth-grade students.

Eisenberg, Michael B., and M.K. Brown. "Current Themes Regarding Library and Information Skills Instruction: Research Supporting and Research Lacking." *School Library Media Quarterly* 20 (Winter 1992): 103-110.

Focuses on the value of library media instruction programs, their scope and integration into the curricula, and what methodologies to use. Reviews research in support of assumptions held about user instruction and analyzes implications for research and practice.

Employment-Related Key Competencies for Post-Compulsory Education and Training. ERIC Reproduction Service, 1992. ED 353 964.

Defines the collection, analysis, and organization of ideas as a part of information literacy. Information literacy is defined as a key competency for the development of skills required for workplace efficiency.

Gold, Judith, et al. "Whole Language and Teacher/Librarian Partnerships." *Phi Delta Kappan* (March 1992): 536-537.

Describes a teacher-librarian collaboration at Bank Street School in New York to help students from age three to eighth grade gain better reading skills.

Goltz, Carol. "Stacks and Macs at West Anchorage High." *PNLA Quarterly* 56 (Winter 1992): 19-20.

Describes Hypercard as a part of an interactive multimedia library skills program for high school students.

Goodman, Roz. "Media Specialist Helps Alaskan Students Research Rock 'n Roll." *PNLA Quarterly* 6 (Winter 1992): 18-19.

Describes an innovative way to teach research and library techniques to high school students.

Helmick, Aileen. "Analysis of Selective Research." *School Library Media Annual* 10 (1992): 77-82.

Analyzes research related to school libraries including information literacy.

Hill, Maggie, et al. "The New Literacy." *Electronic Learning* 12 (September 1992): 28-34.

Discusses literacy for the 21st century using the example of the Norristown, Pennsylvania area school district where a restructured curriculum focuses on thinking and communication skills.

"Into the Curriculum." *School Library Media Activities Monthly* 8 (May 1992): 17-25, 28-29.

Describes six fully developed library media activities in different subjects with activities, evaluations, and follow-ups.

Irwin, Marilyn. "Library Media Specialist as Teacher for Students Who Are Disabled." *Indiana Media Journal* 14 (Spring 1992): 19+.

Describes user instruction for handicapped students.

Jay, M. Ellen, et al. "Designing Instruction for Diverse Abilities and the Library Media Teacher's Role." *Emergency Librarian* 19 (March/April 1992): 44.

Johnson, Glenn. "A Process to Help Develop Your Picture." *School Library Media Activities Monthly* 8 (February 1992): 33-34.

Describes broad-based information skills program that encompasses classroom-integrated units.

Kirk, Deborah H., and L. Welborn. "The Impact of Outcome-Based Education on the Library Media Program." *Colorado Libraries* 18 (March 1992): 5-9.

Students must demonstrate what they have learned in the way of library and information skills before they graduate.

Knudsen, Carmelle, and J. Orpinela. "Preparation High School, or What Students Should Know about Libraries When They Leave High School." *Emergency Librarian* 19 (May/June 1992): 12-14.

Reports a workshop in which participants learned how to teach information skills to students. Emphasizes the need for practical application.

Kuhlenschmidt, Eden, et al. "Ms. K., There Is a Tiger in the Computer." *Indiana Media Journal* 14 (Spring 1992): 6-7.

Describes science lessons for seventh graders in special education classes.

"Local Attractions: A Timely Research Project." *The School Librarian's Workshop* 12 (June 1992): 1-2.

Discusses how elementary and junior high school students create travel brochures.

Love, Glenda. "Sharing Skills: Dictionary Discovery." *School Library Media Activities Monthly* 8 (May 1992): 37-38.

Mancall, Jacqueline, et al. "Searching Across the Curriculum." *Phi Delta Kappan* (March 1992): 526-528.

Discusses the importance of teaching students how to access and use information in every curricular area and the integration of information skills teaching as part of all classes.

Martin, Ron. "The Random House Children's Encyclopedia." *School Library Media Activities Monthly* 8 (March 1992): 44-46.

Provides guidance in teaching elementary school students to use encyclopedias. (See other issues of this journal for practical hints to teach elementary library skills.)

Martinez, Carole. "Teachers and Technology: Making the Connection." *Colorado Libraries* 18 (March 1992): 24-25.

Describes the establishment of networked teacher workstations at Cherry Creek High School in Colorado.

Moinet, Jo Ann, and E.D. Hart. "Research Skills for College-Bound Seniors." *LLA Bulletin* 54 (Spring 1992): 207-216.

Presents a summary of a survey of library and information skills for high school students in Louisiana.

Montgomery, Paula K. "Integrating Library, Media, Research and Information Skills." *Phi Delta Kappan* (March 1992): 529-531.

Advocates the integration of library, media, research, and information skills into the school curriculum to ensure students' acquisition of information skills.

Montgomery, Paula K. "Sources for Selecting Reference Sources." *School Library Media Activities Monthly* 8 (June 1992): 46-47.

Morgan, Jennifer. "Me—Today and Tomorrow." *The School Librarian's Workshop* 12 (April 1992): 14.

Describes a project to integrate research skills into the fifth-grade language arts curriculum.

Morin, Melinda J. *Teaching Library Skills: A Source or Process Approach? A Research Study.* ERIC Reproduction Service, 1992. ED 345 738.

This dissertation was designed to determine the dominant approach to library skills instruction in the schools of the DeKalb County School System in Georgia and any relationships with demographics.

Nicholson, Nowana. "Instructional Consulting in the Inclusive School: A New Role for Media Specialists." *Indiana Media Journal* 14 (Spring 1992): 3-5.

Describes library skills education programs for students with disabilities.

Norton, Sally. "Primary Sources in the Classroom." *Ohio Media Spectrum* 44 (1992): 25-29.

Provides a list of primary information sources to be used with high school students in library skills instruction, and criteria to help students evaluate these sources.

O'Connell, Sharon. "Welcome to the Jungle." *School Library Media Activities Monthly* 8 (May 1992): 32-34.

Outlines a sixth-grade media center orientation in the media center.

Ohlrich, Karen B. "Flexible Scheduling: The Dream versus Reality." *School Library Journal* 38 (May 1992): 35-38.

Describes the implementation of flexible scheduling in an elementary school library media program. Integrates library skills into the library curriculum.

"A Panoply of Presidents." *The School Librarian's Workshop* 12 (February 1992): 1-2.

Describes a research project on U.S. presidents for gifted fourth graders.

Pappas, Marjorie L. "Report on Treasure Mountain Research Retreat Two." *School Library Media Library Annual* 10 (1992): 213-219.

Provides an overview of the retreat for school library media specialists where they discussed information literacy issues.

Pinkston, Alfreda J. "Sharing Skills: Super Snoops Use the Library Media Center." *School Library Media Activities Monthly* 8 (January 1992): 35-37.

Describes how students learn to locate information in print or in CD-ROM versions of encyclopedias.

Rankin, Virginia. "Pre-Search: Intellectual Access to Information." *School Library Journal* 38 (March 1992): 168-170.

Describes the pre-search process where junior high school students explore and refine a topic. Using this method helps them relate research to their prior knowledge of a given topic and leads to further investigation.

Reis, Sally M., and J.S. Renzulli. "The Library Media Specialist's Role in Teaching Independent Study Skills to High Ability Students." *School Library Media Quarterly* 21 (Fall 1992): 27-35.

Presents a twelve-step program for library media specialists to use in teaching independent study skills. Provides chances for gifted students to create a variety of products.

Reum, Debby. "This Library Is for You: Empowering Students with Information." *Colorado Libraries* 18 (March 1992): 10-13.

Describes a resource-based learning plus program at Weld County School in Colorado.

Ricker, Sandra L. "Sharing Skills: Final Lesson of the Year." *School Library Media Activities Monthly* 8 (June 1992): 38+.

"Shamrock Subject." *The School Librarian's Workshop* 12 (March 1992): 10-11.

Outlines a curriculum-related project to introduce primary grades to widening or narrowing a topic.

"Sharing Skills: Focus on the Use of Tables of Contents and Indexes of History Sources." *School Library Media Activities Monthly* 8 (February 1992): 35+.

Describes a library skills unit on the topic of slavery.

Soash, Richard L. "Bibliographic Instruction in a Step-By-Step Approach." *Book Report* 10 (January/February): 37-40.

Outlines an information search process based on Kuhlthau's model to teach user instruction to ninth graders. Includes forms for helping students narrow topics and evaluate materials.

Stein, Gayle. "The Perfect Mix: Art and the Media Center." *The School Librarian's Workshop* 12 (January 1992): 10.

Shows how a fifth-grade sculpture project can teach library skills.

Stripling, Barbara. "The Instructional Program in School Libraries." *Arkansas Libraries* 49 (October 1992): 4-7.

Provides components of an effective instructional program in school libraries. Gives advice on working with teachers to integrate media and information skills into the curriculum.

Thomas, James L., and A.E. Goldsmith. "A Necessary Partnership: The Early Childhood Education and the School Librarian." *Phi Delta Kappan* (March 1992): 533-536.

Discusses the importance of teacher/school librarian partnerships to provide young children with access to developmentally appropriate materials.

Todd, Ross J., et al. *The Power of Information Literacy: Unity of Education and Resources for the 21st Century*. ERIC Reproduction Service, 1992. ED 354 916.

Describes an integrated information skills program at Marist Sister's College, a secondary school in Sydney, Australia, where information literacy has been placed at the center of the curriculum.

Walker, H. Thomas, and P.K. Montgomery. *Library Media and Information Skills*. Santa Barbara, CA: ABC-CLIO, 1992.

Discusses bibliographic instruction for elementary and high school students based on material published in *School Library Media Activities Monthly* from 1984-1990.

Whitney, Karen A. "Response Three to Ann Irving." *School Library Media Annual* 10 (1992): 52-55.

Addresses three issues raised by Irving (see above) and discusses information literacy under the influence of information technologies.

Woodward, David B. "So You Want to Host a Teacher Inservice Workshop Series." *Ohio Media Spectrum* 44 (Spring 1992): 35-37.

Describes the workshop that informed teachers about library resources and services with an emphasis on library skills instruction.

SPECIAL LIBRARIES

Frasca, Michael A., et al. "A Multi-Disciplinary Approach to Information Management and Critical Appraisal Instruction: A Controlled Study." *Bulletin of the Medical Library Association* 80 (January 1992): 23-28.

Describes a collaborative course at the University of Illinois College of Medicine to teach critical evalua-tion and library skills to third-year medical students. Using a control group it was found that the group in the course performed substantially better on an assessment test.

Ikeda, Naomi R., and D.G. Schwartz. "Impact of End User Search Training on Pharmacy Students: A Four Year Follow-up Study." *Bulletin of the Medical Library Association* 80 (April 1992): 124-130.

Reports on the study at the University of Michigan to provide pharmacy students with online search training.

Janto, Joyce M. "Teaching Legal Research: Past and Present." *Law Library Journal* 84 (Spring 1992): 281-297.

Provides a comprehensive report on teaching research methodology to law students.

Lee, R.G., and Philip A. Thomas. "Librarians as Teachers: Academic and Practitioner Views." *The Law Librarian* 23 (March 1992): 37-38.

Discusses librarians' work in teaching bibliographic instruction to law students.

Levy, Sandra R., and P.G. Hinegardner. "Teaching Pro-Cite: Classroom Instruction and Consultations." *Medical Reference Services Quarterly* 11 (Spring 1992): 31-38.

Relates experience of librarians teaching a Pro-Cite course in the Health Sciences Library at the University of Maryland. Provides practical ways to prepare and teach such a course.

Potter, Laurie A. "Measuring Library Staff Time Spent Training Patrons to Use Health-Related CD-ROM Databases." *Bulletin of the Medical Library Association* 80 (July 1992): 299-300.

Measures the time consumed in training patrons to use the MedLine CD-ROM at the University of Nevada School of Medicine Library.

Shipman, Barbara L., et al. "End-User Searching and New Roles for Librarians." *Medical Reference Services Quarterly* 11 (Fall 1992): 1-16.

Discusses the changing role of librarians due to the proliferation of databases and other technological information sources based on the Medical Library at the University of Michigan. Describes the impact on the reference department and how the staff is being prepared to deal with these changes.

Smith, Doreen L. "Basic Library Skills for Health Sciences." *PNLA Quarterly* 56 (Winter 1992): 16.

Describes a library school's program for hospital staff and nursing students as part of a continuing education program.

Smith, Philip J., and Virginia Tiefel. "The Information Gateway: Designing a Front-End Interface to Enhance Library Instruction." *Reference Services Review* 20, no. 4 (1992): 37-48.

Describes the Gateway, a computerized library system for undergraduate students to teach them integrated access to information sources.

Steele, Alena, and G. Tseng. "End-User Training for CD-ROM MEDLINE: A Survey of UK Medical School Libraries." *Program* 26 (January 1992): 55-61.

Summarizes a survey of 31 UK medical school libraries to assess user instruction methods for CD-ROM MEDLINE.

Stigleman, Sue, and C. White. "A MicroComputer Teaching Lab for Information Management Education." *Medical Reference Services Quarterly* 11 (Spring 1992): 67-73.

Describes a hands-on microcomputer teaching lab at the University of North Carolina at Chapel Hill, Health Sciences Library, to instruct students in information management.

ALL LEVELS

Burton, Melody. "The Paper Chase: How to Manage CD-ROM Documentation." *Database* 15 (April 1992): 102-104.

Presents a guide to libraries to help them in writing documentation on assisting users in using CD-ROM databases.

Condic, Kristine S. "Reference Assistance for CD-ROM Users: A Little Goes a Long Way." *CD-ROM Professional* 5 (January 1992): 56-57.

Provides guidelines to help reference librarians provide effective, friendly, and cost-effective use instruction for CD-ROM databases.

Doyle, Kristina S. "Outcome Measures for Information Literacy within the National Education Goals of 1990." ERIC Reproduction Service, 1992. ED 351 033.

This is the final report and summarizes findings from 46 national organizations regarding their concern with information literacy.

Drake, Frances. "Training for National Online Manpower Information System." *BURISA* 102 (February 1992): 5-7.

Discusses primary training requirements for online system and on-site courses, distance learning, and computer-assisted learning.

Harris, Roma M. "Bibliographic Instruction: The Views of Academic, Special and Public Librarians." *College and Research Libraries* 53 (May 1992): 249-256.

Identifies positions taken by academic, special, and public librarians regarding user instruction and reference services. Reveals that academic librarians would like to achieve user independence, special librarians favor information delivery, and public librarians fall somewhere in between.

McCrank, Lawrence J. "Academic Programs for Information Literacy: Theory and Structure." *RQ* 32 (Summer 1992): 485-497.

Discusses the importance of information literacy in relation to public relations and the library's place in the creative realm of information providers. Argues that information literacy should not be limited to libraries. Offers components for a comprehensive information literacy program encompassing all educational levels.

PARTICIPANTS

ROSTER OF PARTICIPANTS

Diana Accurso
Library
Denison University
Granville, OH 43023
accurso@max.cc.denison.edu

David W. Allan
Memorial Library
Mankato State University
Mankato, MN 56001
dwallan@msusi.msus.edu

Tony Amodeo
Von der Ahe Library
Loyola Marymount University
Los Angeles, CA 90045
fmod@lmuacad.Bitnet

Sarah Anderson
Library
North Park College
Chicago, IL 60625
npcts@class.org

Lori Arp
Library
University of Colorado-Boulder
Boulder, CO 80309

Rayonia Babel
Library
Aurora University
Aurora, IL 60506

Andrea Bartelstein
Library
University of Washington
Seattle, WA 98195
andi@u.washington.edu

Lisa Baures
Memorial Library
Mankato State University
Mankato, MN 56001

Rick Bean
O'Hare Campus Library
DePaul University
Des Plaines, IL 60018

Barbara Beaton
Hatcher Library
University of Michigan
Ann Arbor, MI 48109
barbara@umich.edu

Jean Beccone
DeWitt Wallace Library
Macalester College
St. Paul, MN 55105

Jeff Beck
Library
Eastern Washington University
Cheney, WA 99004
jb@ewu.vms

Cheryl Becker
Health Sciences Library
University of Wisconsin
Madison, WI 53706
cbecker@macc.wisc.edu

Richard A. Bell
Library
University of Wisconsin-
Eau Claire
Eau Claire, WI 54701

Pat Berge
Science Library
Marquette University
Milwaukee, WI 53233
9360Bergep@vms.csd.mu.edu

Kathleen Betchkal
Ralph M. Besse Library
Ursuline College
Pepper Pike, OH 44124

Goodie Bhullar
158 Ellis Library
University of Missouri
Columbia, MO 65201

Marilee Birchfield
Library
Northwestern University
Evanston, IL 60208

Cheryl Blackwell
Stockwell-Mudd Libraries
Albion College
Albion, MI 49203

Lisa Blankenship
Michener Library
University of Northern
Colorado
Greeley, CO 80639
lblanken@goldng8.univnorth-
co.edu

Barbara Bowley
Library
Union County College
Elizabeth, NJ 07087

Jane T. Bradford
Library
Stetson University
DeLand, FL 32720
jbradfor@stetson

Virginia Brohard
Central Campus Library
Houston Community College
Houston, TX 77004

Nancy Broughton
Idaho State University
Pocatello, ID 83209
brounanc@isu.edu

Patti S. Caravello
University Research Library
UCLA
Los Angeles, CA 90024
ecz5psc@mvs.oac.ucla.edu

Patricia Carroll-Mathes
Ulster County Community
College Library
Stone Ridge, NY 12484

Sandra Cary
Library
Wartburg College
Waverly, IA 50677

Marybeth Charters
Mississippi State
University Library
Mississippi State, MS 39762
umfc1@ra.msstate.u.edu

Susan Clarke
Library
DePaul University
Chicago, IL 60614
libsmc@orion.depaul.edu

Margit Codispoti
Helmke Library
Indiana University-Purdue
    University-Fort Wayne
Fort Wayne, IN 46805

Kathleen Conley
Milner Library
Illinois State University
Normal, IL 61790

Jeff Coon
Library
Indiana University-Kokomo
Kokomo, IN 46904
jcoon@indiana.edu

Carole Cragg
Bethel College
LRC
St. Paul, MN
cracar@bethel.edu

John Culshaw
Library
University of Colorado-Boulder
Boulder, CO 80309

Peter Cupery
Library-IMC
University of Wisconsin-Madison
Madison, WI 53706
cupery@macc.wisc.edu

Paula Dempsey
Library
DePaul University
Chicago, IL 60614
libprd@orion.depaul.edu

Maria Dittman
Library
Marquette University
Milwaukee, WI 53233

Sandra Duling
Library
Castleton State College
Castleton, VT 05735

Tina Eger
Library
Carthage College
Kenosha, WI 53140

Eugene Engeldinger
Library Director
Carthage College
Kenosha, WI 53140

Valerie Feinman
Swirbul Library
Adelphi University
Garden City, NY 11530
feinman@adlibv.adelphi.edu

Marsha Forys
Main Library
University of Iowa
Iowa City, IA 52242
marsha-forys@uiowa.edu

Cynthia Foulke
Staley Library
Millikin University
Decatur, IL 62522
cfoulke@mail.millikin.edu

Paul Frantz
282 Knight Library
University of Oregon
Eugene, OR 97403

Linda Fratt
Library
Trinity College
Deerfield, IL 60015

Jack Fritts
Library
National-Louis University
Evanston, IL 60201

Donna Gagnier
Library
Illinois Institute of Technology
Chicago, IL 60616
libgagnier@minna.acc.iit.edu

Margaret Gardner
Library
Wheaton College
Norton, MA 02766
mgardner@wheatonma.edu

Christy Gavin
Library
California State University
Bakersfield, CA 93311

Jayne Germer
Cloud County Community
College Library
Concordia, KS 66901

Donna Goodwyn
Library
Elmhurst College
Brookfield, IL 60513

Gail Gradowski
Orradre Library
Santa Clara University
Santa Clara, CA 95053
ggradowski@scu.bitnet

Eunice Graupner
Business Library
University of Wisconsin
Madison, WI 53706
graupner@macc.wisc.edu

Marcia Grimes
Wheaton College Library
Norton, MA 02766
mgrimes@wheatonma.edu

Mark Haber
Gill Library
College of New Rochelle
New Rochelle, NY 10805

Carrie M. Hackney
Founders Library
Howard University
Washington, DC 20059

Doreen Harwood
Alverno College Library
Milwaukee, WI 53234

Marilyn Hautala
Library
St. Michael's College
Colchester, VT 05439

Anne Hedrich
Merrill Library
Utah State University
Logan, UT 84322
annhed@cc.usu.edu

Terese Heidenwolf
Skillman Library
LaFayette College
Easton, PA 18042
ht#o@lafayacs

Patricia Herrling
Steenbock Library
University of Wisconsin
Madison, WI 53706
pherrling.macc.wisc.edu

Susan Hopwood
Memorial Library
Marquette University
Milwaukee, WI 53233
hopwoods@vms.csd.mu.edu

Sue Huff
Lewis Towers Library
Loyola University
Chicago, IL 60611

Janet Hurlbert
Library
Lycoming College
Williamsport, PA 17701

Sandra R. Hussey
Lauinger Library
Georgetown University
Washington, DC 20020
shussey@guvax.georgetown.edu

Rebecca Jackson
Gelman Library
George Washington University
Washington, DC 20052
rjackson@gwuvm.bitnet

Esther Jen
Library
Lake Forest College
Lake Forest, IL 60045
jen@lfmail.lfc.edu

Melba Jesudason
College Library
University of Wisconsin
Madison, WI 53706
jesuda@macc.wisc.edu

Carolyn Johnson
Library
Arizona State University
Tempe, AZ 85287
lccrj@asuvm.inre.asu.edu

Carole Kabel
Library
National-Louis University
Chicago, IL 60603

Elys L. Kettling
Wayne College Library
University of Akron
Orville, OH 44667
elkettling@uakron.edu

Olive King
Library
Ryerson Polytechnical Institute
Toronto, Ontario
Canada M5B 2K3
libr8504@ryevm.ryerson.ca

Lynn Klekowski
Loop Campus Library
25 East Jackson
DePaul University
Chicago, IL 60604

Janice Kragness
Minneapolis Campus Library
University of St. Thomas
Minneapolis, MN 55403

Leslie Kent Kunkel
Library
Fielding Institute
Santa Barbara, CA 93105
lkkunkel@fielding.edu

Kristie Lange
Library
University of Wisconsin-
     Platteville
Plattville, WI 53818

Abigail Loomis
443D Memorial Library
University of Wisconsin
Madison, WI 53706

Kathleen Lovelace
Library
Barat College
Lake Forest, IL 60045

Michelle McCaffrey
Library
Saint Michael's College
Colchester, VT 05439

Brent McClintock
Economics Department
Carthage College
Kenosha, WI 53140

Susan R. McMillan
Schmidt Library
York College of Pennsylvania
York, PA 170403
mcmillan@marvin.yorkcol.edu

Sharyl A.McMillian-Nelson
Miller Nichols Library
University of Missouri-Kansas
     City
Kansas City, MO 64110

Sharon Mader
Library
DePaul University
Chicago, IL 60614

Beth Mark
Messiah College Library
Grantham, PA 17027
bmark@meis.messiah.edu

Patrick Max
Library
Castleton State College
Castleton, VT 05735

Vanaja Menon
Library
Lake Forest College
Lake Forest, IL 60045

M. Ann Miller
Library
College of the Mainland
Texas City, TX 77591

Donna Miller
Library
Lebanon Valley College
Annville, PA 17003
miller@acad.lvc.edu

Sally Jo Milne
Good Library
Goshen College
Goshen, IN 46526

Carol Moulden
Library
National-Louis University
Evanston, IL 60201
cmou@nlu.bitnet

Theresa Mudrock
Library
University of Washington
Seattle, WA 98195
mudrock@lib.washington.edu

Diane Nahl
School of Library and Information
    Studies
University of Hawaii
Honolulu, HI 96822
nahljak@uhunix.uhcc.Hawaii.edu

Emilie Ngo-Nguidjol
Memorial Library
University of Wisconsin
Madison, WI 53706
ngo@macc.wisc.edu

Monica Norem
Library
North Harris College
Houston, TX 77073

Daniel Norstedt
Library
University of Wisconsin-Eau
Claire
Eau Claire, WI 54701
norsteda@uwec.edu

Rose P. Novil
Library
National-Louis University
Evanston, IL 60201
rnov@nlu.bitnet

James Olson
Lincoln Park Campus Library
DePaul University
Chicago, IL 60614

Jan Orf
O'Shaugnessy-Frey Library
University of St. Thomas
St. Paul, MN 55105
jmorf@stthomas.edu

Bill Orme
University Library
IUPUI
Indianapolis, IN 46202
orme@indycms.iupui.edu

Kate Owen
Library
University of Wisconsin-Parkside
Kenosha, WI 53141

Amy Parentheau
Media Center
Alverno College
Milwaukee, WI 53234

Aimee Patterson
Library
Houston Community College
Houston, TX 77004

Karen B. Pearson
Library
St. Xavier University
Chicago, IL 60655

Ann Pederson
Chester Fritz Library
University of North Dakota
Grand Forks, ND 58202
auaap@undjes2

Jim Pegolotti
Western Connecticut State
University Library
Danbury, CT 06810
pegolotti@wcsu.ctstateu.edu

Mary Jane Petrowski
Undergraduate Library
University of Illinois
Urbana, IL 61801
petrowski@ux1.cso.uiuc.edu

Linda Piele
Library Learning Center
University of Wisconsin-
    Parkside
Kenosha, WI 53141

Nancy Piernan
Library
University of Detroit-Mercy
Detroit, MI 48221

Linda Pierschalla
Library
Illinois Benedictine College
Lisle, IL 60532

Carol Pike
Helm Library
Western Kentucky University
Bowling Green, KY 42101

Michael Poma
Reinert Alumni Library
Creighton University
Omaha, NE 68178

Bonnie Preston
Catonsville Community
    College Library
Baltimore, MD 21228
aabp@catcc

Alice Primack
Marston Science Library
University of Florida
Gainesville, FL 32611
aliprim@nervm.ufl.edu

Diane Prorak
Library
University of Idaho
Moscow, ID 83844
proak@idui1.csrv.uidaho.edu

Cristine Prucha
Murphy Library
University of Wisconsin-La Crosse
La Crosse, WI 54601

Judith Pryor
Library learning Center
University of Wisconsin-Parkside
Kenosha, WI 53141
pryor@cs.uwp.edu

Jing Qiu
Wise Library
West Virginia University
Morgantown, WV 26506
jqiu@wvnvm

Martin Raish
Library
Binghamton University
Binghamton, NY 13902
mraish@bingvmb

Rocky Ralebipi
St. Mary's Campus
College of St. Catherine's
Minneapolis, MN 55454
mdralebipi@alex.stkate.edu

Harriet Ranney
Mansfield Library
University of Montana
Missoula, MT 59812
ims_her@lewis.umt.edu

Dan Ream
Library
Virginia Commonwealth University
Richmond, VA 23284-2033
dream@ruby.vcu.edu

Carol Reed
Carlson Library
University of Toledo
Toledo, OH 43606
creed@ioft02.utoledo.edu

Trish Ridgeway
Handley Library
PO Box 58
Winchester, VA 22604

Eleanor Rodini
Memorial Library
University of Wisconsin-Madison
Madison, WI 53706

Ann Roselle
Library
Lake Forest College
Lake Forest, IL 60045
roselle@lfmail.lfc.edu

Sr. Margaret Ruddy
Library
Cardinal Strich College
Milwaukee, WI 53217

Diane Ruess
Library
University of Alaska-Fairbanks
Fairbanks, AK 99775

Marilyn Russell-Bogle
Library
University of Minnesota-Duluth
Duluth, MN 55812
mrussell@ua.d.umn.edu

Michele Russo
Library
IU-South Bend
South Bend, IN 46615
mrusso@iubacs.bitnet

Bruce Sajdak
Neilson Library
Smith College
Northampton, MA 01060
bsajdak@smith.edu

Jennie Sandberg
MIT Library
Cambridge, MA 02139
jssandbe@athena.mit.edu

Ann Scholz
Library
University of Wisconsin-Parkside
Kenosha, WI 53141
scholza@cs.uwp.edu

Sally Scott
Library
University of Wyoming
Laramie, WY 82071
sscott@corral.uwyo.edu

Julia Shaw-Kokot
Health Sciences Library
University of North Carolina
Chapel Hill, NC 27514
jsk@med.unc.edu

Rena Sheffer
Library
University of Arkansas-Medi-
    cal Science
Little Rock, AR 72205
sheffer@liblan.uams.edu

Linda Shirato
LOEX
Eastern Michigan University
Ypsilanti, MI 48197
lib_shirato@emunix.emich.edu

Greg Sidberry
Library
University of North Texas
Denton, TX 76203
gsidberry@library.unt.edu

Arlie Sims
Library
Columbia College
Chicago, IL 60605
axvclas.uicvmc.bitnet

Vaswati Rani Sinha
Skillman Library
Lafayette College
Easton, PA 18042
sv#3@lafayacs

Susan Skekloff
Helmke Library
Indiana University-Purdue
Fort Wayne, IN 46805

Monica Smith
Plaza Library
Pepperdine University
Culver City, CA 90230
msmith@sun.pepperdine.edu

Donna Soltermann
Library
St. Louis Community College
St. Louis, MO 63114

Victoria Spain
Axinn Library
Hofstra University
Hempstead, NY 11550

Keith Stanger
Eastern Michigan University Library
Ypsilanti, MI 48197
lib_stanger@emunix.emich.edu

Leslie Stebbins
Goldfarb Library
Brandeis University
Waltham, MA 02254

Jeanne Stevens
De Witt Wallace Library
Macalester College
St. Paul, MN 55105

Randi Stocker
IUPUI Library
Indianapolis, IN 46202
rstocker@indycms.iupui.edu

Louisa Straziuso
OSU-Newark Library
Ohio State University
Newark, OH 43055
lstraziu@magnus.acs.ohio-state.edu

Kay Tavill
Funding Information Center
Marquette University
Milwaukee, WI 53233
tavillk@vms.csd.mu.edu

Terry Taylor
Library
DePaul University
Chicago, IL 60614
libtat@orion.depaul.edu

Debbie Tenofsky
Library
Loyola University
Chicago, IL 60626
zlzlb30@luccpua.it.luc.edu

Carol Tenopir
School of Library and Information
    Studies
University of Hawaii
Honolulu, HI 96822

Dot S. Thompson
Bertrand Library
Bucknell University
Lewisburg, PA 17837
dthompsn@bucknell.edu

Ron Titus
Library
Marshall University
Huntington, WV 25705

Josie Tong
Education Library
University of Alberta
Edmonton, Alberta
Canada T6G 2J8
jtong@vm.ucs.ualberta.ca

Lilly Torrez
University of Texas-Pan American
    Library
Edinburg, TX 78539
lt238d@panam

Rose Trupiano
Memorial Library
Marquette University
Milwaukee, WI 53233
9414trupiano@vms.csdmu.edu

Jan Tudor
Hatfield Library
Willamette University
Salem, OR 97301
jtudor@willamette.edu

Patrick Tweedy
Undergraduate Library
University of California at San
Diego
La Jolla, Ca 92093

Dennis Unterholzner
Library
Carthage College
Kenosha, WI 53140

Sarah Vasse
Library
Orange County Community
    College
Middletown, NY 10940

Mary Jane Walsh
Case Library
Colgate University
Hamilton, NY 13346
mwalsh@colgate.center.edu

James E. Ward
Library
David Libscomb Library
Nashville, TN 37204-3951

Marjorie Warmkessel
Ganser Library
Millersville University
Millersville, PA 17551
mwarmkes@mu2.millersv.edu

Barbara E. Weeg
Donald O. Rod Library
University of Northern Iowa
Cedar Falls, IA 50613
weeg@uni.edu

Katherine M. Weir
Milner Library
Illinois State University
Normal, IL 61761

Marilyn Wells
Cullom-Davis Library
Bradley University
Peoria, IL 61625
wells@bradley.bradley.edu

Sharon West
Rasmuson Library
University of Alaska-Fairbanks
Fairbanks, AK 99775
fnsmw@acad3.alaska.edu

Charles B. Wenger
Oboler Library
Idaho State University
Pocatello, ID 83209

Marcia Whitehead
Boatwright Library
University of Richmond
Richmond, VA 23173
whitehead@urvax.urich.edu

Timothy Williams
Library
J.Sargeant Reynolds
	Community College
Richmond, VA 23285

Betsy Wilson
Library
University of Washington
Seattle, WA 98195

Robert Woodley
Library
Philadelphia College of Pharmacy and
	Science
Philadelphia, PA 19103

Peggy Wright
Library
Western Kentucky University
Bowling Green, KY 42101

Kris Wysick
Library
Albuquerque Technical Vocational
	Institute
Albuquerque, NM 87111

Devon Yoder
Library
Goshen College
Goshen, IN 46526

Cathleen Zange
Library
Judson College
Elgin, IL 60123

Frances Zeigler
Founders Library
Howard University
Washington, DC 20059

Michael C. Zeigler
User Services
Lebanon Valley College
Annville, PA 17003
zeigler@admin.lvc.edu